IMISCOE Research Series

This series is the official book series of IMISCOE, the largest network of excellence on migration and diversity in the world. It comprises publications which present empirical and theoretical research on different aspects of international migration. The authors are all specialists, and the publications a rich source of information for researchers and others involved in international migration studies.

The series is published under the editorial supervision of the IMISCOE Editorial Committee which includes leading scholars from all over Europe. The series, which contains more than eighty titles already, is internationally peer reviewed which ensures that the book published in this series continue to present excellent academic standards and scholarly quality. Most of the books are available open access.

For information on how to submit a book proposal, please visit: http://www.imiscoe.org/publications/how-to-submit-a-book-proposal.

More information about this series at http://www.springer.com/series/13502

Marie Louise Seeberg · Elżbieta M. Goździak
Editors

Contested Childhoods: Growing up in Migrancy

Migration, Governance, Identities

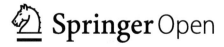

Editors
Marie Louise Seeberg
NOVA
Oslo and Akershus University College
Oslo
Norway

Elżbieta M. Goździak
ISIM
Georgetown University
Washington, DC
USA

ISSN 2364-4087   ISSN 2364-4095 (electronic)
IMISCOE Research Series
ISBN 978-3-319-44608-0   ISBN 978-3-319-44610-3 (eBook)
DOI 10.1007/978-3-319-44610-3

Library of Congress Control Number: 2016948767

© The Editor(s) (if applicable) and The Author(s) 2016. This book is published open access.
Open Access This book is licensed under the terms of the Creative Commons Attribution-NonCommercial 2.5 International License (http://creativecommons.org/licenses/by-nc/2.5/), which permits any noncommercial use, sharing, adaptation, distribution and reproduction in any medium or format, as long as you give appropriate credit to the original author(s) and the source, provide a link to the Creative Commons license and indicate if changes were made.
The images or other third party material in this book are included in the book's Creative Commons license, unless indicated otherwise in a credit line to the material. If material is not included in the book's Creative Commons license and your intended use is not permitted by statutory regulation or exceeds the permitted use, you will need to obtain permission directly from the copyright holder.
This work is subject to copyright. All commercial rights are reserved by the Publisher, whether the whole or part of the material is concerned, specifically the rights of translation, reprinting, reuse of illustrations, recitation, broadcasting, reproduction on microfilms or in any other physical way, and transmission or information storage and retrieval, electronic adaptation, computer software, or by similar or dissimilar methodology now known or hereafter developed.
The use of general descriptive names, registered names, trademarks, service marks, etc. in this publication does not imply, even in the absence of a specific statement, that such names are exempt from the relevant protective laws and regulations and therefore free for general use.
The publisher, the authors and the editors are safe to assume that the advice and information in this book are believed to be true and accurate at the date of publication. Neither the publisher nor the authors or the editors give a warranty, express or implied, with respect to the material contained herein or for any errors or omissions that may have been made.

Printed on acid-free paper

This Springer imprint is published by Springer Nature
The registered company is Springer International Publishing AG
The registered company address is: Gewerbestrasse 11, 6330 Cham, Switzerland

The original version of this book has been revised. For detailed information please see the erratum at 10.1007/978-3-319-44610-3_11

Acknowledgements

This book is a product of the IMISCOE Research Group "Contested Childhoods in Times of Crises," established in 2013. We would like to thank IMISCOE for supporting the establishment and for awarding seed funding to the group, and the Research Council of Norway for generous funding of our cooperation and activities. We would also like to express our appreciation of the whole IMISCOE network, which constitutes a most inspiring environment. IMISCOE has facilitated the publishing of this book through allocation of time slots to our group at the annual conferences and, of course, through editing the book series. At IMISCOE, we would especially like to thank the editorial committee for reviewing and accepting our book and managing editor Warda Belabas for her invariably patient and competent assistance. Our thanks also go to our employers, ISIM at Georgetown University and NOVA at Oslo and Akershus University College (HiOA), and to our colleagues at these two institutions for support and encouragement and for creating the necessary working conditions for the editing of this book. We are very grateful to the three anonymous external reviewers and to IMISCOE's internal reviewer for their thorough, challenging, and constructive comments on the manuscript. We would also like to thank research assistants Michael Sliwinski and Charles Jamieson for their thorough language editing and assistance. Finally, we extend our thanks to our co-creators of this book, the authors of the chapters to follow. Cooperating with you on this project has been a genuine pleasure.

Oslo, Norway
Washington, DC, USA
June 2016

Marie Louise Seeberg
Elżbieta M. Goździak

Contents

1 Contested Childhoods: Growing up in Migrancy 1
Marie Louise Seeberg and Elżbieta M. Goździak

Part I International Migration

2 Forced Victims or Willing Migrants? Contesting Assumptions About Child Trafficking 23
Elżbieta M. Goździak

3 Child Refugees and National Boundaries 43
Marie Louise Seeberg

4 South Sudanese Diaspora Children: Contested Notions of Childhood, Uprootedness, and Belonging Among Young Refugees in the U.S. 61
Marisa O. Ensor

Part II Governance

5 Lost Between Protective Regimes: Roma in the Norwegian State 81
Ada I. Engebrigtsen

6 When Policy Meets Practice: A Study of Ethnic Community-Based Organizations for Children and Youth 99
Marianne Takle and Guro Ødegård

Part III Identities

7 Identity Development Among Youth of Vietnamese Descent in the Czech Republic 121
Andrea Svobodová and Eva Janská

8 Mixed Parentage: Negotiating Identity in Denmark 139
Helene Bang Appel and Rashmi Singla

9 "I Think of Myself as Norwegian, Although I Feel that I Am from Another Country." Children Constructing Ethnic Identity in Diverse Cultural Contexts in Oslo, Norway 159
Mari Rysst

10 Looking Ahead: Contested Childhoods and Migrancy 179
Elżbieta M. Goździak and Marie Louise Seeberg

Erratum to: Contested Childhoods: Growing up in Migrancy E1
Marie Louise Seeberg and Elżbieta M. Goździak

Index 189

Editors and Contributors

About the Editors

Marie Louise Seeberg is Research Professor at the Department of Childhood Studies and co-ordinates the Research Group on Migration and Transnationality at NOVA, Oslo, and Akershus University College. A social anthropologist, she has conducted fieldwork in a wide array of settings. In her Ph.D. thesis, she explored and compared the ways in which Dutch and Norwegian schools deal with ethnic and other differences. Her research topics also include the meanings of home and homeland among Vietnamese refugees in Norway, Swedish welfare institutions' interactions with refugees from Vietnam, and conditions for asylum-seeking children in Norway. More recently, her research focuses on the immigration of care workers to Norway. From 2013, she has led the IMISCOE research cluster "Contested Childhoods in times of Crises." Amongst her publications are *The Holocaust as Active Memory: The Past in the Present* (Ashgate Academic 2013, co-edited with Irene Levin and Claudia Lenz), "Immigrant care workers and Norwegian gender equality: institutions, identities, intersections" in the *European Journal of Women's Studies* (2012), and "No Place: Small children in Norwegian asylum-seeker reception centres" in *Childhood—A Global Journal of Child Research* (with Cecilie Bagge and Truls Enger 2009).

Elżbieta M. Goździak is Research Professor at the Institute for the Study of International Migration (ISIM) at Georgetown University, Washington D.C., and former editor of *International Migration*. In fall 2016 she is the George Soros Chair in Public Policy at the Central European University in Budapest, Hungary. Formerly, she held a senior position with the Office of Refugee Resettlement (ORR) and the Substance Abuse and Mental Health Services Administration (SAMHSA) in the U.S. Department of Health and Human Services. She has taught at the Howard University's School of Social Work and managed a programme area on admissions and resettlement of refugees in industrialized countries for the Refugee Policy Group (RPG). Prior to immigrating to the U.S., she was Assistant Professor of Anthropology at the Adam Mickiewicz University in Poznań, Poland.

She is a recipient of several Fulbright grants to teach and conduct research in Poland, Thailand, and Indonesia as well as a residential fellowship at the Rockefeller Center in Bellagio, Italy. Current research projects include facilitating local integration of Central American children and adolescents in the United States; research on adults trafficked to the United States; and a study of returned victims of trafficking in Poland, Moldova, Nepal, and Thailand. Her book *Trafficked Children and Youth in the United States: Reimagining Survivors* (Rutgers University Press 2016) is the newest addition to her long list of publications. Forthcoming (with Marisa O. Ensor) is a new volume on *Children and Forced Migration: Durable Solutions during Transient Years,* sequel to their book *Children and Migration. At the Crossroads of Resiliency and Vulnerability* (Palgrave 2010).

About the Contributors

Helene Bang Appel is a lecturer at the Metropolitan University College in Copenhagen, Denmark. Her research and teaching focus on culture, language, pedagogy, and identity. She earned her MA in 2010 in English and Psychology from Roskilde University and her BA in Teaching from Zahle's Seminary, now a part of University College Capital (UCC) in Denmark, and worked for several years as a teacher. She has presented her research on "Negotiating identity among children of mixed parentage" at several international conferences.

Ada I. Engebrigtsen social anthropologist, is Research Professor at the Department of Childhood Studies and part of the Research Group on Migration and Transnationality at NOVA, Oslo and Akershus University College. Her work focuses on migration, mobility and ethnic relations with a particular emphasis on relations between Somalis, Roma and the Norwegian society. She is a trained kindergarten teacher and was head of the kindergarten for Roma children in Oslo in the 1980s. She received her Ph.D. from the University of Oslo in 2000. Her doctoral research culminated in the book *Exploring Gypsiness: Power, exchange and interdependence in a Transylvanian village* (Berghahn Books 2007). Recently, she has been studying migrating Romanian Roma, their conditions in Norway, and their relations with the Norwegian public. She currently leads the Norwegian Network on the Anthropology of Mobilities. Among her publications are "Culture, networks and social capital: Tamil and Somali immigrants in Norway" (with Øivind Fuglerud, *Ethnic and Racial Studies 2006*), "The child's—or the state's—best interests? An examination of the ways immigration officials work with unaccompanied asylum seeking minors in Norway" (*Child & Family Social Work 2003*), and "Relations between the State and ethnic minorities in Norway" (*Cultural Identities and Ethnic Minorities in Europe* 1999).

Marisa O. Ensor received her Ph.D. in Anthropology from the University of Florida, also holds a Masters of Law (LLM) in International Human Rights Law from the University of Essex, UK, and a certificate in Refugee Studies from the University of Oxford, UK. She is currently based at Georgetown University's

Justice and Peace Program in Washington DC, and is a Research Associate at the International Institute for Child Rights and Development. Her current research focuses on the link between child protection, social cohesion and non-violent forms of conflict resolution in Burundi and Chad. She recently completed a study of youth's role in processes of transitional justice, peacebuilding and reconciliation in Northern Uganda and South Sudan. Dr. Ensor is the author of numerous publications on humanitarian crises and childhood issues, including the edited volumes *African Childhoods: Education, Development and Peacebuilding in the Youngest Continent* (Palgrave Macmillan, 2012), *Children and Migration: At the Crossroads of Resiliency and Vulnerability* (Palgrave Macmillan, 2010), with Elżbieta M. Goździak, and *The Legacy of Hurricane Mitch: Lessons from Post-Disaster Reconstruction in Honduras* (The University of Arizona Press, 2009).

Eva Janská is Assistant Professor of Social and Regional Geography at the Faculty of Science and a member of the research team at Geographic Migration Centre (GEOMIGRACE), a research institute at the Department of Social Geography and Regional Development, Charles University in Prague, the Czech Republic. Her research interests include various aspects of international migration, including labour and irregular migration, immigrant integration policies and processes in different European countries. She teaches courses on geographic aspects of international migration and integration of foreigners for master level students, and recently led the 3-year research project "Migratory relations of foreigners (and majority) in the Czech Republic: concentration of diffusion processes?" awarded funding by the Grant Agency of the Czech Republic.

Guro Ødegård holds a Ph.D. in Sociology and is Head of the Department of Youth Studies at NOVA, Oslo and Akershus University College. Her research interests include social and political integration among young people and ethnic minorities. Her doctoral dissertation from 2009 was titled *Dejected youth? New political engagement in an old democracy*. In recent years, she has evaluated the Norwegian trial in lowering the voting age to 16 years in the local election of 2011. Her areas of expertise also include civic engagement among young people in the aftermath of the terror attacks in Norway, July 22 2011, as well as young people and civil society, integration and social capital in multicultural communities.

Mari Rysst holds an MA in Political Science and a Ph.D. in Social Anthropology from the University of Oslo, Norway. Currently, she is Associate Professor at Lillehammer University College, and is leader of the Ph.D. programme Children and Youth Participation and Competence Development from August 2016. She also holds a part-time position as senior researcher at the National Institute for Consumer Research in Oslo. She has conducted research and published on children, youth and childhood, gender and body, migration, and consumer studies. She is presently working on a project looking at children and sports related to migration and integration.

Rashmi Singla holds a Ph.D. in Psychology from the University of Copenhagen and a M.Sc. from the University of Delhi. Currently, she is Associate Professor at the Department of Psychology & Educational Research at Roskilde University in Denmark. She is part of the NGO Transcultural Therapeutic Team for Ethnic Minority Youth and Families and participates in international projects about health, globalization, and contested childhoods. Her own migration from India to Denmark in 1980 has contributed to her academic interest in movements across borders, transnationalism and diaspora, family and peer relations, ethnicity, inclusion/exclusion processes and psychosocial intervention. Interplay between Eastern and Western Psychology such as meditation, yoga, organizational diversity management are also areas of interest. Her recent book *Intermarriage and Mixed Parenting, Promoting Mental Health and Wellbeing: Crossover Love* (Palgrave 2015) deals with ethnically intermarried couples and mixed parenting in relation to mental health and well-being.

Andrea Svobodová, social anthropologist, is currently finishing her postgraduate study at Geographic Migration Centre (GEOMIGRACE), a research institute at the Department of Social Geography and Regional Development, Charles University in Prague. In her Ph.D. project, she explores the questions related to the integration and identity of Vietnamese youth. Previously, she worked at the Integration Centre for Foreigners in Belgium, where she conducted research on refugee women. In the Czech Republic, she has also worked at the Ministry of Labour and Social Affairs where she was responsible for the foreign nationals' integration agenda. She is currently engaged in a project concerning online hate speech at the non-profit organization Multicultural Center Prague.

Marianne Takle is Research Professor at the Department of Health and Welfare Studies at NOVA, Oslo and Akershus University College, and participates in NOVA's Research Group on Migration and Transnationality. She holds a Ph.D. in Political Science from the University of Oslo. Her research interests include European integration, EU migration policy, national migration policy in selected European countries, national identity, urban studies, immigrant organizations, and the integration of immigrants in the light of nationalism and cultural studies. She recently completed a 3-year postdoctoral project on how immigrant organizations in Oslo participate in local democracy.

Chapter 1
Contested Childhoods: Growing up in Migrancy

Marie Louise Seeberg and Elżbieta M. Goździak

Changed Realities Require New Conceptual Tools

Marie Louise: I was born in Oslo, Norway, in 1963. When I was growing up, having a foreign parent was an individual thing, not part of a political issue. My mother was foreign. She did all she could to assimilate, but she was still different. However, there was no specific, politicized, ready-made category for people like her, or people like us except perhaps the "foreigner" or (in my case) "half-foreigner" category. "Immigrants" had not been invented yet, let alone "migrants." Had I been born in the 1990s instead of the 1960s, this would have been very different. From 1997, "the immigrant population" was a category in Statistics Norway's main publication, the Statistical Yearbook. I would have been "from an immigrant background" in the widest definition of the category, that of having "one foreign-born parent." I might have been targeted for tuition in courses for Norwegian as a second language, and my school would then have received "extra resources" for having been able to count me as "a pupil from an immigrant background." This hypothetical, alternative autobiography illustrates a change that has taken place all over the world. People are on the move and, increasingly, children are growing up where their parents did not. The change has been summed up in sweeping terms such as "globalization" and a "new paradigm of mobility."

Elzbieta: The change takes different forms in different parts of the world. I come from Poland, but when I sought refuge in the United States in the early 1980s, I was

---

M.L. Seeberg (✉)
NOVA-Oslo and Akershus University College, Oslo, Norway
e-mail: marie.l.seeberg@nova.hioa.no

E.M. Goździak
ISIM, Georgetown University, Washington, DC, USA

© The Author(s) 2016
M.L. Seeberg and E.M. Goździak (eds.), *Contested Childhoods: Growing up in Migrancy*, IMISCOE Research Series,
DOI 10.1007/978-3-319-44610-3_1

immediately called "New American." I did not like this label at first, as my Polish identity was still very strong, but I learnt to appreciate it as my migration journey unfolded. I took my oath to become a U.S. citizen in 1998 in front of an African American judge alongside 97 other New Americans representing several dozen countries of origin. My daughter, Marta, is a Washington DC-native, holds dual citizenship, and knows no Polish, but speaks fluent Spanish with an Argentine accent. Despite having a foreign-born mother, she has never been perceived as an immigrant by mainstream society. She is a second-generation U.S. citizen. The Latino children she teaches in an inner city school in Austin, Texas call her *gringa* (foreigner), but are proud that their teacher—although not a Latina—speaks Spanish. Despite the fact that, like Marta, many of them were born in the United States, they are often thought of as immigrants. Birthright citizenship accords both Marta and her students U.S. citizenship at birth regardless of the immigration status of their parents, but white privilege protects Marta from being labelled an immigrant while her students of colour, unfortunately, continue to be "othered" no matter their place of birth.

In this book, we are not so much interested in finding one word that grasps the *zeitgeist*—such as "globalization" or "mobility"—as we are in paying closer attention to some aspects of larger contemporary processes. We are especially interested in changing ideas and practices of childhood as part of such on-going developments, and propose the twin concepts of "contested childhoods" and "growing up in migrancy" as tools for the investigation of these specific aspects. We are also interested in how public policies affect these concepts and how contesting these notions may lead to significant policy changes.

In order to be able to speak about "twin concepts", there must be a close resemblance or at least a close relationship between the two concepts. We hope to convince the reader that this is indeed the case and that the concepts are close enough to belong together, yet different enough to be complementary. Twins, of course, also come from the same womb while "contested childhoods" and "growing up in migrancy" have separate origins. When we have decided to bring them together, it is because children are as much part of migration as adults are, and the time has come to explore the connections between two traditionally separate fields of study.

Childhood studies and migration studies meet in research on children who form part of migration processes. In the field of childhood studies, the significance of migration and of migrancy as defining elements in children's lives is often absent. Similarly, the field of migration studies has only to a limited extent taken on board insights from childhood studies. Although migration scholars often write about children and adolescents, especially using the label "second generation", they less frequently contest the appropriateness of using the Western framework of an idealized "normal" childhood to frame experiences of all minors, regardless of background and belonging. Conversely, childhood scholars often include ethnically and racially diverse groups of children and adolescents in their scholarship and writing without fully recognizing the implications of migration and migrancy on the minors. As we shall see, there are notable exceptions to this dichotomized picture, especially among migration scholars with training in anthropology and childhood scholars with training in geography or anthropology.

This book is part of a contemporary development where several endeavours are being made, from different empirical and theoretical points of departure, to build a new, synthesized field on a platform that combines the two previously separate research agendas. Some of this work is ongoing, while other studies have already been published and inform our own work in various ways. In the following sections of this introductory chapter, we present some studies and thoughts that we have found especially valuable in developing the perspectives of this book. We first present approaches to migration as developed primarily in childhood studies and then approaches to research on children within migration studies.

Childhood Studies and Approaches to Migration

Meanings, values and practices related to childhood vary and are constitutive of different social and cultural groups—groups that may form minorities or majorities within national states, as well as transnational or diasporic networks. As migration scholars, we bring different conceptualisations of childhood to centre stage in migration contexts by recognizing the multiplicity of childhoods with all of their complexities. We acknowledge the constant evolution the concept is undergoing (James et al. 1998; Wells 2009) in complex and changing environments (Castles 2010; Morin 2008). This means that "children are active, creative social agents who produce their own unique children's cultures while simultaneously contributing to the production of adult societies." At the same time, however, childhood is a structural form, a part of society "that never disappears even though its members change continuously and its nature and conception vary historically" (Corsaro 2011, 3). As society changes, individual childhoods change, leading to changes in childhood as a social, political and cultural category. Conversely, as children's lives and the category of childhood change, so does society. Certain types of childhood fit into, are shaped by, and shape certain types of society while other types of childhood go with other types of society. This metonymic relationship of childhood and society also forms the dynamic link between childhoods at the ideological, normative level and childhoods at the level of practice.

Common views of childhood as a universally similar, biologically determined phase of human development have been overwhelmingly rejected in childhood studies, building on the seminal insights of Aries (1962). Aries demonstrated that childhood is a social and therefore historically changing category. Key texts such as

Theorizing Childhood (James et al. 1998) foregrounded children as agents in changing contexts and laid the foundations for analyses of childhood in terms of structure and agency, identity and difference, change and continuity, the local and the global. Significantly, they describe their own contribution as an epistemological shift from a study of children as primarily "becoming", with adulthood as the goal of development, to studying children's "being", their own experiences of lived childhoods (James et al. 1998, 207–8).

Karen Wells' work further expands the horizon of childhood studies from still predominantly western-centric preoccupations to the field of globalization. She does not address migration as such, but contributes with valuable analyses of the many connections and intersections of childhood with processes of globalization, migration included. In the book *Childhood in a Global Perspective* (Wells 2009), she shows how children's lives and adult understandings of childhood interplay across the globe, as part of larger political, legal and economic processes. Especially concerned with the (re)production of inequalities, Wells brings into view how tensions between different understandings of childhood should be understood as dynamics of power where children are simultaneously agents and objects.

In 2013, the journal *Childhood* lent its pages to a special issue bringing the concept of "becoming" back into childhood studies with a new twist: contrasting "becoming" not just to "being" but to a concept of "belonging" regarded as overly and ideologically fixated on stable and localized social units. The issue "Fixity and Fluidity—Circulations, Children, and Childhood" was edited by U.S. anthropologists Stryker and Yngvesson (2013). They used the metaphor of circulation (not synonymous with migration, but partly overlapping) as a way to illuminate childhood as a form of "non-determinative, social becoming", where children are seen as navigators through unstable social landscapes. This new concept of belonging was worked out in contrast to the prevailing emphasis on children as agents of their own "belonging." The special issue also highlighted tensions between a child-centred perspective on becoming and the approach of state agents who are authorized to intervene in the lives of children, particularly children who are understood to be displaced, lost, living on the margins, or in some other way "at risk." Especially valuable is the theoretical advance on a concept of "becoming" which foregrounds the navigations of children and young people in their own lives and helps us view children's agency as "an interrelation between proper action and the conditions of possibility in the contexts where children navigate" (Leifsen 2013, 309). Such an approach is what we are aiming at by way of exploring the interplay of structure and agency, building on the premise that social structures are historically and spatially specific. In our view, history does not determine agency any more than social structures do. But structures do enable and constrain agency, and neither agency nor structure can be understood independently of their historical and localized context (cf. Danermark et al. 2002).

The multiplicity of contemporary childhoods is demonstrated through the empirical scope of another special issue, this time in the journal *Global Studies of Childhood*, entitled "Children on the Move: The Impact of Involuntary and Voluntary Migration on the Lives of Children." Edited from Hong Kong and Australia by Lai and Maclean (2011), the issue is quite general in scope and describes the situations and responses of migrant children in many different settings. While five of the six articles focus on the importance of learning and schooling for migrant children, the issue as a whole contributes empirically rather than theoretically, placing itself within the prevalent notions of migrant children as somehow "between" victimhood and agency.

Contested Childhoods

Understanding childhood as a metonymic part of society also implies recognition that how we raise our children, and the choices our children make, do not only shape the future of the children themselves. They also shape the societies in which the children take part and the societies in which they will participate in the future.

The critical reader may well ask who "we" are in this context. Whose children are we talking about? This is where the contestation comes in. Children and young people may be regarded as primarily representing the future of the societies into which they or their parents have migrated, the future of their families, of their societies of origin, or their own present and future lives as autonomous, transnational individuals. Diverging concerns may be reflected in different ideas and practices of childhood and negotiated in different social fields. In the chapters that follow, we address some outcomes of such negotiations in the short and longer term and changes that migration may bring about in how we understand childhood and how childhoods play out in the real world.

Children and childhood play important roles in constituting the nation and are thus symbolically significant to the state. As "childhood is a concept which lies at the intersection of multiple frames of reference and languages" (Ní Laoire et al. 2010, 156), governmental policies as well as societal conceptualizations of childhood are based on ideal images of children and childhood that vary culturally. Different conceptualizations and ideals of childhood thus prevail within different national states, in Europe and beyond, and are closely interrelated with ideas of the family. National populations tend to comply with official understandings of what childhood should be like, while migrants, whatever their countries of origin, are more likely to form families and childhoods discrepant from such official understandings. This leads to emerging contestations and negotiations over childhoods, and a rising feeling of crisis—a "crisis of values"—at the intersection of family and state. Although everyone seems to agree that "children are the future", there is less consensus on *whose future they are*. A long heralded weakening of the nation-state paired with the increasing transnational situation of many families makes such questions essential. An increasingly "omniphobic Europe" (Ozkirimli 2012)—connected to economic, cultural or moral crises, to a perceived problematic role of Islam in many migrants' family lives, and to extensive commercialization of childhood (Rysst 2010)—strengthens the motivation of governments to control family life and childhood not least among migrants. How such motivations play out in practice is an empirical question.

At the most fundamental level, contestations may arise around the question "what is a child?" Currently, as laid down in the Convention on the Rights of the Child and in most other legal contexts, the term "children" includes everyone up to the age of eighteen, which means that it also includes adolescents. However, in most other contexts definitions and delimitations of children and of childhood are relative. This is because "hard" criteria, such as biological age or the lawful rights and duties accorded to different age groups are often less important for choices and opportunities than "weak" criteria such as cultural expectations, social relations and structural positioning. Applying flexible definitions of children and childhood in research is supported by the fact that youth is often regarded as a transitional phase between childhood and adulthood, thus weakening the rigid dichotomy of "childhood" and "adulthood." Furthermore, because life phases are defined not only by individual biological age but also relative to each other as social categories of meaning, childhood and youth are closely knit and define each other mutually.

Families, national states, and civil society organisations as well as children themselves are central actors engaged in contesting the many meanings and practices of childhood. Childhoods thus become fields of conceptual, moral and political contestation, where "battles" may range from minor tensions and everyday negotiations of symbolic or practical importance involving a limited number of people, to open conflicts involving violence and law enforcement.

Migration Studies and Approaches to Childhood

Although children have not been entirely neglected in migration studies, the approach to children's place in migration processes and policies in this field provides a rather different perspective. Partly this is because the field of migration studies is not a consolidated disciplinary field, but comprises the mainstream theoretical and methodological approaches of disciplines from statistics, law, and economics to social geography, cultural anthropology and social psychology. This book has grown out of the qualitative branches of migration studies, but even here, as we have noted above, concepts deriving from the "harder" branches of the field such as "first" and "second" generation immigrants have prevailed. In addition, a significant trait in migration studies, as opposed to childhood studies, is the preoccupation with structure rather than with agency. In combination with a predominant view of adults as the drivers of migration, this has led to an image of children as dependent and dependants, as victims, or as simply not part of the main picture at all.

In their edited volume *Children and migration: at the crossroads of resiliency and vulnerability* anthropologists Marisa O. Ensor and Elżbieta M. Goździak directed attention to the growing numbers of migrant children (Ensor and Goździak 2010). One of the first books taking the perspective of migrant children themselves, this volume offered a comprehensive analysis of the increasingly common, but poorly understood, phenomenon of children in migratory circumstances. Global in scope, it presented research on migrant children in different circumstances and regions of the world and framed the understanding of their circumstances at the intersection of agency and victimhood. We build on this understanding in the present book, while taking into account the structural frameworks that form the various circumstances described in the different chapters.

A group of contributors to the emerging field of childhood/migration studies focused on children's agency and their experiences of migration, as well as on the concept of belonging. The book *Childhood and migration in Europe: portraits of mobility, identity and belonging in contemporary Ireland* (Ní Laoire et al. 2011), scrutinizes the case of Ireland as a European country of immigration and emigration. This book also emphasises children's subjectivity and agency in constructing identity and belonging. In contrast, our aim is to direct more attention to the interplay of structures, contexts, and relations of power in forming different modes of being, becoming, and belonging.

In a special issue of the *Journal of Ethnic and Migration Studies*, called "Transnational Migration and Childhood" (White et al. 2011), the same group of scholars challenge adult-centric studies in migration research by focusing on the experiences of children in migratory contexts. This issue also disputes ethno-centric notions of childhood and of child migration, advocating the agency and subjectivity of children as a mode of understanding and of gaining new knowledge about the diverse field of child migration and about the roles children play in their own migration processes. Again, we find this perspective invaluable—indeed, necessary —when combined with insights into structural aspects of both childhood and migration.

In another special issue of the *Journal of Ethnic and Migration Studies*, anthropologist Katy Gardner brings to the fore the intersection of childhood and migration. The issue, entitled "Transnational Migration and the Study of Children," was published in 2012, just a year after the one just mentioned, demonstrating the growing interest in this burgeoning field. Gardner takes children's agency and the social construction of childhoods as points of departure, and aims to explore the insights the study of children and their experiences may throw on processes of transnational movement, cultural identity, and the dynamics and inequalities of global capitalism. With this aim, the mutual workings of structure and agency are brought together through empirical studies of "transnational children" and their lives.

The book *Child and youth migration. Mobility-in-migration in an era of globalization*, edited by Veale and Donà (2014) picks up several of the threads laid down by preceding work on childhood and migration, and adds the dimension of mobility. This complements the larger picture of children and young people engaged in transnational and global migration by including the many smaller, more short-term and dynamic patterns of movement. Such "mobility-in-migration" includes young people and children who are "left behind" in their parents' larger migration project and move to their grandparents for a shorter or longer period of time, as well as children who move back and forth between countries during the holidays or at different stages of their education. The book aims to highlight the connections between such mobilities as part of the larger migration patterns. In doing so, it has much in common with the special issue of *Childhood* on the circulation of children, mentioned above (Stryker and Yngvesson 2013), indicating that the two fields of study may be converging.

Growing up in Migrancy

Where you grow up shapes your experiences, your life chances, your identity, and your personality. We use the phrase "growing up in migrancy" inspired by the classic "Growing up in New Guinea" (Mead 1930/1975). Growing up, Mead says, comprises "The way in which each human infant is transformed into the finished adult, into the complicated individual version of his city and his century" (Mead 1930/1975, 9). Our claim is that increasing numbers of children are growing up, not primarily in a place or a period, but within a social space that we call migrancy. We regard migrancy not simply as the "the state or condition of being a migrant; the existence of a migrant population; migrants as a class or group" (Oxford English Dictionary, cited in Näre 2013). Rather, with Näre (2013, 605), we view migrancy as "the socially constructed subjectivity of 'migrant' (…), which is inscribed on certain bodies by the larger society in general and legislative practices in particular. (…) Very often the inscribed subjectivity of migrancy is not only attributed to those who have migrated" but also to children of immigrants, children who have never moved away from their place of birth. "[M]igrancy has become as important a social category as those classics of the modern era: gender, social class, 'race' and nationality" (Näre 2013, 605). Migrancy is not only a category, not quite a social field, but perhaps something in between: it may constitute a social space. Increasing numbers and proportions of the world's children are growing up in this space, even when they are not migrants, but because their parents or even grandparents once were. In the chapters to follow, we bring different conceptualisations of childhood and of migrancy to centre stage in research on migration and on post-migration integration and transnational lives.

Issues regarding childhood and migration have been addressed more indirectly within the IMISCOE research network of which this book, too, is part—especially through studies of the integration of families and of the second generation (e.g.

Grillo 2008; Crul et al. 2012). However, in a migration context we find the concept of "childhood" more fruitful than that of the "second generation." Often "the first generation" is taken to mean people who are the first of their family to have immigrated, "the second generation" is applied to people who have immigrant parents, and "the third generation" to people whose grandparents were immigrants. However, in some parts of the world the term "second generation" often comprises members of the first as well as the third generation of transnational, ethnic minority or migrant families. Originally a statistical category aimed at counting the proportion of children of immigrants, "second generation" is inaccurate at best, and constitutive of ascribed migrancy and racialization at worst.

Statistical categories are an important basis for policy-making and political discourse, and as such influence the approaches and assumptions underlying analyses. Statistical data on immigration stems from these diverse frameworks and may or may not include statistics on emigration and immigration as well as integration measures. For example, the category "second generation" is applied differently in different national contexts. In Europe, the concept of "second generation immigrant" is widely criticized for ascribing migrancy to people who have not themselves migrated. As Gardner points out, "by describing young people first and foremost as the descendants of immigrants, it racialises them" (Gardner 2012, 900). In the U.S., in contrast, wide use of the term "second generation American" escapes the ascription of migrancy, but not the problem of finding a concept that is refined to fit a reality where the country of birth is not the most significant factor influencing life chances and experiences.

"Childhood" as a social category does not ascribe migrancy to any group or category of people, and it overrides the problem of separating and refining ever-new sub-categories in order to be able to categorize every member of a society who is a migrant or a child or grandchild of an immigrant. "Childhood" spans all of humanity, rather than separating people into "us" and "them" based on geographical origins. That said, like all social categories, "childhood" might itself be an instrument of another kind of "othering", where adults and children appear to be qualitatively different categories of people, based on differences in age and generation.

To the profound insights from childhood studies, we use the concept of migrancy to add a geographical dimension both directly and indirectly. Directly, we examine transnational families where children are part of more than one geographically located society and experience transnational social fields (Gardner 2012). Indirectly, we explore how migrancy is an attributed characteristic of children and their families whether or not the children themselves have migrated (Näre 2013).

Changing Realities, Adaptable Methodologies

The contributors to this volume represent a wide range of disciplines, including cultural and social anthropology, political science, social psychology, sociology, and geography. In the research that informs the chapters, the authors used several, mostly qualitative, methodologies, including ethnographic interviews with Sudanese refugee children resettled in the United States, children and adolescents trafficked to the United States, schoolchildren and leaders of youth organizations in Norway, and children born to South Asian and Danish parents in Denmark. Many of these interviews were combined with participant observation and "deep hanging out." The methodologies also include analysis of media accounts and court documents pertaining to a child welfare case of Roma children as well as close reading of historical and contemporary narratives of refugee children's experiences. This was combined with analysis of past and present policies towards refugee children in the UK and in Norway, and analysis of life-stories of Vietnamese youth in the Czech Republic.

The methodologies deployed in the different chapters in this book may be described as "ethnography," yet not necessarily as ethnography in the traditional sense of the word. "When ethnography was first established as a way of researching and writing about other people's lives," writes Kirin Narayan, "'the field' as a site of research for anthropologists referred to a culturally different and out-of-the-way bounded place. As ideas of which places might appropriately be considered the field has shifted, so too have techniques for fieldwork and modes of representation. Ethnographers now find the field in the familiar and the metropolitan, in archives, markets, corporations, laboratories, media worlds, cyberspace, and more. Moreover, as places are more complexly connected to other places through the intensifying forces of globalization, the field can stretch across networks of sites" (Narayan 2012: 26).

The authors who present their research in the present volume mainly carried out their research in large modern cities. Some, like Marisa O. Ensor, Mari Rysst, Rashmi Singla and Helene Bang Appel, and Marianne Takle and Guro Ødegård focused on one city—Omaha, Nebraska, Oslo, Norway, or Copenhagen, Denmark. Others, like Elzbieta M. Goździak, Andrea Plackova and Eva Janská, and Marie Louise Seeberg carried out multi-sited ethnography. Goździak's research took her to ten states in the United States and the District of Columbia. Plackova and Janská too ventured to several parts of the Czech Republic, while Seeberg's research explores four different spatiotemporal sites through the stories of four children, one at each site.

The encounters with the studied populations varied in length and frequency. Some authors were fortunate to interact with the children and adolescents they studied over a longer period and were able to interview them multiple times, while others did not have such opportunities and had to limit their interactions to one interview. Mari Rysst's field methods included in-depth interviews and what Clifford Geertz calls "deep hanging out" (1998). "Deep hanging out" describes the anthropological research method of immersing oneself in a cultural, group, or social experience on an informal level. Observations gleaned from "deep hanging out" typically end up being the most poignant insights of one's anthropological research. In contrast to anthropological practices of conducting short interviews with subjects or observing behaviour, "deep hanging out" is a form of participatory observation in which the anthropologist is physically or virtually present in a group for extended periods of time or for long informal sessions. Rysst had the benefit of "deep hanging out" with a group of children born in Norway to parents hailing from Turkey, Afghanistan, Iraq, Iran, Morocco, Somalia, Gambia, Nigeria, Norway, and Vietnam. She spent time with them in classrooms and during recess over a three months period. As she writes in her chapter, "[o]ne of the methodological advantages of long-term participant observation is a good chance of achieving relations based on trust." The author posits that building rapport with the studied children and developing a considerable level of trust also increased the reliability of data she collected once she conducted more formal interviews.

Marisa O. Ensor interacted with members of the South Sudanese diaspora, both youngsters and adults, through her attendance at a variety of different events, such as academic conferences, social occasions and community celebrations, as well as more informal gatherings of younger South Sudanese and their non-South Sudanese friends. She also conducted in-depth, semi-structured interviews with youth ranging in age from 14 to 21 years of age. These interviews took place in community centres, cafes and restaurants near participants' homes in different parts of Omaha, Nebraska. She used an interview guide aimed at eliciting reflections on younger people's experiences growing up in South Sudan or in exile, the challenges and opportunities of life in the U.S., and their hopes and expectations for their future. She interviewed the majority of her study participants at least two or three times, with interviews lasting for a variable length of time, typically around two hours. Ensor maintained close contact with some of the South Sudanese youngsters and their families, and has had regular updates on their activities and experiences.

Elzbieta M. Goździak began her research by "studying up"—looking at decision-makers, policies, and programmes set up to prevent child trafficking, protect trafficked children, and prosecute perpetrators (Nader 1972; Gusterson 1997). When she initiated her research access to trafficked minors, guarded by their protectors almost as closely as by their traffickers, was impossible. Many service providers contested the value of doing research with trafficked children and adolescents and argued that participation in research would further traumatize victims. She disputed this assumption and underscored the empowerment that could be derived from involvement in research. As she gained the trust of service providers, she was able to meet a few survivors of child trafficking and begin "studying down,"—eliciting stories from survivors of child trafficking—and "sideways," comparing experiences of various survivors and assistance programmes (Bowman, n.d.; Stryker and Gonzalez 2014). These ethnographic encounters varied in duration and intensity, but rarely allowed for prolonged participant observation of a singular programme or individual survivor. There are no communities of trafficked children and youth (Brennan 2005); many of the study participants lived with foster families and were scattered around the country, often miles away from the locality where they were first rescued. In her chapter, Goździak underscores the fact that research with survivors of child trafficking to the United States is complicated and does not always follow the more traditional ethnographic trajectory. While unable to spend more than two or three days at each programme and just a couple of hours with each survivor, she nevertheless characterizes her study as ethnographic. She travelled to "the field" to see the programmes in action and participated in or organized working meetings with a variety of case workers, attorneys, and law enforcement representatives working with survivors of child trafficking. She conducted focus group discussions and individual in-depth interviews with programme staff, and interviewed many of the survivors in their place of residence, at their worksite, or at the programmes where they were being served. Goździak's aim was to listen to the trafficked girls and boys in order to present their points of view and convey how the survivors conceptualized their trafficking experiences and their traffickers. She also attempted to explore what they perceived as their most urgent needs, and how these perceptions differed from the conceptualizations and the approaches of the service providers. Case files and court documents, where included, inform and add the narratives of service providers and child advocates whose voices she also wanted to capture.

Marianne Takle and Guro Ødegaard studied and compared the Norwegian government's criteria for funding to children and youth organisations, and how the ethnic-community based organisations adapted to these criteria. While the discussion of government policies is based on policy document analysis, the authors also visited the organisations' webpages, Facebook profiles and their written statutes, as well as conducting semi-structured interviews with the leaders of the organisations. They followed an interview guide with questions and topics they wanted to cover and started each interview by asking personal questions about the leaders' motivations for using their spare time to work for their respective organisations. They then followed up these with questions related to the organisations' aims, main activities, and the members' engagement. Each interview was concluded with a question about each the organisation's future. While they mainly followed the interview guide, other questions were also discussed when they felt it appropriate. Both authors worked together in all the interviews—while one researcher asked the questions, the other transcribed the interview. Unlike many studies where interviews are conducted by research assistants, this provided a valuable familiarity with the material and with the different perspectives represented in the material that would otherwise have been unattainable. This was strengthened by the fact that the authors also took part, as observers, in meetings for youth organisations in Oslo.

In Helene Bang and Rashmi Singla's chapter about mixedness in a Danish context, the first author conducted all the interviews herself, again providing an irreplaceable closeness to the material. The interviewees were chosen in an interesting "match" with the authors' own Asian origins, which facilitated empathy and the building of trust between the researchers and the participants. The participants were also selected on the basis of age, building on the premise that young people in the age group 11–18 are both able to reflect verbally on their experiences and emotions and find themselves in a period of life where experiences and emotions are often more intense and significant for identity processes than at any other point in life.

In Andrea Plackova and Eva Janska's chapter, the empirical basis differs from Bang and Singla's research, although the thematic focus on identity processes is closely related. Here, the participants' perspective is more retrospective, with young people aged 16–29—a later phase of the overlapping stage between childhood and adulthood where individuals are in the process of consolidating identities that for younger people may be more fluid. The interviewing method here was that of "collecting" life histories, or of creating more or less coherent personal narratives out of the experiences, emotions, and reflections of earlier years. Through their analysis of this material, they show how young Czech Vietnamese, or Vietnamese Czech, are—not unlike their Danish Asian or Asian Danish counterparts—creatively navigating amongst stereotypes and ascribed identities.

Both Ada I. Engebrigtsen and Marie Louise Seeberg relied on secondary data sources. Ada I. Engebrigtsen used her involvement as an expert witness for the defence in legal cases of Roma children forcibly placed in the foster care. She used her involvement in the lawsuit, analysis of court documents, and media accounts to analyze one of the cases closely. In addition, her previous work and research among the Roma in Oslo, Norway and in a village in Romania gave her a thorough historical understanding of the social and policy contexts as well as of the cultural underpinnings of the case study she writes about in her chapter.

In her chapter, Marie Louise Seeberg uses the stories of four individual children as cases representing each of her four sites of investigation: the boundary crossings of refugee children into Norway and the UK in the 1930s and the 2010s. Although the children are not representative of refugee children at the four sites in any statistical sense of the word, they and their stories are typical for their time and place in the sense that they could only have happened in the way that they did, at these particular points in time and place. In other words, they provide useful points of departure for investigating specific, historical policies and possibilities for refugee children. Rather than basing the chapter on research interviews, Seeberg has delved into autobiographical material published by the children themselves in books and on the internet, as well as examining policies through archival material, media items, and published research. The four case studies are her points of departure for studying the contexts in which the cases are located. Precisely through this creative combination of methods and sources adapted to the matter of investigation, and reflecting the words of Narayan above, they are *ethnographic* case studies in spite of the absence of traditional, first-hand ethnographic research. In this way, she creates a methodological approach to sites where direct access is difficult or impossible, for reasons as different as the disappearance of an older generation and the current vulnerability of asylum seeking children.

About This Book: Migrancy and Contestations of Childhood

As this brief review indicates, childhood and migration studies differ not so much in their empirical foci as they do in their emphases and theoretical base—the lenses used to view the subject matter. While childhood studies during the last few decades have emphasized the importance and even primacy of children's agency and subjectivity (James and James 2012), migration scholars have predominantly paid attention to structural issues in their search for drivers and consequences of migration (Brettell and Hollifield 2014). Combining the two fields, therefore, also implies finding theoretical approaches that explore the interdependencies of structure and agency. Gardner (2012: 892) suggests that the concept of "social fields" may be useful here, as it directs attention to relationships as sites both of agency and emotions and of hierarchy and power. As suggested above, if we regard the concept of "migrancy" as something between a category and a field, we may direct attention both to the power/resistance of definition and to relationships of agency, emotions, and hierarchy. The childhoods of children growing up in migrancy are contested childhoods.

Presenting material from Europe and America, this book covers a wide geographical area within the global North, and presents quite different childhoods and societies. The United States, Norway, Denmark, the Czech Republic, and the United Kingdom are countries representing diverging engagement with migrant children. The U.S., for example, has always portrayed itself as a country of immigrants whereas a country like the Czech Republic was historically a source of emigrants that now experiences immigration. These countries also represent different levels of formal support for migrant children. At the one end of the spectrum, we have the U.S., which bars legal immigrants from accessing public programs in the first five years upon arrival (an exception is made for refugee families who receive assistance from the federal government and immigrant children who, regardless of their immigration status, have access to public education). At the other extreme, we find welfare states such as the Scandinavian countries, where the independent status of children means that migrant children often have more extensive rights than adults. The chapters to follow thus present cases at each end of the welfare dimension, and show how welfare provisions play directly into the lives of children and young people. The Czech Republic takes a third position. Its recent history as a socialist state forms the backdrop of current conservative-liberalist policies, but is also characterised by historically embedded state structures in a country that is in many ways still in transition.

The overall questions we address are: Which normative assumptions of childhood and migrancy inform societies' efforts to include the children of immigrants and "migrant" children? How do children and young people seek to establish their positions, and how may these efforts interplay or conflict with families' struggles to preserve ethnic heritage and transnational belonging? A related topic, which we also explore, is what kind of changes migration brings to the understandings and practices of childhood in different countries and how these changes impact upon the lived experience of childhood. Conversely, we also examine how local and national understandings and concepts of childhood influence the understanding and definitions of mobile children, and of trafficking and other border crossings undertaken by children (Goździak 2008).

Based on these questions and explorations, the book is structured into three parts. In the first part, we present three chapters that address the questions in different contexts of international migration. The second part brings together two chapters that describe attempts to establish means of providing governance of childhood in the context of migrancy. The three chapters that form the third part bring to the fore how children may challenge assumptions in their own processes of identity formation.

Human trafficking continues to capture the imagination of the global public. In her chapter, Elżbieta M. Goździak contests the media's gut-wrenching narratives about children sold into servitude. Public discourse emphasizes the particular vulnerability of trafficked children, related to bio-physiological, social, behavioural, and cognitive phases of the maturation process and underscores the necessity to act in the children's best interest. Goździak argues that while trafficked children are overwhelmingly portrayed as hapless victims forced into the trafficking situation, they are usually also actors with a great deal of volition participating in the decision to migrate. She contrasts the image of "the forcibly trafficked child" whose childhood has been lost and needs to be reclaimed with a diversity of experiences and voices that need to be heard in order to facilitate long-term economic and social self-sufficiency of survivors of child trafficking.

Child refugees embody a moral and political dilemma, as national sovereign rights and universal children's rights demand opposite paths of action, argues Marie Louise Seeberg in the following chapter. Child refugees also pose a challenge to current scholarship in childhood studies, refugee and migration studies and studies of nations and nationalism. In each field, important aspects of the experiences and structural conditions forming the lives of child refugees are marginalized. Seeberg asks: Why are some children allowed to cross the boundaries into particular national states, and others denied the right to do so? Which of their multiple statuses —as a child, a refugee, or an asylum seeker—may give them access to different spaces within specific national states? How may child refugees be regarded as different from adult refugees, and how may such differences affect their rights and possibilities? Such questions bring to light the combined underlying premises of nationhood and of childhood, with changing notions of personhood at the very core. This chapter focuses on comparing and analysing the specific criteria for national boundary crossing as they apply to four children: two from the UK, two from Norway. Two crossed national boundaries in the 1930s and two crossed boundaries in the 2010s. Refugee children's access to the physical, social and symbolic spaces of Norway and the UK in the two periods of the 1930s and 2010s indicate a changing pattern of similarities and differences.

In war-torn nations where youngsters constitute the majority of the population, children often play a pivotal role in many of the processes taking place in their societies, both in their country of origin and in the diaspora. This is the point of departure for Marisa O. Ensor's chapter about South Sudanese refugees in the United States. Omaha, Nebraska is currently home to approximately 10,000 South Sudanese refugees, amongst other displaced groups. Mirroring demographic trends in their home country, the South Sudanese population in the U.S. is very young. Some of them came to the U.S. as refugees, as was the case with the close to four thousand famous "Lost Boys of Sudan" who arrived in the U.S. in 2001; others are the U.S.-born children of refugee parents and have never been anywhere in Africa. Their life experiences have often been quite diverse and disparate depending on their migratory trajectories, among other factors. The categories "child", "youth", "refugee", "migrant", and "South Sudanese" are similarly quite situational, fluid and contested. This has led to tensions and even violence, with some youth allegedly joining the many street gangs that have recently arisen in the area. Against this background, the diasporic identities and cultural practices of children and youth are being translated, appropriated, and creolized to fit into local social contexts and structures.

In the second part of the book, which focuses on policies and governance, Ada E. Engebrigtsen describes how after World War II, a group of Roma gypsies settled in Norway, constituting a minority that now comprises a population of around 700 persons. Several of their elders had travelled in Norway between the 1880s and 1930s, but were refused entry to Norway when they sought refuge from Germany in the 1930s. In the 1970s and 1980s, a massive project was launched to integrate the remaining Roma into Norwegian society. Engebrigtsen explains how this instead led to clientification of the Roma, and social segregation did not decrease. Since 2000, public childcare services have been strongly involved in Norwegian Roma families and approximately five per cent of the children have been taken into custody and raised in foster-families. Foster-families are non-Roma and siblings grow up with little contact with each other and their Roma families, in spite of the fact that Norwegian Roma are granted status as a National Minority under the European Convention for the Protection of Minorities. Under the Convention, they are protected from discrimination and are granted a right to develop their native language and minority culture or heritage. Engebrigtsen discusses the dilemmas and contradictions between two different protective national regimes—Child Protection laws and the Convention for the Protection of Minorities —and explores how these different protective regimes affect the current meanings and practices of Roma childhoods in Norway.

In the following chapter, Takle and Ødegård scrutinise the identifications and practices of ethnic community based youth organisations in Norway. Although many of their members were born in Norway, the organisations are firmly placed within a migrancy framework by the state's financial support system and other instruments of governance. Yet, the government's policy is not to establish these organisations as ethnic enclaves for the perpetuation of homeland cultures; on the contrary, the government regards these organisations as bridges to learning individual democratic participation in society outside the ethnic community. The leaders of the organisations, themselves young people, do not define their task in terms of democracy, but as helping their peers to maintain their families' and ethnic communities' cultural heritage. Paradoxically, then, they do not contest the migrancy ascribed to them by the government, but appear to have internalized it, thus perpetuating the status of themselves as "migrants".

In the third and final part of the book, the authors direct attention to the processes of identity of young people growing up in migrancy. Adolescence is a turbulent time during which many young people reflect on their identities, and identity development may be particularly challenging for children and young people from a migrant background. Andrea Svobodová's and Eva Janská's chapter focuses on the dynamics of identity formation and the construction of a sense of self among youth of Vietnamese origin in the Czech Republic. The chapter shows how these young people contest ascribed identities and talk about their feelings of belonging while trying to come to terms both with the influences that formed their socialization processes within an immigrant community and with the way of life of the majority society. The authors examine how identities develop over time, what factors influence identity construction, and show how the youth they met were active agents in the process of defining their position "between the two cultures" rather than passively accepting labels—ethnic or others—used by members of the majority.

Globalization has led to an increase in the number of children of mixed parentage, due to more transnational marriages and the formation of intimate relationships across national and ethnic borders. However, European research often overlooks mixed couples and children of mixed parentage. This omission should be viewed in the light of the facts that, historically, children of mixed parentage have been pathologized, and that the term "race" is a taboo in public discourse, probably due to the negative associations with Second World War eugenics (King-O'Riain et al. 2014). Nevertheless, race matters, as hybrid space continues to expand and interconnections across nations result in increasingly international family patterns. In their chapter, Helene Bang Appel and Rashmi Singla deal with ethnicity, race and visible differences between children of mixed parentage and the majority of the Danish population. They investigate how children of mixed parentage construct identities, which are contested in their environments as they challenge the stereotypical notions of belonging and identifying with only one ethnic group. With its point of departure in the history of "mixedness" in Denmark, the chapter provides empirical answers to questions about identity formation among the children who belong to the contested category "children of mixed parentage" and discusses how a new paradigm may be emerging that renders an earlier pathologization of mixed children obsolete.

Mari Rysst's chapter also bears upon silent European discourses of "race" when she discusses identity construction among children living in the Grorud Valley in Oslo. Compared to other parts of Norway, a large proportion of diverse immigrants —visually different from ethnic Norwegians—settled in this valley. Currently, the majority of the residents are of foreign origin. Rysst describes how, as they grow up, they have to navigate between the cultural values from their families' countries of origin and the cultural values of the Norwegian society regarding ethnic/national identity construction. This has implications, she argues, both for their feelings of belonging and for their well-being. The fact that children and youth participate in many social contexts raises high demands on their ability to master complex surroundings. This chapter presents aspects of these processes from the children's point of view, contesting earlier research presuming that youth from migrant background had "one foot in each culture", and that this was problematic. Rather, she takes inspiration from studies that view youth of migrant background as creative *bricoleurs* and competent navigators of more than one culture, in line with the "new paradigm" of childhood in which children and youth are viewed as active participants in their socialization (James et al. 1998). Rysst discusses how youth living in migrancy in Norway construct national/ethnic identity at the intersection of age, gender, ethnicity, religion, and sexuality. The chapter shows that youth growing up in diverse cultural settings seek primary identification other than Norwegian identity in a narrow sense. These processes are closely intertwined with gender construction.

In the final chapter, we return to and weave together theoretical and practical implications of the research presented in this volume. We share with the readers our parting thoughts against the backdrop of our personal experiences with conceptualizing and applying some of the themes explored by the book's contributors. We discuss the implications of these studies for further research, practice, and policy developments. We are optimistic that this book forms a solid foundation for building on the contestations presented in the chapters ahead.

References

Ariès, P. (1962). *Centuries of childhood: A social history of family life*. New York: Vintage Books.
Brennan, D. (2005). Methodological challenges in research with trafficked persons: Tales from the field. *International Migration, 43*(1–2), 35–54.
Brettell, C. B., & Hollifield, J. F. (2014). Migration theory: Talking across disciplines. London: Routledge.
Castles, S. (2010). Understanding global migration: A social transformation perspective. *Journal of Ethnic and Migration Studies, 36*(10), 1565–1586.
Corsaro, W. A. (2011). *The sociology of childhood*. Los Angeles, Calif.: Sage.
Crul, M., Schneider, J., & Lelie, F. (2012). *The European second generation compared: Does the integration context matter*. Amsterdam: IMISCOE research. Amsterdam University Press.
Danermark, B., Ekstrom, M., & Jakobsen, L. (2002). *Explaining society: Critical realism in the social sciences*. London: Routledge.
Ensor, M. O., & Goździak, E. M. (2010). *Children and migration: At the crossroads of resiliency and vulnerability*. Basingstoke: Palgrave Macmillan.
Gardner, K. (2012). Transnational migration and the study of children: An introduction. *Journal of Ethnic and Migration Studies, 38*(6), 889–912.
Geertz, C. (1998). Deep hanging out. *The New York review of books*.
Goździak, E. M. (2008). On challenges, dilemmas, and opportunities in studying trafficked children. *Anthropological Quarterly, 81*(4), 903–924.
Grillo, R. (2008). *The Family in question: Immigrant and ethnic minorities in multicultural Europe*. Amsterdam: IMISCOE Research. Amsterdam University Press.
Gusterson, H. (1997). Studying up revisited. *PoLAR: Political and Legal Anthropology Review, 20* (1), 114–119.
James, A., & James, A. (2012). *Key concepts in childhood studies*. Thousand Oaks: Sage.
James, A., Prout, A., & Jenks, C. (1998). *Theorizing childhood*. Cambridge: Polity Press.
King-O'Riain, R. C., Small, S., Mahtani, M., Song, M., & Spickard, P. (Eds.). (2014). *Global mixed race*. NYU Press.
Lai, A., & Maclean, R. (2011). Children on the move: The impact of involuntary and voluntary migration on the lives of children. *Global Studies of Childhood, 1*(2), 87–91.

Leifsen, E. (2013). Child circulation in and out of the secure zone of childhood: A view from the urban margins in Ecuador. *Childhood-a Global Journal of Child Research, 20*(3), 307–322. doi:10.1177/0907568213483147.

Mead, M. (1930/1975). *Growing up in New Guinea*. London: Penguin Books.

Morin, E. (2008). *On complexity (Advances in systems theory, complexity, and the human sciences)*. Cresskill, New Jersey: Hampton Press.

Nader, L. (1972). Up the anthropologist: Perspectives gained from studying up. In D. Hymes (Ed.), *Reinventing anthropology* (pp. 284–311). New York: Vintage Books.

Narayan, K. (2012). *Alive in the writing: Crafting ethnography in the company of Chekhov*. Chicago: University of Chicago Press.

Ní Laoire, C., Carpena-Méndez, F., Tyrrell, N., & White, A. (2010). Introduction: Childhood and migration—mobilities, homes and belongings. *Childhood: A Global Journal of Child Research, 17*(2), 155–162.

Ní Laoire, C., Carpena-Méndez, F., Tyrrell, N., & White, A. (2011). *Childhood and migration in Europe: Portraits of mobility, identity and belonging in contemporary Ireland*. Farnham: Ashgate Publishing.

Näre, L. (2013). Migrancy, gender and social class in domestic labour and social care in Italy: An intersectional analysis of demand. *Journal of Ethnic and Migration Studies, 39*(4), 601–623.

Ozkirimli, U. (2012). 'And people's concerns were genuine: Why didn't we listen more?': Nationalism, multiculturalism and recognition in Europe. *Journal of Contemporary European Studies, 20*(3), 307–321.

Rysst, M. (2010). 'I am only ten years old' feminilities, clothing-fashion codes and the intergenerational gap of interpretation of young girls' clothes. *Childhood, 17*(1), 76–93.

Stryker, R., & Gonzalez, R. (Eds.). (2014). *Up, down, and sideways. Anthropologists trace the pathways of power*. Oxford: Berghahn Books.

Stryker, R., & Yngvesson, B. (2013). Introduction: Fixity and fluidity–circulations, children, and childhood. *Childhood, 20*(3), 297–306.

Veale, A., & Donà, G. (Eds.). (2014). *Mobility-in-migration in an era of globalization: Child and youth migration*. New York: Palgrave Macmillan.

Wells, K. (2009). *Childhood in a global perspective*. Cambridge: Polity.

White, A., Ní Laoire, C., Tyrrell, N., & Carpena-Méndez, F. (2011). Children's roles in transnational migration. *Journal of Ethnic and Migration Studies, 37*(8), 1159–1170.

Open Access This chapter is licensed under the terms of the Creative Commons Attribution-NonCommercial 2.5 International License (http://creativecommons.org/licenses/by-nc/2.5/), which permits any noncommercial use, sharing, adaptation, distribution and reproduction in any medium or format, as long as you give appropriate credit to the original author(s) and the source, provide a link to the Creative Commons license and indicate if changes were made.

The images or other third party material in this chapter are included in the book's Creative Commons license, unless indicated otherwise in a credit line to the material. If material is not included in the book's Creative Commons license and your intended use is not permitted by statutory regulation or exceeds the permitted use, you will need to obtain permission directly from the copyright holder.

Part I
International Migration

Chapter 2
Forced Victims or Willing Migrants? Contesting Assumptions About Child Trafficking

Elżbieta M. Goździak

In the film *Taken,* Liam Neeson plays a retired government agent whose daughter Amanda, on vacation in Paris, is captured by two mobsters running a slavery-prostitution ring. What follows—predictably—is a frantic father on a transatlantic quest to rescue his daughter. In reality, trafficking scenarios do not follow Hollywood scripts. Trafficked children are rarely taken by force. Parents of "trafficked" children do not have to search for them because they know exactly where they have taken their children or whom they have paid to smuggle their children across international borders.

In this chapter, I contest some of the prevailing assumptions about trafficked children and adolescents, especially issues of volition and agency, vulnerability and resiliency, victimhood and survivorship. I contest some of the myths "woven from solid data, conjecture, cultural assumptions, and organizational and political agendas" (Frederick 2005, 127–128) about the forced nature of the trafficking process and juxtapose them with the realities, as expressed by the survivors of child trafficking. I contrast the image of "the forcibly trafficked child" whose childhood has been lost and needs to be reclaimed with the diversity of experiences and voices of children and adolescents trafficked into the United States. These voices need to be heard in order to facilitate the long-term economic and social self-sufficiency of survivors of child trafficking.

E.M. Goździak (✉)
ISIM, Georgetown University, Washington, DC, USA
e-mail: emg27@georgetown.edu

© The Author(s) 2016
M.L. Seeberg and E.M. Goździak (eds.), *Contested Childhoods: Growing up in Migrancy*, IMISCOE Research Series,
DOI 10.1007/978-3-319-44610-3_2

Studying Trafficked Children and Youth

I have been researching child trafficking for over a decade. I began by "studying up"— looking at decision-makers, policies, and programmes set up to prevent child trafficking, protect trafficked children, and prosecute perpetrators (Nader 1969; Gusterson 1997). Access to trafficked minors, guarded by their protectors almost as closely as by their traffickers, was impossible and research funds scarce; most of the money appropriated by the U.S. Congress for anti-trafficking activities was spent on direct services to victims or information campaigns. Many service providers contested the value of doing research with trafficked children and adolescents and argued that participation in research would further traumatize victims. I disputed this assumption and underscored the empowerment that could be derived from involvement in research.

As I gained the trust of service providers, I was slowly able to meet a few survivors of child trafficking and begin "studying down," eliciting stories from survivors of child trafficking, and "sideways," comparing experiences of various survivors and assistance programmes (Bowman 2015; Stryker and Gonzalez 2014). In 2005, I received a grant from the National Institute for Justice (NIJ) and started interviewing survivors of child trafficking and their helpers in earnest. My team and I travelled to many cities and towns around the United States to meet trafficked minors, their foster parents, and caseworkers. These ethnographic encounters varied in duration and intensity, but rarely allowed for prolonged participant observation of a singular programme or individual survivor. There are no communities of trafficked children and youth (Brennan 2005); many of the study participants lived with foster families and were scattered around the country, often miles away from the locality where they were first rescued.

I have written about this research elsewhere—providing the anatomy of the research project that spearheaded this study and discussing the trials and tribulations this research entailed (Goździak 2008, 2012). Nonetheless, I do want to stress that research with survivors of child trafficking to the United States is complicated and does not always follow the more traditional ethnographic trajectory of endless hours and days spent in the company and community of those the ethnographer wishes to study.

The bulk of the fieldwork was conducted between 2005 and 2007 with follow-up visits and conversations with survivors of child trafficking and service providers in 2013 and early 2014. In the end, I researched fifteen programmes in ten states— Arizona, California, Florida, Maryland, Massachusetts, Michigan, New York, Pennsylvania, Texas, and Virginia—and the District of Columbia. This chapter is based on the analysis of interviews with forty survivors and thirty-five service providers.[1] These were in-depth ethnographic interviews focused on eliciting the

---

[1]These children and adolescents are part of a larger group of minors officially recognized by the U.S. federal government as victims of child trafficking. When the study commenced the group included 142 minors. Here I base my analysis on a smaller sample. As I write this chapter in the spring of 2015, the number of children and adolescents under the age of 18 officially recognized by the federal government as victims of child trafficking hovers around 880 individuals.

survivors' conceptualization of their trafficking experiences and their traffickers, understanding what they perceived as their most urgent needs, and how these perceptions differed from and contested the conceptualizations and the approaches of the service providers. I wanted to tell *their* stories. The ethnographic details come from their narratives, not my analysis of court documents and case files.

What is Child Trafficking? Who is a Child?

The *UN Protocol to Prevent, Suppress and Punish Trafficking in Persons, especially Women and Children* (2000) defines child trafficking as "the recruitment, transportation, transfer, harbouring or receipt of any person under the age of eighteen for the purposes of sexual or labour exploitation, forced labour, or slavery" Palermo Protocol. The U.S. Trafficking Victims Protection Act (TVPA) of 2000 concurs with the general agreement in the international community that, in the case of minors, the trafficking term applies whether a child was taken forcibly or voluntarily (Miko 2004). This is because—in the eyes of the law—children are seen as not having agency and thus are considered unable to consent to being smuggled.

The UN Protocol and the TVPA law use the definition of a child promulgated by the UN Convention on the Rights of the Child (CRC) , which states that "every human being below the age of 18, unless under the law applicable to the child, majority is attained earlier" is considered a child. While the CRC takes into account "evolving capacities" of the child to exercise the rights on his or her behalf, policy-makers and service providers concerned with child trafficking often use chronological age as the sole measure of biological and psychological maturity. They frequently do not distinguish between a ten and a seventeen-year-old. They define both as children who need special safeguards and care. Many social workers reject cultural and social meanings attached to local systems of age ranking (La Fontaine 1978).

And yet, cross-culturally the concepts of "child" and "childhood" vary according to social, cultural, historical, religious, and rational norms as well as according to one's personal circumstances. There are tremendous differences between a ten and a seventeen-year-old. There are also often considerable differences between two different seventeen-year-olds, particularly individuals coming from different cultural, social, and economic backgrounds. Gender differences need to be accounted for as well.

The cohort of trafficked "children" in my study ranged in age from two to seventeen years, with the vast majority (83.3 %) falling between 14–17 years of age when they were trafficked. Approximately two-thirds of all the youngsters were concentrated in the age range of 16–17 when trafficked.[2] Not surprisingly, many considered themselves adults. Several of the girls were mothers with children of

---

[2]These statistics are based on the sample of 142 minors.

their own. Some of these babies were the result of romantic relationships that the girls had back in their country of origin. They strongly contested being labelled "children." Gabriela said: "I am not a child. I have a child. I have a son back in Honduras. I came here to earn money so he can have a better life." Seventeen-year-old Pablo, who was trafficked with two of his younger brothers, introduced himself as the guardian and protector of his siblings: "I am all they got here. I have to make sure they are cared for properly." Gabriela and Pablo's self-image stood in sharp contrast with the childhood ideals championed by their caseworkers.

Conceptualizing these teenagers as on the brink of adulthood, instead of as helpless kids, is important not only in terms of self-identity but also in terms of the girls' and boys' wants and needs. They wanted to migrate to the United States, they wanted to work instead of going to school, they wanted to become emancipated rather than to live in foster families, and they balked at curfews and limitations imposed on them by well-meaning — but often culturally misinformed—social workers who wanted the young people to "reclaim their childhoods."

Passive Victims Duped by Criminals or Capable Decision-Makers Aided by Family Members?

Journalists and service providers often portray trafficked children and adolescents as hapless victims forced into the trafficking situation and hardly ever as actors with a great deal of volition. I do not want to minimize the suffering many of these young people experienced, but I do want to acknowledge the evidence that speaks to their capacities to make independent decisions.

With few exceptions, the youngsters in my study were highly motivated to migrate to the U.S. in the hope of earning money. Some acted independently, others made the decision to go to the United States together with their parents. When Belen was ten years old, her father committed suicide. Within a few months, the family fell apart. Belen's mother abandoned her children and Belen and her siblings had to fend for themselves. Belen's uncles and aunts took two of the older children in, but Belen and her younger brother were left in the family home. Some of her father's relatives tried to take possession of the house and turn Belen and her brother out, but Belen fought back and on her fourteenth birthday, the court ruled in her favour and she became the legal owner of the house. She provided for herself and her brother by getting food from her friends. At some point she also obtained a job in a factory. Unfortunately, her brother got into drugs and, as she said, "I lost control of him." At seventeen years of age she decided to go to the United States. She tried to travel legally, but was refused a tourist visa. She contacted an uncle in Pennsylvania and asked him for help. Belen's uncle arranged for a *coyote* (a smuggler) to get her across the U.S.-Mexican border. Belen exhibited a great deal of agency and independent decision-making at various times both before her journey to *el Norte* and after she arrived in the United States. Raped and made pregnant by the smuggler, she escaped what U.S. Immigration and Customs Enforcement (ICE) called a "house of prostitution" and using a stolen Medicaid (health insurance) card went to Planned Parenthood and had an abortion.

Catalina first heard about the "opportunity" to go to the U.S. from her grandparents. Her mother arranged a meeting with a *coyote* and her father paid him $10,000. Poor as the family was, Catalina's father decided to mortgage the family farm to raise the cash. Apparently, Catalina's grandfather later changed his mind and advised her not to travel to *el Norte*, but she decided to go regardless. In case files, this kind of family involvement was often described as "colluding with the traffickers," although, according to Catalina and other girls in this study, parents genuinely believed that they were improving their children's prospects for the future and were unaware that the smuggling might turn into severe exploitation and trafficking.

Twin sisters, Flora and Isa, came to Texas to join their mother and work in a cantina owned by their uncle. They were shocked when Immigration and Customs Enforcement (ICE) raided the cantina and charged their mother with child trafficking. U.S. law enforcement's conceptualizations of who is a trafficker and what constitutes acceptable working conditions for adolescents stand in sharp contrast with the cultural and familial notions of helpers facilitating better lives abroad.

Although girls like Belen made the decision to migrate on their own—by the time she was planning to join her uncle in Pennsylvania, Belen's father was deceased and her mother nowhere to be found—they were told by the U.S. law enforcement and child advocates that they were not capable of making independent decisions. Although the Convention on the Rights of the Child (CRC) emphasizes the evolving capacities of children, in practice U.S. law, especially anti-trafficking law, does not consider underage minors as having the ability to make their own decisions. This stance is especially strong in cases of trafficking for sexual exploitation. Parents who smuggled their children across the border were described by law enforcement as greedy adults who sold their unsuspecting, innocent daughters into a life of prostitution. The persistent view of the trafficked girls as "sex slaves" was even more surprising since in many cases there was no evidence of sexual abuse. But stories about the irrevocable loss of sexual innocence are a particularly potent symbol that works well in many courtrooms.

The image of a passive, exploited victim went hand-in-hand with the conceptualization of human trafficking as a phenomenon dominated and controlled by organized crime. In reality the picture is much more nuanced (Williams 2008). Smaller operations based on kinship or friendship ties may, of course, be part of larger criminal networks. In my research, however, I have not uncovered any direct evidence of such connections. Moreover, the trafficked girls did not speak of criminal networks. Flora and Isa were astounded and saddened when police dragged their mother away in handcuffs. Rather, they focused on the close relationships between themselves and those who helped them cross the U.S. border and find employment. "This is my mother," cried Isa, "where are you taking her?" Despite this reality, policy makers, child advocates, and service providers maintained a studied blindness towards the complicated role family and kin play in facilitating and financing migration journeys of children and adolescents to the United States.

ICE agents often did not recognize that children and youth migrate or are smuggled partly to seek out economic opportunities to support their families. When they talked about migrant children, it was usually in the context of children migrating in the shadows of parents whom the police officers considered the primary migrants. They regarded the children and youth "exclusively as victims, 'lured' or 'duped' by the 'false promises' ostensibly made by traffickers of a better and more prosperous life elsewhere" (Kapur 2008, 119). Yet, in order to engage more critically in debates about and analyses of child trafficking, the processes around child labour migration require a more careful examination. Marisa O. Ensor and I wrote about this issue in our book *Migrant Children*. Citing the work of other anthropologists, we concluded: "(…) an excessive focus on migratory processes that are imposed, difficult, and traumatic may lead to the erroneous assumption that all forms of child migration are necessarily exploitative" (Ensor and Gozdziak 2010, 3). There is growing empirical research from many parts of the world on the reasons why children migrate, which should help dispel the notion that child labour migrants are always passive victims trafficked or forced to migrate because they are young, naïve, and do not know any better (Whitehead and Hashim 2005). Heissler posits that "given the emphasis on trafficking at the global policy level," the processes of facilitating child labour migration "are rarely seen as benign, especially when others reap material benefits" (Heissler 2013, 90). Suppositional perceptions such as these have resulted in a certain ambiguity of the label "trafficker," which as a result is used to describe many different types of individuals who assist adolescents and young adults in crossing international borders and finding employment in the destination country.

Acknowledging that minors—especially older teens—possess agency does not take away from the suffering they experienced at the hands of traffickers. However, depriving them of the recognition that they are rational human beings capable of making independent decisions perpetrates the myth that child development is solely based on biological and psychological structures that are fairly uniform across history, class, and culture. In contrast to the notion of the universal model of childhood, anthropological research shows that childhood and youth are social and cultural rather than biological constructs (Boyden and de Berry 2005).

Children and adolescents are people, and therefore they do have agency. Agency is an intentional action that encompasses both intended and unintended consequences, according to Anthony Giddens (1993). Trafficking was certainly an unintended consequence of the girls' and boys' decision to migrate in search of work. Had they known that they would be maltreated, insufficiently compensated, and isolated from the outside world, they most likely would not have agreed to leave even the most poverty-ridden native village. Without a crystal ball to show them the future, they made the best decisions they could under the circumstances. They owned these decisions even when they desperately wanted to leave the trafficking situation. It is worth mentioning that some of the adolescents did not find their circumstances as dire as child advocates would have the public believe. Several of the Peruvian boys trafficked to work in the construction industry wanted to stay with the same employer, but hoped that service providers would be able to ensure that the boss paid them what he promised, gave them cigarette and lunch breaks regularly, and treated them with respect.

Law enforcement alleged that sixty per cent of the adolescent girls were trafficked for sexual exploitation despite the fact that many of the girls were adamant that they were neither involved in sex work nor sexually abused. One ICE agent told me: "Look, when I see young girls with lots of make-up wearing low cut blouses and the shortest skirts you can imagine, of course I am going to conclude that they were trafficked for sex. Maybe nothing happened yet, but whether they realize it or not, the intent was obvious…" In interviews, the girls presented different assessments of the situation. Magdalena said: "A short dress accentuating my figure does not mean I am a prostitute!" They liked pretty and revealing clothing. Tight and low-cut blouses made them feel sexy and sophisticated, they said. I thought that there was a lot of cultural misunderstanding, both on the part of the law enforcement and on the part of the young girls, about what was age-appropriate attire and what was not. The girls also said they had certain freedoms to make decisions. Naya claimed: "If I wanted to go upstairs with the men, I could earn a lot more money, but I didn't want to sell myself. I made the boss lots of money dancing with the customers and selling them high price drinks." The police did not believe the girls and the girls said the police lied. Both parties contested each other's perceptions of the situation.

While many anthropologists theorizing agency (Tsing 2000; MacGaffey 2000) have a very celebratory view of the concept, Julia Meredith Hess and Dianna Shandy (2008) suggest that, at the juncture of migrant children and the state, this view is more constricted. The same can be said about trafficked children. The politics of compassion governing the lives of trafficked (and other unaccompanied) children tempered the agency of the trafficked girls and boys in my study. The decisions law enforcement and service providers were making were glossed over as "being in the best interest" of the youth. Perhaps it was in the best interest to classify the trafficked girls and boys as "victims" in order to provide them with the legal assistance and social services they needed to stay in the United States.

30   E.M. Goździak

However, stripping them of decision-making abilities did not serve the youth well. How were they to make decisions that were in their best interests if they were not recognized as human beings with volition?

What is in the Best Interest of the Trafficked Child? Who Decides?

In the United States, the system of care for trafficked children has been developed within a framework based on middle-class Western ideals about childhood as a time of dependency and innocence during which children are socialized by adults in order to become competent social actors. Adults generally mediate economic and social responsibilities so that children can grow up free from pressures of responsibilities such as work and childcare. Children who are not raised in this way are considered "victims" who have had their childhood stolen from them. The realities experienced by the "children" in my study, even before the trafficking ordeals, were very different from these ideals. Extreme poverty drove most of them to migrate. In some situations, parental illness compounded already dire economic circumstances and placed even more pressure on the youngsters to contribute to the family's income. Family members who facilitated their migration often presented it as an opportunity to help the young person to "pay back" or support parents. Also, although many of these children worked in their countries of origin—they took care of their siblings, did house work, worked on family farms, or sold wood or foodstuffs in the street—they seldom earned wages for their labour. Thus, a chance to work for wages was seen as an opportunity not to be missed.

The frameworks that conceptualized child labour migration within legal and child protection categories such as "child trafficking," "unaccompanied minors," and "child exploitation" (Mai 2011) are based on the principle of the "best interest of the child" but frequently fail to understand the mix of vulnerability and resiliency of young migrants in its full complexity.[3] This, in turn, ends up further exacerbating their vulnerability. The protectionist narratives of child advocates and service providers too often stand in sharp contrast with the narratives of the youth that emphasize their own agency and resiliency.

Let me turn back to Flora and Isa, introduced earlier in this chapter. Flora and Isa never thought they were trafficked; they explained their migration to the U.S. as an escape from the poverty of Honduras after the ravages of Hurricane Mitch. They came to the U.S. to join their mother, who managed a bar owned by one of her brothers. The girls ended up working in the bar as well. On the basis of a tip-off from a local resident, ICE raided the bar and Flora and Isa, along with several other

---

[3]It is worth noting that while many of the children studied by other contributors to this volume could not shed the label of "migrancy" even when they never migrated, many of the young people in my study wanted to be categorized as migrants, but the system of care denied them this identity.

girls, were "rescued" and referred to a foster care programme to begin a process of restoration and rehabilitation. Prosecutors said that the young women were subjected to long and dangerous smuggling routes and that at least one was raped during the journey. Some of the defendants and their attorneys disputed the forced labour allegations, saying it was more a situation of poor people helping poor relatives affected by a natural disaster. "If it was a family business," Assistant U.S. Attorney Richard Roper said, "it was a hell of a way to treat your family; smuggling them through dangerous routes, misrepresenting to them what they were going to do here."

Shortly after the raid, Special Agent George Ramirez, formerly with the Immigration and Naturalization Service (INS), testified in court that the smuggling ring, called the Molina Organization, forced some of the young women into prostitution to pay off smuggling fees. The young ladies, however, did not corroborate this view. Prosecutors and defence attorneys offered sharply differing opinions about accusations of forced labour and forced prostitution. According to the defence attorney Mick Mickelsen, "There were 52 girls interviewed, and there was only one that said anything about prostitution." Flora and Isa consistently emphasized that they were not pressured to provide sexual services to any of the bar clients or, for that matter, to any of the men that smuggled them from Honduras through Guatemala and Mexico to Texas. In the end, the twenty-four count indictment did not mention any prostitution allegations. Assistant U.S. Attorney Roper said that the allegations were dropped because the victims did not want to testify. Without their cooperation, he said, the allegations would have been impossible to prove to a jury. Eighty-eight people, including Flora and Isa's mother, were detained, mostly on immigration violations.

Flora did not want to be placed in foster care; she wished to return to Honduras. Her pro bono attorney counselled Flora that it was not in her best interest to return home because some of the relatives involved in her trafficking were deported to Honduras and might try to traffic her again. Flora did not think her uncles posed a threat, but did concede that it might be best to stay in the United States. She was mainly afraid of the poverty she would need to face if she returned to Honduras.

Flora also decided to stay because she wished to visit her mother, who was in jail on charges of smuggling underage girls. Again, Flora was counselled against visiting her incarcerated mother. Flora's caseworker told her that it was not in her best interest to see her "abuser." Despite the advice, Flora kept in touch with her mother through letters and phone calls. Persistence paid off and in the end she and Isa, accompanied by their caseworker, travelled to California where their mother was incarcerated. A note in Flora's file described the trip as very successful: "The trip went well. The girls' mother was supportive, encouraging, and very appropriate with her daughters during the visit. She encouraged her daughters to work hard in school and put Christ first in their lives." The caseworker was able to talk to the mother and upon hearing more of her story she determined that, despite the mother's involvement in her daughters' trafficking, "contact with the mother was not detrimental to the girls' safety."

While in foster care, Flora's "best interests" were determined mainly by her middle-class, non-Spanish speaking foster mother who thought that an obedient child should stay home and study, not go out with friends or watch TV. Flora's caseworker sided with the foster mother. However, the foster mother's dissonant views on the "proper behaviour" of a seventeen-year-old girl led to even more rebellion on Flora's part. Flora thought she should have fun. She wanted to have a boyfriend and she started dating a young Latino man. When she became pregnant, she left her foster family to live with the baby's father and moved into a group home after they broke up. Whether the pregnancy was a conscious choice to have a baby or a result of unprotected sex is unclear. What was obvious was Flora's dedication to her son. As her situation changed—from being in the care of a foster mother to being responsible for herself and her baby in a group home—the social worker's assessment of Flora changed as well. The caseworker noted, "Flora is a very outgoing and confident young woman. Very strong-willed and determined. Though these traits created difficulties when she was in foster care, she now is applying them to planning for the future and is showing much more understanding of living independently and using the responsibilities she has." It seemed that the social worker had a complete change of heart, from denying Flora's ability to make her own decisions by supporting the foster mother's rules to advocating for Flora's rights to determine her own best interests and the interests of Alejandro, her infant son. Flora welcomed this change in attitude, but could not articulate the reason for this transformation. The social worker put it simply: "I was wrong. I should have listened more carefully to Flora."

The "best interest" standard is a widely used ethical, legal, and social basis for policy and decision making involving children (Kopelman 1997). The origins of the "child's best interest" principle date back to the late 19th century when the European public became aware of the plight of exploited, abused, and neglected children through popular novels such as those penned by Charles Dickens. In 1989, the principle became part of the Convention on the Rights of the Child. In the intervening years, the notion of "best interest" has come under attack as self-defeating, individualistic, unknowable, vague, dangerous, and open to abuse (Veatch 1981, 1995; Ruddick 1989; McGough 1995; Rodham 1973).

Despite criticisms, the best interest principle remains the dominant legal standard in actions concerning children, including migrant and trafficked children. Attorneys, social workers, and therapists working with trafficked youth frequently and fervently invoke the concept. However, because the concept is broad and rarely defined, it is open to idiosyncratic interpretations (Kelly 1997). Flora's caseworker, for example, changed her opinions about what was in Flora's best interest several times, eventually realizing that Flora's resiliency meant independent decision-making was in the girl's best interest. These subjective assessments can result in an inconsistency in service provision, and may hamper post-migration transition efforts. Moreover, the best interest principle sometimes seems to contradict the right of the minor to participate in determining what is best for them. The question thus remains: Who determines the best interests of the trafficked minor, and how? How does the determination of the child's best interests correspond with the child's right to express their wishes? There is consensus in the literature that Western policy-makers and caretakers tend to prioritize children's perceived best interests over their right to express their wishes and feelings (Bluebond-Langner and Korbin 2007). In the course of this research, I have seen many examples of service providers deciding the child's best interest rather than advocating for their wishes and feelings.

The criteria used by foster parents and service providers for determining a child's best interests were based on a culture-specific understanding of children as "nurtured" by their caretakers. As indicated earlier, the TVPA does not distinguish between ten and seventeen-year-olds. It does, however, make a clear distinction— ideological, strategic, and operational—between children and adults. Taking issue with this dichotomy, Sanghera explains: "This distinction is based on the principle that the development of children as human beings is a process and is not complete as long as they are minors. Children are deemed "innocent" and in need of special protection and assistance in making decisions. It is believed that minors cannot be expected to act in their own best interest as their ability to exercise full agency is not yet entirely developed" (Sanghera 2005, 13). These attitudes produce the system that ignores the voice of the minor, the system where "all persons under the age of 18 constitute a homogenous category—children, devoid equally of sexual identity and sexual activity, bereft equally of the ability to exercise agency and hence in need of identical protective measures" (Sanghera 2005, 6).

My research team and I accepted the young people's assertion that they had wanted to come to the U.S. while recognizing that, at the time of making the decision to migrate, they might have had no idea about the abuse and exploitation they would face once they crossed the border, and, had they known, consequently might not have agreed to come to the United States. The bigger challenge was related to where "to draw a line between coercion and consent for young people under the age of eighteen and how best to promote their rights and agency while still protecting them" (Kempadoo 2005, xxv). The dilemma was whether to consider them as vulnerable victims the way the U.S. law does, stipulating who is a victim and thus who is eligible for services, or as survivors with a great deal of resiliency to overcome the adverse circumstances and hardships, or both. Identifying vulnerabilities is important in order to facilitate access to appropriate services. However, focus on vulnerability and victimhood without recognition that many of these minors were resilient survivors is detrimental to recovery, as it creates unnecessary dependency on support programmes.

Victimhood

Understanding youth's perception of the trafficking experiences as victimization and their identity as victims plays an important role in post-trafficking adjustment, according to social workers and clinicians working with young people. However, this understanding is widely contested, especially by social and behavioural scientists wanting to understand subjects—adults and minors—as agentive, sensuous, and intentional (Jensen and Ronsbo 2014). Given the programmatic importance of seeing trafficked children and youth as victims, let me unpack and contextualize them both within the theoretical frameworks and the narratives put forth by the youth and the service providers in this study.

We have seen a surge in victim-oriented politics in the last few decades (Cole 2006). Theorists such as Diana Meyers identify at least two kinds of victims: heroic and hapless (Meyers 2011). The first category encompasses "martyrs and heroes, who, through their own agency, choice, or strength, are made into victims in the service of a greater good." Descriptions of these hero victims can be found in both revolutionary and religious discourses (see Fanon 2005; Guevara 2006; Khalili 2007). Evelyn, a survivor of domestic servitude, has embraced her own suffering to become an advocate. She often shares very painful memories publicly in the service of a greater good.

The victims of the second category are often seen as passively suffering bodies, and this view is especially prevalent in discourses of humanitarianism, forced migration studies, and discussions of trafficking of women and children for sexual exploitation. "Humanitarian victimhood is produced as a host of different agents, such as donors of international aid (Pupovac 2001), clinicians (Young 1995), and social movements and NGOs, and deploy the victim as a way to forge solidarities and relatedness across different social and geographical spaces" (See Fassin and Rechtman 2009; Jensen and Ronsbo 2014). The martyr is often perceived as a much more agentive victim than the hapless victim of humanitarian disaster or the victim of human rights violations because they take it upon themselves to become a victim.

It is noteworthy that victim status gives priority of concern to certain sufferers over others, argues (Bayley 1991). The youth identified as victims of child trafficking by the federal government were indeed given a special status. Equipped with "letters of eligibility" from the Office of Refugee Resettlement (ORR), they could now access immigration relief and other forms of assistance, including education, healthcare, social services, and counselling. At the same time, Central American minors fleeing violence and poverty in Honduras, Guatemala, and El Salvador and arriving in the United States in unprecedented numbers are considered to be undocumented migrants and put in detention centres (Gonzalez-Barrera 2014).

In judging some sufferers as victims, we risk the paternalistic devaluation of these individuals by transforming resilient and agentive actors into dependent and hapless people (Bayley 1991). As indicated above, the girls and boys in this study did not identify as victims. Admittedly, they may not have been living in the most idyllic conditions, but many did not see themselves as abused or taken advantage of. Faced with poverty and a lack of opportunities to improve their livelihoods, the youngsters were not very happy back at home either. In imagining childhoods spent in tropical climates among extended family, some service providers thought otherwise. The girls did speak about the natural beauty of their native lands, but in the same conversations often described the abject poverty that left them going to bed hungry and unable to feed their babies. Living in multigenerational families provided emotional comfort, but often meant that there were many more mouths to feed. While child advocates vilified parents who sent or brought their children and teens to the United States, the youngsters saw their experiences as labour migration undertaken voluntarily and their parents as helpers, not villains.

That girls' and boys' did not identity as victims was closely related to their expectations about coming to the United States. Almost all of the youth had been highly motivated to migrate to the U.S. in the hope of earning money, as many had compelling reasons to send remittances, such as sick parents and younger siblings or their own babies to support. They did not equate labour migration with victimhood.

Education or Waged Employment

Typically, the youngsters' desire to earn money did not change once they were rescued. When Angela stripped in a bar in New Jersey, she earned good money— about $400 or $500 a night. She paid her *coyote* half of the $15,000 she owed him for bringing her from Honduras to New Jersey and was still able to send money home to her family. The million Honduran lempira (approximately $48,000 USD) she sent to her grandparents allowed them to build a nice house. When *la migra* "rescued" Angela, she had a few thousand dollars in savings, but the money was confiscated. Angela was very angry that the money was gone. "It would have come in handy," she said, "especially now that I am pregnant." She could not understand why she was being punished when she had earned the money fair and square. Frankly, neither could I. Yes, the money was earned performing a job that law enforcement did not approve of for a seventeen-year-old, but it was still Angela's money. Moreover, the anti-trafficking law provides for restitution to victims of trafficking, but few survivors receive what is rightly theirs. Neither did Angela. She did not think her financial interests were taken into consideration at all by law enforcement that claimed to be helping her.

The desire to get a job and make money conflicted with programmes' focus on formal schooling. Following U.S. laws requiring minors to attend school, the programmes assisting trafficked youth focussed more on education and less on employment. Social workers cited regulations defining the age of employment, the number of hours minors are allowed to work, and rules about work permits whenever the youth asked for assistance with finding work. These restrictions ran counter to many goals of young people and resulted in adjustment challenges; they affected girls' commitment to education and their desire to remain in care. Cecilia, for example, told her caseworker she did not want to go to school: "I need money! How am I going to support myself?" After much persuading, Cecilia stayed in school, but kept on asking whether she could leave high school and enrol in a vocational programme that would give her tangible skills. "What am I going to do with all this reading and writing?" she kept on asking. "I need to be able to do something concrete to get a job." In her junior year, when her academic advisor mentioned college, Cecilia again rejected the idea. She told me: "How many years do they think I have to wait to get a good job?" Without access to decent jobs, and indeed requirements that restricted their ability to find work, the youth did not see the assistance as helpful.

Therapeutic Interventions

The contrast between programmes' perceptions of children's best interests and the girls' wishes was strongest surrounding the psychological consequences of trafficking and culturally appropriate responses. Most programmes used the Western concept of "trauma" both as the basis to imagine the trafficked children's experiences and to promote a therapeutic model of rehabilitation services.

A relatively small number of children in this study met the criteria of post-traumatic Stress Disorder (PTSD). Some children presented no psychological disturbance, while others exhibited symptoms of depression. Indeed, depression was the most common diagnosis.[4] To mitigate the psychological consequences of trafficking, children were offered a wide range of mental health services: individual or group therapy, counselling by a torture treatment specialist, and art therapy. Initially, the majority of the youth refused to avail themselves of psychological services but programme staff were persistent. Two girls, with suspected sexual victimization, were referred to a bilingual counsellor. They participated in five counselling sessions, but refused to continue. Several survivors were concerned that going to therapy would stigmatize them further and label them as "crazy." One girl joked that she was "too lazy to go to counselling every week." She also added that she did not know what she would talk about in the sessions. Caseworkers often commented that the "girls went into therapy kicking and screaming," but mental health services were considered in the children's best interests.

Therapy caused "retriggering" for Catalina; she reported having nightmares after her sessions. Upon consultation with a different clinician, a decision was made not to ask questions that did not relate to concrete aspects of the present as such discussions re-opened the pain of the trafficking experience. The therapist instead engaged with Catalina around an art project, thinking this approach would be less

---

[4]The "diagnoses" were performed by case managers who referred the survivors to clinical social workers, psychologists, or psychiatrists.

threatening. However, Catalina was still reluctant to participate. Programme staff tried many different tactics to convince the survivors about the efficacy of mental health programmes. One girl was told that if she did not go to counselling and did not take her medication she would be separated from her baby. Many programmes clearly wanted all youth to participate in therapy and were convinced about the efficacy of this treatment. Some followed their agency's protocol as to the appropriate use of therapy and the children's interest and willingness to attend sessions, but the pressure was on the young people to participate in counselling. Eventually, most children and youth were in treatment. Again, the service providers' assessment of what was in the girls' best interests prevailed.

With one exception, programmes did not consider indigenous healing strategies, social justice, or human rights approaches. For most programmes, cultural competence was limited to finding a Western-trained therapist who could communicate with the survivor in her native language. The Peruvian children and their families who insisted on seeing a Catholic priest were the only exception; the local Hispanic congregation embraced them and provided necessary support.

The push for mental health services was consistent with strategies employed to deal with other victimized populations. The number of programmes established to provide psychological help to refugees, victims of wartime violence, and more recently trafficked victims has grown exponentially (Bracken et al. 1997). The expansion of such programmes indicates the prominence of mental health concepts in the forced migration field. Particularly prominent is the discourse of "trauma" as a major articulator of human suffering (Summerfield 2000, 417). This prominence is based on the premise that trafficking, ethnic cleansing, war, and civil strife constitute mental health emergencies and result in post-traumatic stress, which has in turn led to the use of treatment modalities based on the Western biomedical model. At the same time, other models, building on the victims' own resilience, indigenous coping strategies, and spirituality, are not being explored as much as they could or should. The expansion of trauma programmes is directly related to what Kleinman calls "medicalization of human suffering" (Kleinman et al. 1997).

Undeniably, most of the children and youth in my study had suffered incredible ordeals and, without safe environments in which to recover, they were at risk for re-trafficking. Indeed, there were a couple of instances where the traffickers, pretending to be relatives of the children, contacted the girls. Marianela was one of those girls. Her abuser called her on the phone in the convent where she was staying awaiting placement in a group house. They arranged to meet in a nearby park and the programme staff never heard back from her. However, vigilance of the staff protected many other youngsters from re-victimization. The programmes' unprecedented dedication to the protection of the children in their care was admirable. At the same time, by focusing so much on the children's vulnerability, the programmes often lost sight of the youth's resiliency. Preoccupied with Western standards of child welfare, staff did not have adequate resources to tap into culturally relevant healing strategies.

Towards Solutions and Resolutions

Studies of children and childhoods increasingly see children as "at once developing beings, in possession of agency, and to varying degrees vulnerable" (Bluebond-Langner and Korbin 2007). Developments occurring in the field of childhood studies parallel developments in women's studies, which consider women as social actors and contextualize them in theories of behaviour, culture, and society. Unfortunately, the discourse on child trafficking focuses mainly on the vulnerability and victimization of trafficked children, even though recognition of the coexistence of agency and vulnerability is particularly important in the child trafficking domain. As Diane M. Hoffman, who studied *restavek*[5] children in Southwest Haiti, observes,

> Recognizing their agency is not denying that they suffer; nor is it to sanction the social structural inequalities that make the restavek system possible in the first place. Rather, it is to point the way to a reconceptualization of the restavek child in a more positive light, to portray the child as a person who has real capacities, skills, intelligence, and personal fortitude that can make him or her an asset to the society, rather than a victim or a drain on a society that is itself in chaos (Hoffman 2010, 48).

I acknowledge the legal necessity to use the term "victim." The services that trafficked youth were eligible for were paid with money earmarked for "victims of crimes" and adjustment of their immigration status was also linked to being victimized. I am, however, opposed to extending this label beyond the legal realm. Therapeutically speaking, assigning the identity of a forcibly trafficked victim is often counter-productive to young people's integration into American society or re-integration into their home country, should they choose to return. Recognition of the coexistence of vulnerability and resiliency influences the way we conduct research with trafficked children and affects our ethical responsibilities to the studied youngsters. This recognition is important because it affects—or should affect—institutional responses to survivors of trafficking. While there is no denying that trafficked children and youth have often been severely abused and exploited, one must also consider questions of agency and resiliency while analysing this phenomenon, designing services for trafficked minors, crafting policy responses aimed at preventing child trafficking, and prosecuting perpetrators. Well-informed rehabilitation approaches must consult children's voices, experiences, and perspectives to explicitly inform and shape policy decisions and programmatic responses. Listening to the voices of children has become a powerful mantra for activists and policymakers worldwide. Yet, despite such pronouncements, many of the trafficked girls and boys found their voices silenced or ignored in the name of their "best interests."

---

[5]A restavek (or restavec) is a child in Haiti who is sent by his or her parents to work for a host household as a domestic servant because the parents lack the resources required to support the child. The term comes from the French language rester avec, "to stay with."

Programmes need to be flexible. The youths' perceptions of the nature of their experiences and their families' involvement in trafficking may be at odds with the perceptions held by law enforcement and service providers. Despite these differences, it is essential that law enforcement and service providers are flexible enough to allow the trafficked youth to have a unique, and perhaps differing, assessment of what happened to them and who wronged them. Minors should also be educated about their rights and about U.S. and international conventions protecting children. "Know your rights" sessions are commonplace for migrant children in detention centres; similar training should be provided for trafficked minors, especially adolescents. Trafficked minors need to be educated about the way the law views certain actions of adults as criminal. This kind of training should focus on the legal aspects of child trafficking, not moral assessments of parents' actions. Hopefully, a rights-based service model taking into account young people's resiliency and agency will empower them sufficiently to continue rebuilding their post-trafficking lives long after they leave assistance programmes.

References

Bayley, J. (1991). The concept of victimhood. In D. Sank & D. I. Caplan (Eds.), *To be a victim* (pp. 53–62). New York: Springer.

Bluebond-Langner, M., & Korbin, J. E. (2007). Challenges and opportunities in the anthropology of childhoods. *American Anthropologist, 109*(2), 241–246.

Bowman, D. (2015). Studying up, down, sideways and through: situated research and policy networks. https://www.tasa.org.au/wp-content/uploads/2015/03/Bowman-Dina.pdf.

Boyden, J., & de Berry, J. (2005). *Children and youth on the front line: Ethnography, armed conflict and displacement.* Oxford and New York: Berghahn Books.

Bracken, P., Giller, J., & Summerfield, D. (1997). Rethinking mental health work with survivors of wartime violence and refugees. *Journal of Refugee Studies, 10*(4), 431–442.

Brennan, D. (2005). Methodological challenges in research with trafficked persons form the field. *International Migration, 43*(1–2), 35–54.

Cole, A. (2006). *The cult of true victimhood: From the war on welfare to the war on terror* (1st ed.). Stanford, California: Stanford University Press.

Ensor, M. O., & Goździak, E. M. (Eds.). (2010). *Children and migration. At the crossroads of resiliency and vulnerability.* New York: Palgrave.

Fanon, F. (2005). *The wretched of the earth (Richard Philcox, Trans.)* (Reprint ed.). New York: Grove Press.

Fassin, D., & Rechtman, R. (2009). *The empire of trauma: An inquiry into the condition of victimhood.* New Jersey: Princeton University Press.

Frederick, J. (2005). The myth of nepal-to-india sex trafficking: its creation, its maintenance, and its influence on anti-trafficking interventions. In K. Kempadoo, J. Sanghera, & B. Pattanaik (Eds.), *Trafficking and prostitution reconsidered: New perspectives on migration, sex work and human rights* (pp. 127–128). Boulder, Colorado: Paradigm Publishers.

Giddens, A. (1993). *The giddens reader.* Redwood City, California: Stanford University Press.

Gonzalez-Barrera, A. (2014). Record number of deportations in 2012. Pew Research Center. http://www.pewresearch.org/fact-tank/2014/01/24/record-number-of-deportations-in-2012/. Accessed 15 May 2015.

Goździak, E. M. (2008). On challenges, dilemmas, and opportunities in studying trafficked children. *The Anthropology Quarterly, 81*(4), 903–923.

Goździak, E. M. (2012). Challenges, dilemmas and opportunities in studying trafficked children in the United States. In Course Reader eBooks. Belmont: Wadsworth Cengage Learning.

Guevara, C. (2006). *Radical writings on guerrilla warfare, politics and revolution*. London: Filiquarian.

Gusterson, H. (1997). Studying up revisited. *PoLAR: Political and Legal Anthropology Review, 20* (1), 114–119.

Heissler, K. A. (2013). Rethinking "trafficking" in children's migratory processes: the role of social networks in child labour migration in Bangladesh. *Children's Geographies, 11*(1), 89–101.

Hess, J. M., & Shandy, D. (2008). Kids at the crossroads: Global childhood and the state. *Anthropological Quarterly, 81*(4), 765–776.

Hoffman, D. M. (2010). Migrant children in haiti: Domestic labor and the politics of representation. In M. O. Ensor & E. Goździak (Eds.), *Children and migration: At the crossroads of resiliency and vulnerability*. New York: Palgrave Macmillan.

Jensen, S., & Ronsbo, H. (2014). *Histories of victimhood*. Philadelphia: University of Pennsylvania Press.

Kapur, R. (2008). Migrant women and the legal politics of anti-trafficking interventions. In Cameron, S., & Edward Newman, E. (Eds.), *Trafficking in humans: Social, cultural and political dimensions*. Tokyo: United Nations University Press.

Kelly, J. B. (1997). The best interests of the child: A concept in search of meaning. *Family Court Review, 35*(4), 377–387.

Kempadoo, K. (Ed.). (2005). *Trafficking and prostitution reconsidered. New perspectives on migration, sex work and human rights*. Boulder: Paradigm Publishers.

Khalili, L. (2007). *Heroes and martyrs of palestine: The politics of national commemoration*. Cambridge: Cambridge University Press.

Kleinman, A., Veena, D., & Lock, M. (1997). *Social suffering*. Oakland: University of California Press.

Kopelman, L. M. (1997). The best-interests standard as threshold, ideal, and standard of reasonableness. *Journal of Medicine and Philosophy, 22*(3), 271–289.

La Fontaine, J. (1978). *Sex and age as principles of social differentiation*. London: Athlone Press.

MacGaffey, J. (2000). *Congo-paris: Transnational traders on the margins of the law*. Bloomington: Indiana University Press.

Mai, N. (2011). Tempering with the sex of "angels": Migrant male minors and young adults selling sex in the EU. *Journal of Ethnic and Migration Studies, 37*(8), 1237–1252.

McGough, L.S. (1995). Children V. Child custody. In W.T. Reich, (Ed.), *Encyclopedia of bioethics* (pp. 371–378). New York: Simon and Schuster MacMilan.

Meyers, D. T. (2011). Two victim paradigms and the problem of "impure" victims. *Humanity: An International Journal of Human Rights Humanitarianism and Development, 2*(2), 255–275.

Miko, F.T. (2004). *Trafficking in Women and Children: The U.S. and International Response*. Washington, DC: Congressional Research Service.

Nader, L. (1969). Up the anthropologist: Perspectives gained from "studying up". In D. Hymes (Ed.), *Reinventing anthropology* (pp. 284–311). New York: Random House.

Protocol to Prevent, Suppress and Punish Trafficking in Persons, Especially Women and Children, supplementing the United Nations Convention against Transnational Organized Crime. (2000). http://www.ohchr.org/EN/ProfessionalInterest/Pages/ProtocolTraffickingInPersons.aspx.

Pupovac, V. (2001). Therapeutic governance: Psychosocial intervention and trauma risk management. *Disasters, 25*, 358–372.

Rodham, H. (1973). Children under the law. *Harvard Educational Review, 43*(4), 487–514.

Ruddick, W. (1989). Questions parents should resist. In L. M. Kopelman & J. C. Moskop (Eds.), *Children and health care: Moral and social issues* (pp. 221–230). Dordrecht, Netherlands: Kluwewr Academic Publishers.

Sanghera, J. (2005). Globalization, labor migration, and human rights: unpacking the trafficking discourse. In K. Kempadoo, J. Sanghera, & B. Pattanaik (Eds.), *Trafficking and prostitution reconsidered* (pp. 3–24). Boulder, Colorado: Paradigm Publishers.

Stryker, R., & Gonzalez, R. (Eds.). (2014). *Up, down, and sideways. anthropologists trace the pathways of power.* Oxford: Berghahn Books.

Summerfield, D. (2000). Childhood, war, refugeedom and "trauma": Three core questions for mental health professionals. *Journal of Transcultural Psychiatry, 37*(3), 417–433.

Tsing, A. (2000). The global situation. *Cultural Anthropology, 15*(3), 327–360.

Veatch, R. M. (1981). *A theory of medical ethics.* New York: Basic.

Veatch, R. M. (1995). Abandoning informed consent. *The Hastings Center Report, 25*(2), 5–12.

Whitehead, A., & Hashim, I. (2005). *Children and migration: Background paper for DFID migration team.* Brighton: University of Sussex, Development Research Center on Migration, Globalization and Poverty.

Williams, P. (2008). Trafficking in women: The role of transnational organized crime. In S. Cameron & E. Newman (Eds.), *Trafficking in humans.* Tokyo, New York, and Paris: United Nations University Press.

Young, A. (1995). *The harmony of illusions: Inventing post-traumatic stress disorder.* Princeton: Princeton University Press.

Open Access This chapter is licensed under the terms of the Creative Commons Attribution-NonCommercial 2.5 International License (http://creativecommons.org/licenses/by-nc/2.5/), which permits any noncommercial use, sharing, adaptation, distribution and reproduction in any medium or format, as long as you give appropriate credit to the original author(s) and the source, provide a link to the Creative Commons license and indicate if changes were made.

The images or other third party material in this chapter are included in the book's Creative Commons license, unless indicated otherwise in a credit line to the material. If material is not included in the book's Creative Commons license and your intended use is not permitted by statutory regulation or exceeds the permitted use, you will need to obtain permission directly from the copyright holder.

Chapter 3
Child Refugees and National Boundaries

Marie Louise Seeberg

Refugee Children; Child Refugees: Four Situations and a Question

1938: Escaping from Hitler's Germany, seven-year-old Edith leaves her parents and her home as part of the Kindertransport,[1] *organized transportations of mainly Jewish children to the UK from Hitler's Reich, based on private guarantees that they will not be a financial burden. She is taken into a foster family with her older sister (Milton 2006).*

1939: Berthold, aged seven, travels with a group of children from Bratislava to Norway and is taken into a foster family. As Germany invades Norway in 1940, he is transferred to Norway's only Jewish orphanage. In 1942, all the orphanage children are safely conducted to Sweden, from where he returns to Norway in 1945 (Levin 2009; Rothlauf 2008).

2013: Mohammed, fourteen, arrives in the UK from Iran. Smuggled into the country in the fridge compartment of a lorry, he and eight other youngsters climb out of the lorry, walk along the road, and are discovered and arrested. Social workers take him into a residential centre for unaccompanied minors where he waits, wondering what will happen next (Gentleman 2013).

2013: After a series of rejections and appeals, the Jasmin versus Norway case is closed. Jasmin, seventeen, born in Germany to stateless Kurdish parents who have been denied asylum and the right to work, is finally granted residence in Norway

---

[1]Plural: Kindertransporte.

M.L. Seeberg (✉)
NOVA, Oslo and Akershus University College, Oslo, Norway
e-mail: marie.l.seeberg@nova.hioa.no

© The Author(s) 2016
M.L. Seeberg and E.M. Goździak (eds.), *Contested Childhoods:*
Growing up in Migrancy, IMISCOE Research Series,
DOI 10.1007/978-3-319-44610-3_3

with her mother and siblings on the grounds of her social and cultural integration (NOAS 2014).

In this chapter, I compare some criteria for refugee children's crossing of national boundaries at four different socio-temporal sites: the UK and Norway, in the late 1930s and the early 2010s. My comparison is based on a closer look into the cases of the four children introduced above, one from each of the four sites. Their situations and experiences serve to identify key criteria for the crossing of territorial, social, and symbolic boundaries into the two nation states at these different points in time.

In times of crisis, national refugee policies tend to be restrictive, yet the protection of children remains the most broadly recognized of all humanitarian concerns. The presence of refugee children, or child refugees, reveals an Achilles' heel of democratic states: the weaknesses of combined underlying premises of nationhood and of childhood. I argue that these premises connect in ways that provide a key to understanding both nationhood and childhood. As social spaces, nations and childhoods are defined and encompassed by context-specific boundaries. Studying how these boundaries are (re-)enacted in specific cases may help us understand the connections between nationhood and childhood.

Why are some children allowed to cross the boundaries into certain nation-states at particular times, and others denied access? Which of their multiple statuses—as a child, a refugee, or an asylum seeker—may give them access to different spaces within specific nation-states? How may child refugees be regarded as different from adult refugees, and how may such differences affect their rights and possibilities? Such questions bring to light the combined underlying premises of nationhood and of childhood, with changing notions of personhood at the core.

In this chapter, I do not aim to address all these questions, but will focus on comparing and analysing specific criteria for national boundary-crossing as they apply to four children. My concern here is with their entry into the territorial, social and symbolic spaces of UK and Norway. The concept of boundaries cuts across legal, social, or cultural criteria for admission. Although there are significant legal dimensions to the admission policies and processes of refugees, a comprehensive description of the relevant legal frameworks is beyond the scope of this chapter.

Here, my comparison of the UK and Norway in the late 1930s and in the early 2010s aims to throw light on the following question: How may similarities and differences in the criteria for refugee children's crossing of national boundaries throw light on changing and contested notions of childhood? I shall investigate this using the four examples introduced above—Edith, Berthold, Mohammed, and Jasmin.[2]

---

[2]Their names have not been altered, as all the cited material is taken from previously published sources.

Boundaries of Nations, Boundaries of Childhoods

Receiving states may provide refugees with basic protection—the right to legal entry and temporary or permanent settlement—or add social rights to education, work, healthcare and the vote, as well as symbolic admission into the national community. Such differentiation of access depends on the context, including international and national laws. The concept of *boundaries*, the focus of attention for Barth in his work on ethnicity (1969), is useful in studying differential access to social spaces. National boundaries are always, to some extent, porous (Papadopoulos et al. 2008). With Lamont and Molnar's (2002) typology as my point of departure, I distinguish between three main forms of national boundaries. *Territorial* boundaries are the physical borders of the nation-state, *social* boundaries delimit the rights, resources, and duties associated with citizenship as formal membership in the nation-state, and *symbolic* boundaries are the "conceptual distinctions made by social actors…that separate people into groups and generate feelings of similarity and group membership" (Lamont and Molnar 2002, 168). The sum of the three forms of boundaries constitutes the limit of the national community, and crossing a boundary implies a degree of inclusion into this community.

I regard exclusion and inclusion in terms of degrees rather than as absolute opposites. Territorial, social, and symbolic national boundaries have over the past century developed from near congruence towards increasing separateness (Ong 1999). In the 1930s, the sovereignty of nation-states depended on a harmonious relationship between territory (geography), bureaucracy (state), and people (national identity). The concepts of inclusion and exclusion from territory, bureaucracy, and nation were inherent in the citizen/immigrant divide, based on the existence of a physical border (Preuss 1995). The distinction between citizen and immigrant was particularly visible at the border. In the 2010s, European border policies require a revision of this classical border concept (Bigo et al. 2010). Boundaries have shifted: "the line differentiating members from non-members is relocated" (Zolberg and Long 1999, 9). The distinction between citizens and different categories of immigrants is now visible at Europe's outer borders, in practices physically taking place within each European state, and at visa and ticket points well beyond Europe. The criteria for gaining access to Norwegian or UK territory interact with the criteria for gaining access to welfare benefits, in different ways for different categories of people in what Fuglerud (2005) has called processes of "graded sovereignty." Such processes are mediated through policies and practices that in turn interact with media representations of "asylum seekers."

Refugee policies vary between the four sites, yet in all of them protection is granted only to a small minority of those potentially in need of it. Kjeldstadli (2003a) finds the explanation for this similarity in an international game logic where each state competitively reduces its "offers" to refugees in order to prevent as many as possible from seeking asylum. This logic thrives on the ambiguity of the international political situations of the two periods where recognizing a "real refugee" may be complicated. Restrictive policies are strengthened through regulating the rights to social goods. Such strategies, with clear consequences for the life chances of refugee children, have played out quite differently at our four sites.

Along with changes in national boundaries, the boundaries of childhood have also changed considerably since the 1930s. A "belief in the natural innocence of childhood as a world apart" was constitutive of Norwegian nationhood until the 1990s (Gullestad 1997, 33). In a general, nostalgic view, the boundaries of an idealized, paradisiacal childhood have gradually been pushed back (James et al. 1998, 242). This corresponds to a paradigmatic turn towards children's rights and agency, where "Norway tends to be in the forefront when it comes to the child as an actor with participation rights" (Vitus and Liden 2010, 67). In both periods in the UK, childhood remains more implicitly and ambiguously interrelated with the nation, not least because the composite national identity of the UK and the "massive stratification of contemporary Britain" makes it impossible to "write sensibly about an English childhood" (James 2002, 149). The main contemporary difference is that of Norwegian childhoods as symbolically, politically, and individually central to adult society, whereas in the UK, children and childhoods emerge as relatively marginal and subjected to rigid "adult power" (James 2002). As we shall see, this is also evident in our selected cases.

The Four Selected Cases

The four cases introduced initially form the empirical basis for this chapter. The cases are taken from the literature and from Internet sites, published by associations of or for refugee children and by newspapers, featuring the stories of individual child refugees. These are only four of many thousands of cases, and I cannot claim that they are representative in any statistical sense of the word. However, I would hold that each case is in its own way typical for its time and place, and that the four cases, separately and together, form a sound basis for an initial analysis within the theoretical framework of territorial, social, and symbolic boundaries as described above. The critical reader may also rightly point out that I have selected cases that are particularly suited to this kind of analysis.

The four sites have also been purposely selected. Norway and the UK share a close historical affinity as countries of refuge on the north-west geographical margins of Europe, yet there are considerable differences in their ideas and practices of childhood and nation. The 1930s and 2010s are both periods of international crises and of complicated and ambiguous "refugee producing" situations, in contrast to the block alliances of World War II and the Cold War. Ideas and practices of childhood and nation have undergone considerable changes from the first period to the second, making it possible to investigate both changes and continuity.

During my searches for individual accounts, I found hundreds of books and internet pages presenting interviews, biographies, and autobiographies, especially from two of the four sites: the UK in the 1930s and Norway in the 2010s. The *Kindertransporte* were for decades ignored or surrounded by silence. They came to attention during the 1980s, along with many other aspects of the Holocaust (Seeberg et al. 2013); writings and individual testimonies of this spectacular rescue operation have since proliferated. In Norway, similar attention has not been accorded to the few Jewish children who escaped to Norway in the same period. The contrast is especially interesting when juxtaposed with the contrast between the considerable public attention given to individual children denied asylum in present day Norway and the public silence surrounding individual children in the asylum process in the UK. These differences in public attention reflect the differences in how refugee children are perceived and received at the four sites. Methodologically, this means that the material available to me has been much more limited in the cases of the UK in the 2010s and Norway in the 1930s than in the UK of the 1930s and the Norway of the 2010s.

The 1930s: Edith and Berthold

In the 1930s, the legal concept of the refugee was linked to the newly founded League of Nations and its first High Commissioner of Refugees, the Norwegian Fridtjof Nansen, who was appointed in 1921. On Nansen's death in 1930, the Nansen International Office for Refugees continued its work, increasingly for Jews and other refugees from Nazi Germany. In Europe, the 1920s' dominant fear of Communism and Stalin was gradually overshadowed in the decade that followed by the increasing alarm caused by Hitler's national socialism and expansionist ambitions, leading to shifting and ambiguous alliances. British and Norwegian authorities joined other European governments and referred to each other's restrictive immigration policies in legitimizing their own. Although a refugee law was in place —*The Convention Concerning the Status of Refugees Coming from Germany* of 10 February 1938—neither Norwegian nor British authorities recognized Jews as refugees on the grounds of racial persecution (London 2000; Kjeldstadli 2003b). Governments at the time deemed a "strict policy" necessary to "prevent a mass influx" of refugees and rejected most applications for entry.

When Edith arrived in the UK, she was one of nearly 10,000 Jewish children whose lives were saved in spite of this strict policy, through the *Kindertransporte*. She travelled by train with her older sister Ruth as part of a group of children, and remembers the border control between Germany and the Netherlands. In her autobiography, she describes the journey:

[T]he officer in uniform with a swastika armband who collected our papers at the border looked upon me with what I took to be parental concern as he handed back my passport, which under my name—augmented by the Jewish "Sara" mandated by the Third Reich— had been stamped STATELESS...I know that to cross to England we boarded the boat at Rotterdam... But the crossing itself is a blank. Probably we were all asleep. The next day comes to mind as the revelation of a huge London station with massive steel arches overhead. Liverpool Street Station (Milton 2006).

Their travel documents were in order. The double visa requirements—exit visa to leave Germany and entry visa to enter the UK—had been taken care of before the children were put on the train, by parents, Jewish committees and other volunteers. Edith had no idea who facilitated her passage to the UK and where her own journey fits into the larger initiative:

[I]t took me more than forty years to understand that our transposition to England ... was a fragment of a larger and extraordinary history. The Kindertransport ... has been the subject of a fair amount of recent literature and of several films. It could, in fact, be counted as a sort of miracle, and I am still amazed at my own bland passivity and ignorance about my escape (Milton 2006).

The criteria that must be fulfilled for this miracle to happen were laid down by the UK government. In the following citations, I have used bold font in order to highlight the criteria for my subsequent analysis:

In response to the events of November 9 and 10 [Kristallnacht], the British Jewish Refugee Committee appealed to members of Parliament [to rescue Jewish children] and a debate was held in the House of Commons. The already existing refuge aid committees in Britain switched into high gear, changing focus from emigration to rescue. The British government had just refused to allow 10,000 Jewish children to enter Palestine, but the atrocities in Germany and Austria, the untiring persistence of the refuge advocates, and philosemitic sympathy in some high places—in the words of British Foreign Minister Samuel Hoare "Here is a chance of taking the young generation of a great people, here is a chance of mitigating to some extent the terrible suffering of their parents and their friends"—swayed the government to permit **an unspecified number of children under the age of 17 to enter the United Kingdom**. It was agreed to admit the children on **temporary travel documents**, with the **idea that they would re-join their parents when the crisis was over. A fifty Pound Sterling bond had to be posted for each child "to assure their ultimate resettlement."** The children were to travel in **sealed trains**. The first transport left on December 1, 1938 ... the last left on September 1, 1939—just two days before Great Britain's entry into the war ... By that time, approximately 10,000 children had made the trip (The Kindertransport Association 2015).

The phrase "non-Aryan children," rather than "Jewish children," was used in the Parliament discussions (Norton 2010) and, although most of them were Jewish, some non-Jewish children are also said to have been rescued (cf. Gopfert and Hammel 2004). The children had to be under the age of 17. Many were younger. The older children had to look after the younger ones:

It was understood at the time that when the "crisis was over," **the children would return to their families. Parents or guardians could not accompany the children**. The few infants included in the programme were **tended by other children on their transport. A £50 Sterling bond** had to be posted for each child, "to assure their ultimate resettlement" (United States Holocaust Memorial Museum 2015).

3 Child Refugees and National Boundaries

The requirement to post a bond of £50 for each child meant that no child would depend on the British government for subsistence. In practice this requirement limited the number of rescued children to the ones for whom funding could be provided. It also transferred all responsibility for the refugee children to the private sector: individual British citizens as well as non-governmental organizations.

Kindertransport was unique in that Jews, Quakers, and Christians of many denominations worked together to rescue primarily Jewish children (The Kindertransport Association 2015).

Private citizens or organizations had to guarantee to pay for each child's care, education, and eventual emigration from Britain. **In return for this guarantee, the British government agreed to allow unaccompanied refugee children to enter the country** on temporary travel visas (United States Holocaust Memorial Museum 2015).

The British government's contribution was limited to allowing the children to cross the territorial boundaries. Thus, their lives were saved. The crossing of social and symbolic boundaries was left to the children and civil society. Children were taken into Jewish or non-Jewish foster homes, as fostering was considered the best solution. However, there were not enough foster homes, therefore some children were put up in hostels or were sent to the countryside to work on farms. The scheme was organized as an educational one, and schooling was provided. It is unclear what kinds of schools the children attended and who paid for their education. More research is also needed to uncover the services to which the children had, or did not have, access. In terms of symbolic boundaries, the picture is much clearer. Edith describes it well:

(…) my life begins when I am seven going on eight—when I have just set foot in England. It is 1939 (…) It is the fact that I worry so much—the fact that unlike all the others I am afraid—that makes me an enemy alien. This is what worries me most of all—I am an enemy alien, and I am proving that I am an enemy alien by being such a coward about bombs and other things falling from the sky. I would like desperately to disguise myself as a little English girl, but I know that I would convince no one, since the very act of trying to disguise myself proves I am not English. (…) I suspect it is as a first quite unconscious step in my attempt to be less foreign that I am setting about forgetting all my German (Milton 2006).

Separated from parents and homelands and desperately contesting the label of "German enemies," the children rapidly shed their Germanness in favour of English identities. They needed to belong, and there was only one way to achieve this: to become English. Language was the primary marker of national identity. At the same time, Edith describes how her Anglican Church foster family expected and even encouraged her to retain a Jewish identity, incorporating her into a pre-existing British Jewish category.

In Norway, no similar large-scale operations took place. However, a rescue on a very much smaller scale was organized in cooperation between individual Norwegian citizens and non-governmental organizations. In an article about the subsequent rescue of these children to Sweden as Norway came under German occupation, Irene Levin writes:

In spite of the restrictive refugee policy, the Norwegian government accepted around 500 Jews from Germany, Austria and Czechoslovakia during the years immediately preceding the war. Among these were the 21 children from Vienna—aged seven to nine years (...). After some time, two boys from Czechoslovakia arrived. One of them was Berthold Grünfeld (Levin 2009, my translation).

The conditions for accepting the Jewish children were stricter in Norway than in the UK. The children had to be no older than 12 years and their state of health had to be checked and found acceptable by a doctor recognized by the Norwegian government. It was also expected that the children's parents were on their way to migrate to a third country where reunification would happen. The organization *Nansenhjelpen* (the Nansen relief), founded by Fridtjof Nansen's son to provide safe haven and assistance for Jewish refugees in Norway, was to be responsible for all expenses. Given these conditions, the immigration was limited to a maximum of sixty children, and it was specified that any adoptions would not lead to amendments of the quota (Hamkoll 2010, 45–46). There was no expectation these foreign, Jewish children would stay in Norway and "become Norwegians," and with the German occupation, they lost any basis for doing so.

The 2010s: Mohammed and Jasmin

Compared to the images of hardship and poverty in the 1930s in Europe and its colonies, the early 2010s evoke images of an unequally distributed yet previously unimaginable abundance. There has been a global tendency away from mainly inter-state conflicts to an upsurge of civil wars and conflicts that to a lesser extent follow territorial boundaries (Kaldor 2013). Norway was at the pinnacle of wealth, while the UK, still affluent, was struggling in the aftermath of the recent economic crisis. The rest of Europe was marked by economic crisis in different ways and to different degrees. Outside Europe, economic instability was the order of the day in many countries, often linked to a lack of democracy and to war and conflict within and across national borders, causing people to flee from many different countries and for many different reasons.

In the UK, territorial boundaries were not formally open to child refugees. Since 2004, a UK refugee quota scheme (the Gateway Programme) annually provided assistance to 750 refugees designated as especially vulnerable by the United Nations High Commissioner for Refugees (Platts-Fowler and Robinson 2011). However, this scheme had no particular focus on children and was extremely small compared to the numbers of de facto refugees and asylum seekers arriving in the UK. The majority of child refugees were smuggled into the UK hidden in lorries crossing the Channel from France. Journalist Amelia Gentleman stayed for two days in a hostel for unaccompanied child asylum seekers near Dover, and learned as much as she could from them and the staff. She reported:

3 Child Refugees and National Boundaries 51

An Iranian boy, Mohammed—who, like everyone interviewed here, asked that his real name should not be printed, and who says he is 14—describes how his uncle paid for him to be taken from Iran after his brother was arrested. He doesn't know how much his uncle paid, nor precisely what route he took, although the interpreter says it usually goes through Turkey and Greece, taking more than three months, with 10-day breaks from time to time, staying in houses along the way and surviving mainly on biscuits. (...) At Calais, Mohammed was grouped with about eight other young people and hidden in a lorry, late at night. "The traffickers used ladders to get us in through the roof; the driver didn't know we were in there." (...) When the lorry came to a stop somewhere outside Dover, they climbed back out of a vent in the roof and began walking along the road until they were spotted and arrested (Gentleman 2013).

Mohammed had been helped or escorted from Iran to Calais by paid helpers and had travelled for months. Having crossed the territorial boundaries into the UK, the small group of child refugees of which he was part was taken into social care:

The younger boys, and girls of all ages, are immediately found foster carers. Almost none of the children have documents, so determining their age is a complex process; but those boys who seem to be a bit older (15 or above) are sent to (...) a hostel for unaccompanied asylum seekers.

Young children were taken into foster homes, as Edith had been more than 70 years earlier—a strong form of symbolic as well as social inclusion. However, those who seemed "a bit older" than fifteen were placed, together, in a hostel staffed with social workers. Although not immediately allowed across symbolic boundaries, the young asylum seekers were thus given access to some social goods:

This is a peculiar refuge: sparsely furnished bedrooms, along dimly lit corridors painted in faded 1970s institutional colours. The children remain here until their age is confirmed, their health checked, their asylum requests investigated and their educational needs assessed. They are given a few sessions about British life and culture—with a heavy focus on drugs and sexually transmitted diseases—but much of the time they are left to their own devices, allowed to wander into the nearby town or sit in the centre's shabby common room, congregating into huddles of boys with shared languages. (...) the county is under pressure to improve the care they are given. Support workers are on hand from 8 am to 10 pm, trying to help them adjust to their new environment. "They have been on the road for such a long time, getting into all sorts of difficulties with people, that there is a sense of relief at having a roof over their heads, a place that is warm and safe," the Kent official says. "But they quickly move on to the next worry: what is going to happen to me now? (...) A doctor at the practice that looks after the children's home residents says (...) Many are underweight from surviving on one meal a day. "I see young men with terribly painful injuries from their journey," the doctor says. "Many of these young people haven't had any medical care throughout their life" (Gentleman 2013).

This description indicates what the children had access to: beds and meals, basic health services and rudimentary education—it was something, but much less than a foster child would get. Social workers also did most of the age assessment in order to determine whether the asylum seeker was really a child or just pretending to be one:

Social workers consider how they interact with their peers, whether they are reserved or shy, whether they have shaved hundreds of times before or if they have never used a razor. They look at whether children are still growing physically during the time they are at the centre. Dental x-rays can be used. (...) the parliamentary report into the care of migrant children expresses concern that "funding pressures could be incentivising local authorities to assess children either as adults, or as older than would otherwise be the case," because of the huge costs involved—last year, in Kent alone, £14m was spent caring for these children (…)

Children who arrived without their parents were the responsibility of local authorities and, accordingly, there was a considerable body of literature on "unaccompanied minors" and on how to do social work with child asylum seekers in the UK (Kohli 2006; Wade 2011). Much less was known about the children in asylum seeking families in the UK: known as "dependants," they had no separate asylum cases, and constituted no separate category in Home Office statistics.

In Norway, by contrast, children in asylum-seeking families attracted extensive popular support and were symbolically significant as litmus tests of "Norwegian values." A strong national identity built on the ideal and practice of childhood as local belonging (Gullestad 1997) interacted with the central role of children's rights in law and in popular perception and supported the creation of strong local support for many asylum-seeking children (Vitus and Liden 2010).

My fourth case is Jasmin. In 2013, when I first read about her, she was seventeen years old. Born in Germany in 1996, she had come to Norway with her family in 2002. Her parents had previously lived in Turkey, as refugees from Lebanon. The family was stateless. For a decade, Norwegian authorities tried to send the family to Turkey, while Turkish authorities refused to receive them. Crossing the internal Schengen borders from Germany to Norway in the early 2000s had not been particularly difficult. It turned out to be much more difficult to be allowed to stay, and to gain access to the rights that make it possible to lead a normal life: the crossing of social and symbolic boundaries. Jasmin wrote:

The fact that my parents are here now, is not their own fault. My parents were children when they escaped the war in Lebanon. What do you think they should have done? Stayed? Remained there, and died, instead of fleeing? I don't know, but their parents made the decision for them. Later they married and continued onwards with us children. What do you want? That my siblings and I do the same: continue to go from one country to the next?[3]

In the context of Norway in the early 2010s, very little was said about the territorial boundary-crossings into Norway. In a research report, Brekke and Aarset (2009) described a number of journey patterns. All means of transportation were used, which also means different points of entry. A main common denominator here, as case of the UK in the 2010s, was the prominent role of "people smugglers." Norway, too, had a quota of refugees agreed annually with the UNHCR; official government representatives facilitated their admission to Norway. However, as in the UK, quota refugees constituted a very small minority of de facto refugees and there was no special quota for child refugees. In Norway, the mainstream media focused on the "removal" of often quite young children from Norway, usually with their parents and siblings.

---

[3]This and subsequent Jasmin quotations NOAS 2014, my translation.

3 Child Refugees and National Boundaries   53

All children up to the age of sixteen have the right to schooling in Norway, and several reports show that asylum-seeking children were in fact enrolled in schools in this recent period, although in some cases in lower-quality courses than other children (Lidén et al. 2011; Valenta 2008). Schools provide a crucial link between the social and the symbolic, and local communities' actions against the deportation of specific children was to a large extent grounded in the children's belonging to the local community through its school. Jasmin described her situation like this:

> I have many friends. Some of them were allowed to stay in Norway and got the residence permit, and those were moments of great happiness. At the same time, there has been much sorrow because many of my friends were sent back to their home countries.

The friends Jasmin referred to here were friends at the reception centre for asylum seekers, where the family had lived for ten years. Such friendships with other young people living at reception centres may analytically be regarded as inclusion into a temporary community of outsiders. Jasmin also had other, more stable social arenas:

> Out of school, we have activities and at school we are very active. (…) My life has limited freedom. One day I was told that I could not continue to secondary school because I did not have a residence permit. My friends all supported me and said I would be ok. Luckily, the headmaster accepted asylum seekers after all.

These friends were school friends, including young people who were not living in the liminal state of waiting for asylum, but who had more predictable life trajectories in their local communities in Norway. In spite of secondary education not being a right for rejected asylum seeking children, Jasmin was accepted into secondary school. Yet her troubles were not over:

> Over the summer, all my friends have summer jobs because they want to earn some money for themselves. I also wanted to get a job. I applied and applied and in the end I did succeed in finding a job. But unfortunately I was then told that I could not get a work permit because I am an asylum seeker. All I wanted with that job was to earn a little money of my own, like everybody else. (…) I would like to ask if you know what it is like to be at the receiving end of all those "no's". No to work, no to school, no to going abroad on holiday, no to freedom and many no's that I cannot count. It is as if I were tied up with a rope and cannot go on.

In 2013, the whole family was granted residence in Norway.

Comparing the Four Cases

Comparing the three sets of criteria across the four cases may appear to be a daunting task, and a detailed comparison would be beyond the scope of this chapter. However, Table 3.1 summarizes a more general comparison of the three sets of criteria in our four cases.

In the UK in the 1930s, selected children were accepted as refugees when adults were not. Only to a small extent were the children allowed to access social

54   M.L. Seeberg

resources and thereby cross the social boundaries of the nation state. Symbolic boundaries were open to them on the one and absolute condition that they change their national identity, of which language was the main marker. This was the chance to simultaneously and literally "take the young generation of a great people" as the Foreign Minister had argued, by transforming them from German to English and, again quoting the Foreign Minister "to some extent mitigate the sufferings of the adults" by encouraging them to thrive as Jews, but now as *British* Jews.

Jews had been allowed into Norway since a hotly debated constitutional amendment in 1851, and the Jewish community numbered about 2000 individuals at the beginning of the Second World War. Refugee policies were very strict, largely due to a concern with "creating a Jewish problem" in Norway (Mendelsohn 1987). As the historian Kjeldstadli puts it: "For political refugees to enter and stay was possible with some exceptions, while for Jews, entry was very nearly impossible with some exceptions" (2003b, 467, my translation). In the late 1930s, hardly any Jewish children were allowed to cross the territorial boundaries into Norway, let alone the social or symbolic boundaries. This is one of many indications that Jewishness and Norwegianness were widely regarded as irreconcilable identities, and that children were regarded as independent carriers of a Jewish identity.

Table 3.1 A summarized comparison

	UK 1930s	Norway 1930s	UK 2010s	Norway 2010s
Territorial	10,000 children admitted Under 17 £50 bond as economic guarantee	60 children admitted Under 12, healthy, prospect of reunification with parents in third country, economic guarantee	750 quota refugees, some of which were children. Otherwise: Illegal. No reliable statistics—children registered as dependents "Removal" possible at 18 (end of childhood)	A small number of quota refugees, some of which were children. Otherwise: Illegal. Detailed statistics on children "Removal" possible at any time
Social	No government expenses. CSOs and private people covered expenses	No government expenses. CSO Nansenhjelpen responsible	Access to social care—place to stay, food, basic healthcare. Full legal rights to education 5–16 years, unclear whether this reflects practice	Access to social care—place to stay, food, basic healthcare, school. First year of school often separate and not up to standard. Children more rights than adults
Symbolic	Full assimilation expected	Remigration expected	Return expected at end of childhood	Children assimilated, parents rejected

In the early 2010s in the UK, children were hardly visible as refugees in the public domain. If they arrived with their parents, their social and symbolic inclusion as well as their continued territorial inclusion depended on that of their parents. Children who arrived alone were given access to social care and had the right to schooling, but were likely to lose the right to these and the right to stay six months before their childhood was legally over. This was mainly an issue for children who had been granted a limited leave to remain because they had been found not to be in need of international protection, but could not be returned in the absence of adequate reception arrangements in the countries of origin. Until 2012, children were granted leave for three years or until they turned 17.5 years old; after this the leave was limited to "a period of 30 months or until the child turned 17.5 years old, whichever was shorter" (CCLC 2013). The younger they were, the more they were allowed across the symbolic boundaries. Being recognized as a child, then, did give considerable privileges, albeit temporarily.

In the early 2010s in Norway, child refugees found themselves in a highly ambiguous position. As children, they were symbolically included and principally regarded as Norwegians. Socially, they had full rights to schooling and health services and more rights to benefits than did adult refugees. As asylum seekers, however, they might still face removal from Norwegian territory at any time if their individual cases for asylum were rejected. The stark contrast between the support and warmth surrounding them in the local community, especially in school, and the brutality of being picked up by the police—be it in the same school or at home in the small hours of the morning—has been recounted by many former asylum-seeking children and their advocates.

Across the four sites, whereas it is possible to legitimize rejecting adult refugees by framing them as a political or economic burden or as a security problem, the moral and political costs of rejecting child refugees are higher. In the early 2010s, Norwegian media played an important role in mobilizing popular protests against the deportation of child refugees. In the UK, too, as we have seen, age assessment is crucial in deciding the territorial, social and symbolic rights of refugees, giving privileges to children. The exclusive child rescue operations from the Third Reich show that in the 1930s, too, children triggered more sympathetic responses than adults did.

There may be different normative and legal reasons behind the sharp distinction between child and adult refugees at the four sites. One dimension of difference is agency versus victimization. The definition and rights of children, codified in the UN Convention on the Rights of the Child (United Nations 1989), are well incorporated into Norwegian law since 2003; this Convention was signed by the UK but not incorporated into British law. An early predecessor to the Convention on the Rights of the Child was ratified by the League of Nations in 1924. The emphasis then, in the UK and in Norway, was on refugee children as vulnerable and passive victims rather than as agents with individual rights (Eide 2005; Myers 2009). Recent research on refugee children focuses chiefly on their experiences and rights as individual agents rather than on power structures (Finch 2005; Parr 2005).

Paradoxically, however, in the UK of the 2010s, children who express "excessive" agency may be considered not to be children at all (Crawley 2010).

Contesting the Boundaries of Childhood and Nationhood

By their very existence, child refugees contest, try out, bend and change the boundaries of childhoods as well as of nations. How, then, may the similarities and differences we have seen in the criteria for refugee children's crossing of national boundaries throw light on changing and contested notions of childhood?

In the 1930s' UK, an image of children emerges from the *Kindertransport* case as primarily innocent, incomplete human beings in need of adult protection; they were "becoming" rather than "being," and the refugee children were, in terms of national identity, blank slates with the potential of becoming British. In Norway in the 2010s, the corresponding idea of refugee children as blank slates with the potential of becoming Norwegian is also prominent. However, there is also a strong component of children "being" what they are in their own right, and a very concrete emphasis on their agency and individual rights as children. In contrast, the UK in the 2010s and Norway in the 1930s emerge as sites where children were both subordinate to adults and received less adult, public attention. At these sites, rejection was more likely to pass unnoticed, and the attempted boundary-crossings also less likely to be successful.

While the UK's territorial boundaries in the early 2010s arguably remained more porous than Norway's, letting more refugees or asylum seekers in, refugees and especially refugee children appeared to have greater access to social benefits in Norway than in the UK once they managed to cross the physical border. Children in the UK, unless they arrived alone, were registered as "dependants" and did not feature as individuals in statistics. This supports observations of UK perceptions of children as subordinate and "incomplete." In Norway, individual children were especially targeted for public, local support, emerging as vulnerable and somehow more important and valuable than adult refugees, reflecting the importance of childhood in Norwegian society and nation building.

In contrast to the European Jewish refugees during the 1930s, refugees who arrived in Norway and the UK in the early 2010s came from many parts of the world and a majority, though far from all, came from predominantly Muslim countries. Anti-Jewish, anti-Muslim and colonialist-racist attitudes thus, in different ways, form parts of the background for boundary-upholding criteria of national communities at all four sites. Jews were a minority in all their nation states of residence in the 1930s and this is one of several significant differences between their situation and that of Muslims in the 2010s. However, racist-fuelled tensions between transnationally and religiously constituted groups and national sedentary populations are present in both cases (Engebrigtsen 2011). Although none of my examples involve refugees from the war in Syria, as they pre-date the so called "migration crisis" of 2015, the analytical framework is no less applicable to these more recent developments, where concepts, policies, and practices of borders and boundaries are increasingly and acutely relevant.

How inclusion and exclusion processes play out, what the legal criteria and implications may be, how the presence of refugee children may contribute to boundary shifting, and how boundary-crossing and possible boundary-shifting are represented in public debate are questions that need to be researched in more detail. The same applies to investigating how boundary-crossing criteria at all four sites draw on civic and ethnic symbolic resources, enabling us to identify and analyze interlinks between humanitarian and immigration issues and arguments. Finally, the exploration of such questions may bring about new insights into the changing boundaries of childhood and nationhood, the interconnectedness of nationhood and childhood, and the shifting notions of personhood that form their combined premises.

References

Barth, F. (1969). *Ethnic Groups and Boundaries*. Oslo: Universitetsforlaget.

Bigo, D., Guild, E., & Walker, R. B. J. (2010). The changing landscape of European liberty and security. In D. Bigo, S. Carrera, E. Guild, & R. B. J. Walker (Eds.), *Europe's 21st century challenge—delivering liberty*. Surrey: Ashgate Publishing.

Brekke, J. P., & Aarset, M. F. (2009). *Why Norway? Understanding asylum destinations* (Vol. 2009(12), Rapport). Oslo: Institutt for samfunnsforskning.

CCLC. (2013). *Migrant children's project factsheet*. Coram's Children's Legal Centre, April 2013.

Crawley, H. (2010). "No one gives you a chance to say what you are thinking": Finding space for children's agency in the UK asylum system. *Area, 42*(2), 162–169.

Eide, K. (2005). *Tvetydige barn: om barnemigranter i et historisk komparativt perspektiv* [Ambiguous children: On child migrants in a historically comparative perspective] (PhD dissertation, University of Bergen).

Engebrigtsen, A. I. (2011). Ali's disappearance: The tension of moving and dwelling in the Norwegian welfare society. *Journal of Ethnic and Migration Studies, 37*(2), 297–313.

Finch, N. (2005). Seeking asylum alone. In H. E. Andersson, H. Ascher, U. Björnberg, M. Eastmond, & L. Mellander (Eds.), *The asylum-seeking child in Europe*. Göteborg: Centre for European Research at Göteborg University.

Fuglerud, Ø. (2005). Inside out: The reorganization of national identity in Norway. In T. B. Hansen & F. Stepputat (Eds.), *Sovereign bodies: Citizens, migrants, and states in the postcolonial world*. Princeton, NJ: Princeton University Press.

Gentleman, A. (2013). Asylum seekers: Nowhere boys. *The Guardian,* 22 June. http://www.theguardian.com/uk/2013/jun/22/asylum-seekers-nowhere-boys.

Gopfert, R., & Hammel, A. (2004). Kindertransport: History and memory. *Shofar: An Interdisciplinary Journal of Jewish Studies, 23*(1), 21–27.

Gullestad, M. (1997). A passion for boundaries—Reflections on connections between the everyday lives of children and discourses on the nation in contemporary Norway. *Childhood—a Global Journal of Child Research 4*(1), 19–42.

Hamkoll, K. M. (2010). *Den uheldigste form for immigrasjon: jødiske barneflyktninger som kom til Norge i 1938–1939* [The most unfortunate form of immigration: Jewish child refugees who came to Norway 1938–1939] (Master thesis, History. Oslo: University of Oslo).

James, A. (2002). A cultural politics of childhood identities. In N. Rapport (Ed.), *British subjects: An anthropology of Britain*. Oxford: Berg.

James, A., Prout, A., & Jenks, C. (1998). *Theorizing childhood*. Cambridge: Polity Press.

Kaldor, M. (2013). *New and old wars: Organized violence in a global era*. New York: Wiley.

Kjeldstadli, K. (2003a). *Ingenting lært av 30-tallet* [Nothing learned from the 1930s]? *Aftenposten*, 26 June. Retrieved February 3, 2016, from http://www.aftenposten.no/meninger/kronikker/Ingenting-lart-av-30-tallet-6470824.html.

Kjeldstadli, K. (2003b). *Norsk innvandringshistorie* [Norwegian immigration history]. Oslo: Pax.

Kohli, R. (2006). *Social work with unaccompanied asylum-seeking children*. London: Palgrave Macmillan.

Lamont, M., & Molnar, V. (2002). The study of boundaries in the social sciences. *Annual Review of Sociology, 28*(1), 167–195.

Levin, I. (2009). *Det jødiske barnehjemmet og Nic Waal* [The Jewish orphanage and Nic Waal]. *Tidsskrift for norsk psykologforening 46*, 76–80.

Lidén, H., Seeberg, M. L., & Engebrigtsen, A. (2011). *Medfølgende barn i asylmottak— livssituasjon, mestring, tiltak* [Accompanied children in asylum seeker reception centres]. ISF-rapport 1:2011. Oslo: Institutt for samfunnsforskning.

London, L. (2000). Whitehall and the refugees: The 1930s and the 1990s. *Patterns of Prejudice, 34*(3), 17–26.

Mendelsohn, O. (1987). *Jødenes historie i Norge gjennom 300 år: B. 1 1660–1940* [The history of the Jews in Norway through 300 years: Vol 1 1660–1940]. Oslo, Universitetsforlaget.

Milton, E. (2006). *The tiger in the attic: Memories of the Kindertransport and growing up English*. Chicago: University of Chicago Press.

Myers, K. (2009). The ambiguities of aid and agency: Representing refugee children in England, 1937–8. *Cultural and Social History, 6*(1), 29–46.

NOAS. (2014). Lengst lengeværende har fått opphold [The longest long staying now granted residency]. *Norsk Organizasjon for Asylsøkere*. Retrieved February 3, 2016, from http://www.noas.no/lengst-lengevaerende-har-fatt-opphold/.

Norton, J. A. (2010). The Kindertransport: History and memory (Thesis, Sacramento: California State University).

Ong, A. (1999). *Flexible citizenship: The cultural logics of transnationality*. Durham, NC and London: Duke University Press.

Papadopoulos, D., Stephenson, N., & Tsianos, V. (2008). *Escape routes: Control and subversion in the twenty-first century*. London: Pluto Press.

Parr, A. (2005). The deterritorializing language of child detainees—Self-harm or embodied graffiti? *Childhood—a Global Journal of Child Research, 12*(3), 281–299.

Platts-Fowler, D., & Robinson, D. (2011). *An evaluation of the gateway programme*. London: Home Office.

Preuss, U. K. (1995). Problems of a concept of European citizenship. *European Law Journal, 1*(3), 267–281.

Rothlauf, G. (2008). *Die jüdische Präsenz in der Kultur Norwegens nach 1945*. Universität Wien.

Seeberg, M. L., Levin, I., & Lenz, C. (Eds.). (2013). *The Holocaust as active memory: The past in the present*. Farnham: Ashgate Academic.

The Kindertransport Association. (2015). Rising to the moment. *Kindertransport History*. Retrieved February 20, 2015, from http://www.kindertransport.org/history03_rising.htm.

United Nations. (1989). *Convention on the rights of the child*. New York: United Nations.

United States Holocaust Memorial Museum (2015). Kindertransport 1938–1940. *Holocaust Encyclopedia*. Retrieved November 25, 2015 from, https://www.ushmm.org/wlc/en/article.php?ModuleId=10005260.

Valenta, M. (2008). *Asylsøkerbarns rett til skole: kartlegging av skoletilbudet til asylsøkerbarn* [Asylum seeking children's right to school: A mapping of education provided to asylum seeking children]. Trondheim: NTNU samfunnsforskning.

Vitus, K., & Liden, H. (2010). The status of the asylum-seeking child in Norway and Denmark: Comparing discourses, politics and practices. *Journal of Refugee Studies, 23*(1), 62–81.

Wade, J. (2011). Preparation and transition planning for unaccompanied asylum-seeking and refugee young people: A review of evidence in England. *Children and Youth Services Review, 33*(12), 2424–2430.

Zolberg, A. R., & Long, W. L. (1999). Why Islam is like Spanish: Cultural incorporation in Europe and the United States. *Politics & Society, 27*(1), 5–38.

Open Access This chapter is licensed under the terms of the Creative Commons Attribution-NonCommercial 2.5 International License (http://creativecommons.org/licenses/by-nc/2.5/), which permits any noncommercial use, sharing, adaptation, distribution and reproduction in any medium or format, as long as you give appropriate credit to the original author(s) and the source, provide a link to the Creative Commons license and indicate if changes were made.

The images or other third party material in this chapter are included in the book's Creative Commons license, unless indicated otherwise in a credit line to the material. If material is not included in the book's Creative Commons license and your intended use is not permitted by statutory regulation or exceeds the permitted use, you will need to obtain permission directly from the copyright holder.

Chapter 4
South Sudanese Diaspora Children: Contested Notions of Childhood, Uprootedness, and Belonging Among Young Refugees in the U.S.

Marisa O. Ensor

South Sudanese Diaspora Children

Chuol[1] turned 18 in June 2011, just 1 month before the independence of South Sudan, his native country, on 9th July. His 18th birthday signified Chuol's legal transition into adulthood in the United States where he now lives. On the other hand, the occasion would have been barely marked, if at all, in the small rural community where he was born, and where the categories "child," "youth," and "adult" are defined along cultural rather than chronological parameters.[2] "It is rough out there, but not like back in Africa, says my Mom." Chuol is responding to my query about life in Omaha, Nebraska, where I have been working with South Sudanese youngsters like him since 2009. Now in his early twenties, Chuol left war-torn South Sudan as an infant in 1992 when government soldiers from the north attacked their village. With Chuol on her back, his mother fled on foot to a crowded refugee camp in neighbouring Ethiopia. They arrived in the U.S. 3 years later. Having moved out of Africa when he was too young to remember it, Chuol's experiences growing up in the U.S. are illustrative of the complex processes of

---

[1]The names of all study participants have been changed to ensure their anonymity.

[2]Many people in South Sudan, especially in the rural areas, do not mark their chronological age. Asylum applications often list January 1st as the applicant's birthday. This is a random date assigned to all of those who cannot indicate their actual date of birth when first processed by the UN Refugee Agency (UNHCR), whose staff must also estimate people's age.

M.O. Ensor (✉)
Georgetown University, Washington, DC, USA
e-mail: marisaensor@yahoo.com

M.O. Ensor
The International Institute for Child Rights and Development, Victoria, BC, Canada

© The Author(s) 2016
M.L. Seeberg and E.M. Goździak (eds.), *Contested Childhoods: Growing up in Migrancy*, IMISCOE Research Series,
DOI 10.1007/978-3-319-44610-3_4

inclusion and exclusion faced by thousands of South Sudanese-American children and youth.

Like Chuol and his mother, millions of refugees fled the south of Sudan during the Second Sudanese Civil War (1983–2005). They sought shelter in one of the sprawling camps in neighbouring Ethiopia, Kenya, Uganda, or else joined the urban poor in Khartoum or Cairo. The United Nations resettled nearly 31,000 refugees from these camps to the U.S. Many of them were children, often unaccompanied minors who had been orphaned or separated from their relatives during the war. In the 1990s, Omaha, Nebraska, emerged as an unlikely hub for these South Sudanese, both for primary resettlement from camps in Africa, and for secondary resettlement, as refugees placed in other States relocated to Nebraska in search of jobs, affordable housing and a sense of community. Currently, Omaha is home to approximately 10,000 South Sudanese refugees who, along with other displaced groups, represent over 1.7 % of the city's total population. Mirroring demographic trends in their home country, the South Sudanese population in the U.S. is very young. Some of them arrived in the U.S. as refugees, as was the case with the close to four thousand famous "Lost Boys of Sudan" (HRW 1994) who were resettled to various American cities in 2001. Others are the U.S.-born children of refugee parents and have never lived in Africa.

The term "diasporas" is often used, both in Omaha and in South Sudan, to lump both groups together in everyday discourses. Many of these South Sudanese can indeed be seen as fulfilling all the criteria of a "refugee diaspora" (Van Hear 2009). That is, they are groups that are recently displaced due to conflict—or "a well-founded fear of persecution," in accordance with domestic and international legal standards[3]—and that often maintain considerable material connections to the home state. Their life experiences have, on the other hand, often been quite diverse and disparate depending on their migratory trajectories, among other factors. Tensions and even violence among different migrant groups have recently intensified in Omaha, with some youth allegedly joining the many street gangs often composed of refugees and migrants of various nationalities that have sprung up in the area over the last decade.

Against this complex and tumultuous background, the diasporic identities and cultural practices of children and youth are being translated, appropriated, and creolized to fit into local social contexts and structures. Based on on-going

---

[3]The US definition of refugee derives from that established in the 1951 Convention relating to the Status of Refugees, as amended by the 1967 Protocol Relating to the Status of Refugees. More specifically, the US Immigration and Nationality Act defines "refugee" in Sect. 101(a)(42) as:

Any person who is outside any country of such person's nationality or, in the case of a person having no nationality, is outside any country in which such person last habitually resided, and who is unable or unwilling to return to, and is unable or unwilling to avail himself or herself of the protection of, that country because of persecution or a well-founded fear of persecution on account of race, religion, nationality, membership in a particular social group, or political opinion.

ethnographic fieldwork conducted both in South Sudan and in the U.S. since 2009, this chapter examines the contested notions of "childhood," "migration" and "refugee-ness" that frame the experiences of South Sudanese-American children. This analysis seeks to elucidate the relationship between displacement, belonging and the construction of a diasporic sense of self among South Sudanese children growing up in migrancy in Omaha and, by qualified extension, elsewhere in the diaspora. The overarching argument made here is that the development of a sense of being part of a diaspora is frequently conditioned by complex and often violent processes of inclusion and exclusion that transcend fixed understandings of one's social, cultural and generational positioning. This is perhaps more the case for children and youth than for their adult counterparts.

Following this opening section, I present a brief discussion of the methods and conceptual frameworks that guided the research on which this chapter is based. More specifically, I situate the study of childhood and migrancy of South Sudanese refugees within the broader literature on diaspora studies, favouring notions of hybridity and multiple subjectivities. I then examine the historical and recent determinants underlying the arrival of South Sudanese refugees in Omaha, Nebraska, highlighting the geographical and cultural links between Africa and the U.S., past and present. A discussion of identity formation across generations, and issues of diaspora and violence allows me to contextualize the rise of street gangs as important spaces for the critical, if often violent, reinterpretation of fluid notions of identity, membership and belonging. In the concluding section, I suggest that, despite their troubled present and uncertain futures, young South Sudanese in Omaha display remarkable resilience and the ability to navigate multiple social *loci* in their struggle to adapt to challenging local conditions. As their experiences illustrate, understanding the hybrid affiliations that conform their identity formation is critical for a re-conceptualization of diaspora children as part of more than one geographically and socially located society. Simultaneously informing the scholarship on contested childhood(s) as fluid and situational, this perspective, I argue, allows for a more fruitful elucidation of the mechanisms of growing up in exile, and the broader urban refugee experience in Nebraska and elsewhere.

Studying Diaspora Children: A Note on Frameworks and Methods

A number of theoretical constructs have been developed over the years to examine the immigration experiences and the specific circumstances of migrant children (Ensor 2010). Traditional concern with geographical displacement in migrant and refugee population flows has tended to entail a fixation with "origins" and "homelands." The wider African diaspora, in particular, has provided an important site for the production of diasporic imaginaries. These range from a diffuse sense of identification with "blackness" to the appropriation of specific cultural productions, memories and political projects that stem primarily from diaspora movements in North America. This emphasis on African origins has led to a tendency to overlook differences in "black" cultures and ignore the continuities and discontinuities in the historical processes and conditions that have shaped Africans' experiences abroad (Patterson and Kelley 2000, 18).

Offering an alternative perspective, cultural theorist Hall (2003, 244) has postulated that diaspora identities are formed "with and through, not despite, difference; by *hybridity*... constantly producing and reproducing themselves anew, through transformation and difference" (original italics). This approach has also had particular currency in studies of youth and "second-generation" migrants who are especially likely to experience the "contradictory pulls" of cultural difference (Hall 2000, 232). The hybrid affiliations and creolized cultural practices of young people are indeed becoming a rather uncontroversial focus of the cultural studies literature (Ensor 2013a; Skrbiš et al. 2007, 263). Children and young people may be regarded as primarily representing the future of their societies of origin, the societies into which they or their parents have migrated (Ensor 2015), or their own presents and futures as autonomous, hybrid and transnational individuals. Diverging concerns may be reflected in different ideas and practices of childhood and negotiated in different social arenas.

The experiences of younger generations of South Sudanese in Omaha present a particularly good opportunity to bridge some of these analytical silos within diaspora studies. South Sudanese children, whose lifescapes encompass multiple geographically located societies, occupy fluid positionings characterized by both alienation from and affinity with not only the dominant "white" society, but also other "black" diaspora groups. Contesting rigid dichotomies separating children from adults, their experiences illustrate the contextual and relational nature of the definition of childhood as a social construct. They also exemplify the important relationship between migrancy as an attributed characteristic of children and their families (Näre 2013) on one hand, and differences in social position, migration trajectory and cultural practice on the other.

This chapter explores the production of complex and fluid diasporic identifications through an ongoing ethnographic study of the younger generations of South Sudanese in Omaha, NE, initiated in the summer of 2009. I interacted with members of the South Sudanese diaspora, both youngsters and adults, through my attendance at a variety of different events, such as academic conferences, social occasions and community celebrations, as well as more informal gatherings between younger South Sudanese and their non-South Sudanese friends. I also conducted in-depth, semi-structured interviews with fifteen youth (six females and nine males) whose ages ranged from 14 to 21 when the study began. These interviews took place in community centres, cafes and restaurants near participants' homes in different parts of Omaha. I used an interview guide aimed at eliciting reflections on younger people's experiences growing up in South Sudan or in exile, the challenges and opportunities of life in the U.S., and their hopes and expectations for their future. I interviewed the majority of my study participants at least two or three times, with interviews lasting for a variable length of time, typically around

2 h. Furthermore, I have maintained close contact with some of these South Sudanese youngsters and their families, and have had regular updates on their activities and experiences. Their narratives, which simultaneously emphasize multiplicity, cross-cutting affiliations and overlapping identities, allow for a re-examination of prevalent assumptions in diaspora theory about the analytical distinction between "diaspora" and "host society."

From Africa to Nebraska: Historical and Contemporary Factors

Sudan, of which South Sudan was part until its secession on 9th July 2011, has long been a significant contributor to refugee movements globally (Tempany 2009). The two Sudanese Civil Wars—fought from 1955 to 1972 and 1983 to 2005—resulted in the deaths of an estimated two million people and caused massive internal and cross-border displacement. With over four million displaced during the Second Sudanese Civil War, the South Sudanese diaspora remains large in spite of the fact that at least 2.5 million South Sudanese returned to the country since 2005. Outside of Africa, the largest diaspora communities are in North America, Western Europe (UK, France, Italy, and Sweden), Australia and New Zealand, where there are an estimated 400,000–600,000 South Sudanese in total (The Hand Foundation 2014).

The South Sudanese refugees who found their way to the U.S. took a variety of paths. Some went to Khartoum to avoid the war, find work or go to school. However, for those who eventually reached Nebraska, the most common route was through the Itang refugee camp just across the border in neighbouring Ethiopia. This camp was managed by the UN Refugee Agency, the United Nations High Commissioner for Refugees (UNHCR). Many of these southerners "followed the trail of [human] bones eastward" (Hutchinson 1996, 6) to the relative safety of Ethiopian camps.

In the early 1990s, South Sudanese refugees' already precarious conditions in Ethiopia became untenable. Civil War and the overthrow of the regime of Haile Mengistu, who had ruled Ethiopia since deposing Emperor Haile Selassie in the 1970s, caused the camps to be closed. At about the same time, news began to spread of refugee camps in Kenya, which offered an alternative place of safety, away from the deteriorating situation in Ethiopia and continuing troubles in their own country. For many of these refugees, the possibility of obtaining permission in the Kenyan camps to resettle in a third country such as the United States or Canada provided an additional reason to move to Kenya, where permission to re-locate was more likely to be given (Holtzman 2000, 21).

Where South Sudanese refugees initially resettled was generally not under their control. Those sponsored by relatives were sent to join their kin in the same community. For others, however, their placement was selected by resettlement agencies; the criteria used by the resettlement programmes were unknown by the refugees themselves. In early 1997, Nebraska came to be known among South Sudanese refugees as a "hot spot"—a place where many of them were contemplating relocating (Holtzman 2000, 37). They were attracted by cheap housing and employment opportunities in the meatpacking industry, a mainstay of immigrant labour. Their population was comprised mostly of very young people. Very few individuals were older than their mid-thirties, and the majority were considerably younger. Upon arrival in the U.S., they most commonly lived in young families, consisting of a husband, wife, and their young children. The younger refugees had little or no experience of South Sudan, having grown up in refugee camps or otherwise in exile. Their knowledge of the history and culture of their homeland mainly came through relayed information and experience from parents and other adults in the community (Poppitt and Frey 2007).

Adjustment to life in Nebraska has not been easy for many South Sudanese, who have faced a constellation of obstacles unusual in their depth and scope even for immigrants. There are vast differences in the lifestyles and values of Nebraska and South Sudan. Although some males—but hardly any females—had had at least brief experiences in African cities where they had gone to work or study, for most South Sudanese resettlement to the U.S. constituted their first significant stay outside of rural Africa. Most arrived largely unaware of American customs and without basic literacy skills or competence in English. For the large majority, even the most basic aspects of everyday living were completely unfamiliar. Beyond changes in daily routines, South Sudanese needed to re-forge their social worlds, which often proved to be an even more daunting task. The majority of the adult South Sudanese in my study describe their first years in America as "very difficult," "confusing" and even "frightening." Nevertheless, they also noted how relocation was filled with possibilities and hope for a better future. The experiences of these African-born refugees differ markedly from those of their U.S.-born children whose outlook is often less optimistic; they all counter the static notions of "community" and "enculturation" that still dominate prevalent understandings of diaspora.

Identity Formation Across Generations

In 2009 when I first met U.S.-born Biel and his then adolescent friends, I had just returned from a summer field trip to Rumbek, the capital of Lakes State in central South Sudan. The photographs I brought with me depicted scenes of the daily life of some of the *tukul*-dwelling (huts made of grass and mud), cattle-keeping, tall and proud-looking Dinka who constitute the largest ethnic group in the country. Biel and his friends are, however, Nuer. Chuol and most, but not all, of the South Sudanese I met in Omaha, are Nuer as well. Unusually tall agro-pastoralists like the Dinka, the Nuer represent the second largest ethnic group in South Sudan. As many members of the South Sudanese community in Omaha remarked, ethnic differences between Nuer, Dinka and other groups are, typically subsumed under generalizing labels such as "African," or "black" in the U.S.. The deadly pattern of revenge and counter-revenge attacks along Dinka-Nuer ethnic lines currently ravaging South Sudan on the other hand, have transformed ethnic divisions from a source of identity to a matter of life and death (Office of the Coordination of Humanitarian Affairs [OCHA] 2014).[4]

Accustomed to the completely urbanized life that frames the lifescapes of most American teenagers, Biel and his friends looked at my photographs with amused curiosity. Their repeated exclamations of *"no way"* and *"not me"* conveyed their lack of interest in ever adopting the traditional agro-pastoral livelihoods of their African counterparts. As one of them emphatically put it, "this is all very well for them; this is how they grow up. But this is not who I am. I have roots in the old country, but I was born here. I am an American." The large majority of South Sudanese children and adolescents living in Omaha today are U.S.-born and, in a legal sense, neither refugees nor migrants but American citizens. Their national identification and indeed their sense of personal identity are nevertheless often marked by tropes of displacement and non-belonging.

The development of a sense of identity is key to any discussion of diaspora groups. An examination of this process helps us to understand the ways in which South Sudanese diaspora members fit within the particular contours of contemporary American society. First-generation South Sudanese-Americans, as refugees who have fled their homes and lived in camps in Africa, do share problems and concerns with refugees in America from other countries and cultures. Because many are still dependent on welfare or belong to the class of the working poor, they also face many of the same problems that confront poor and working-poor, native-born Americans. South Sudanese identification with one group or the other —or neither—is often fluid and situational for both children and adults, as well as gender-differentiated.

The particular emotional landscape that South Sudanese children currently inhabit sharply contrasts with the conditions faced by their parents as first-generation migrants. Their perceptions of life in the U.S. follow the pattern predicted by Sluzki (1979) who concluded that many newly arrived immigrants experience a sense of euphoria, with high expectations and anticipated possibilities that may seem boundless. Energies are focused on attending to immediate needs, including finding jobs and a place to live. New immigrants had to establish themselves quickly, as all they received from the U.S. government was a loan for the plane ticket from Africa—which they had to start paying back within 6 months[5]—less than three hundred dollars cash, and food stamps. In many of these

---

[4]In a document released on 9 January 2015, the Human Rights Division of the United Nations Mission in South Sudan (UNMISS) reported that there were reasonable grounds to believe that at least 353 civilians had been murdered and another 250 wounded in attacks in the capitals of the South Sudanese States of Unity and Jonglei between 15 April and 17 April of 2014. These attacks involved the deliberate targeting of victims on the basis of their ethnicity, nationality or perceived support for one of the parties to the conflict (UN News Centre 2015).

[5]Refugees traveling to the United States are issued loans by the International Organization for Migration (IOM) to pay for the costs of their transportation from overseas to the U.S. resettlement

South Sudanese families, both spouses worked two shifts, encouraged both by need and by the prevalent belief that if they worked extremely hard for at least 5 years, they would prosper, which many did, at least in comparison to the living conditions they left behind in Africa.

With the new cultural and contextual norms of diaspora life, the public role of South Sudanese females quickly became significantly altered. Many women reported feeling isolated and even resented by their husbands and other males in the family as they assumed new more socially and economically active roles. Women were more readily able to find jobs as domestic workers, or as cleaners at hotels and restaurants; their husbands, on the other hand, with skills more suitable to an agrarian life in Africa than to urban America, remained trapped in menial low-paying jobs or unemployed and unable to provide for their families on their own. Today, marital tensions and even domestic violence are both common and much more frequently reported to the police than would have been the case in the homeland. Women, especially younger ones, are establishing themselves as community leaders, activists and breadwinners, challenging the old male leadership, and protesting against war, violence and racism (Lim 2009). Broad-ranging changes in daily life have brought major transformations not only in how women and men relate to each other, but also in how they see themselves as individuals and as members of their families and their community at large.

While refugee couples recognize that life in the U.S. sometimes requires a shift in gender responsibilities, new and widely-accepted norms concerning the gender division of labour have not emerged among first generation refugees. Instead, most have resorted to making adjustments and one-off changes as the need arises. As first-generation diaspora members often remark, there was far less ambiguity regarding social expectations for females and males, children and adults in South Sudan. In Omaha, it is the lack of well-defined roles, as much as the profound nature of the changes, which has caused tensions within South Sudanese families. The very definitions of childhood and adulthood—manhood and womanhood—are now surrounded by uncertainty, no longer clearly marked by rites of passage and initiation ceremonies.

Among some of the largest ethnic groups in South Sudan (i.e. the Nuer and the Dinka), the initiation of boys into adulthood is traditionally marked by facial scarification, with initiated young men expected to take on adult responsibilities. The Nuer receive facial markings (called *gaar*) of varying patterns. The most common initiation pattern among males consists of six parallel horizontal lines, which are cut across the forehead with a razor, often with a dip in the lines above the nose. Among the Dinka, initiation into manhood similarly involves the cutting of a varying number of parallel lines or V-shaped marks onto the forehead of the

---

(Footnote 5 continued)

sites and for various medical screening costs. The funds to cover the transportation are provided to IOM by the State Department's Bureau for Population, Migration and Refugees. A promissory note is signed by every refugee 18 years and older prior to arrival in the U.S. confirming the refugee's agreement to make regular monthly payments to the sponsoring agency (USCCB 2016).

male initiate, called a *parapool*—"one who has stopped milking"—as boys would no longer do the work of milking cows after initiation. Although far less common, young females may have their faces scarified as well amongst some Nuer and Dinka clans. In the case of females, scarification tends to be more a sign of high status than of initiation into adulthood and, especially among the Nuer, dotted patterns are preferred over deep cuts.

In South Sudan, current constructions of childhood for boys go beyond being non-initiated and include being single, not steadily employed, and still dependent on one's family (Jok 2005, 144–145). The fixed chronological parameters that define childhood and adulthood in the U.S. are seen as alien and confusing by some South Sudanese for whom social criteria and individual's behaviour are more reasonable predictors of one's generational position.

Racialized notions of belonging in or exclusion from other African diaspora groups constitute a further source of ambiguity, as affinity with other "black groups" has been undercut by experiences of racism. As numerous respondents observed, South Sudanese occupy a racially ambivalent position, "labelled 'black' by the whites, but not really accepted by the black community." For many, the idea of "roots" and "origins" is an important aspect of their self-identity and their ability to "fit in." Aweng, a 17-year-old high school male student remarked:

> Being Sudanese is pretty unique. The whole black culture here is dominated by African-Americans who don't know where their roots are… Nigeria, West Africa… African like me, but I am not really like them. And I still couldn't identify with them either. There are different types of Africans and no other African is like the South Sudanese, like me.

His comments illustrate the constant interplay between similarity and difference in the "black diaspora," and evidence the fundamental "instability and mutability of identities which are always unfinished, always being remade" (Gilroy 1993, xi).

Most migrants, especially those in contexts of forced migration like refugees, are required to move across discontinuous social spaces. These discontinuities can be markedly different for first and second-generation Americans. Migrancy and diaspora thus provide a particularly important context for redefining both childhood and inter-generational relations. Those African-born refugees who suffered traumatic experiences and severe conditions in their home country, and often also in transit and subsequently in the host country, harbour grievances and fears that may impact their relationship with younger generations (Vorrath 2012). Childhood memories of the homeland are often constructed through the language and imagery of violence, poverty and displacement, reinforced by media tropes of refugee-ness and war. Many nonetheless speak passionately about their pride in "being African," and praise the customs and traditions that regulated their pre-flight life in South Sudan.

Family or local tensions and conflict may result when parents' traditional attitudes and perceptions are dismissed or met with resentment from children and adolescents, who are often more acculturated than their parents in the new society through their greater access to schooling (Poppitt and Frey 2007). Some youngsters have, however, embraced their South Sudanese origins even if only vaguely familiar with their cultural meaning. Others have sought inclusion and belonging by joining youth groups and local South Sudanese community organizations which, in the hopeful words of Nyadhial, a very socially active and vivacious 15-year-old girl, can "make us proud of who we are, have events about the culture, where we are from, learn more about our history and what's going on in the country."

Riek, Nyadhial's older cousin, is also very politically engaged and has strong opinions about the resurgence of conflict in South Sudan, which he blames squarely on the lack of political will and the "shameful incompetence" of the country's leaders. He described himself as a "proud South Sudanese" and, unlike most of his compatriots, placed his national origins above his ethnic affiliation. As a child, his feelings about South Sudan were somewhat different, as he explained at one of our meetings at a small coffee shop near the church he attends on Sundays. His early memories of school revolved almost entirely around experiences of racism and feeling of exclusion and, as he became older, increasingly tense relationships with other groups of African descent. "White kids called us all 'blacks', but I look different, darker, taller, and felt different too. It was confusing and isolating. I think that it also made me ashamed to be South Sudanese," he explained.

Riek briefly joined a gang when he was in his mid-late teens, yielding to peer pressure, the lure of danger and adventure, and the promise of forging strong bonds of comradery with his South Sudanese "gang brothers." The harsh realities of life as a gang member, he admits, left him "empty and disappointed" and also "scared at how quickly things can go bad, very bad." Riek eventually left the gang and found a job at a local community newspaper. Other gang-affiliated youth find it harder to leave and, indeed, membership in street gangs has reportedly increased in Omaha in the last decade. Violence, both structural and physical, is a pervasive feature in the life of gang members.

Diaspora, Violence and the Rise of Street Gangs

South Sudanese diaspora children inhabit a cultural milieu where patterned inequalities shape social interactions. As is the case with other members of the African diaspora, South Sudanese socially-ascribed identity is largely racialized in homogenizing ways. Popular thinking in the Global North often equates common skin colour with an assumed common African behaviour, language, attitudes and capabilities (Ndhlovu 2009).

In addition to the obvious structural inequalities they face as the younger generation of a racialized minority, they are also targeted for what (De Vos and Suárez-Orozco 1990) have termed "psychological disparagement."

> They become the object of symbolic violence, which stereotypes them as innately inferior (lazier, prone to crime, and so forth). These attributes make these disparaged minorities, in the eyes of the dominant society, less deserving of sharing in the society's dream and justifies their lot in life (Suárez-Orozco 2000, 211).

4 South Sudanese Diaspora Children: Contested Notions of Childhood, Uprootedness … 71

Discrimination and racism are recurring themes discussed by many of the children and youth with whom I spoke. Inspired by the Longitudinal Immigrant Student Adaptation Study conducted by Carola and Marcelo Suárez-Orozco (Suárez-Orozco et al. 2007), I asked my study participants to complete the sentence, "Most Americans think that South Sudanese people are…" The following statements are representative of the kinds of responses I received:

Most Americans think that we are stupid.

Most Americans think that we are members of gangs.

Most Americans think that we are savages and violent.

Most Americans think that we are ignorant.

Most Americans think that we are primitive Africans.

Overwhelmingly, South Sudanese children reported a conviction that Americans had negative perceptions about them—a sentiment most vehemently expressed by boys and male teenagers. Their awareness of the prevailing ethos of hostility of the dominant culture could, at times, be ignored, internalized, or resisted, depending on personal and social circumstances. For most, these circumstances have recently become more hostile, owing, among other factors, to the rise of gang-related violence attributed to disenfranchised South Sudanese young boys. As the "ethos of reception" to South Sudanese diaspora members becomes less welcoming, their outlook on life's prospects has accordingly become dimmer. A prevailing ethos of hostility in the dominant culture makes it extremely difficult for migrant children to maintain an unblemished sense of self-worth (Suárez-Orozco 2000, 213). "Many are torn between the attachment to their parental culture of origin, the lure of the often more intrigued adolescent peer culture, as aspirations to join the American mainstream culture (which may or may not welcome them)" (ibid. 217).

A conflicted "ethos of reception" (Suárez-Orozco and Suárez-Orozco 2001) is often a significant determinant in diaspora life. The ensuing lack of communal trust frames ongoing relationships. It can also negatively impact the way that people in the host country perceive immigrants' homelands, and influence the manner in which children are taught about their own culture, history and other ethnicities or religions. In sum, it can add to the already significant stresses of growing up in migrancy.

Unlike their parents, most second-generation South Sudanese no longer perceive their circumstances in terms of a day-to-day struggle for survival. For them, disappointed hopes and aspirations coupled with a negative reception in the only community they know as "home" have at times led to feelings of distrust, anger, hostility and fear. Concern with violence is indeed a recurring theme that I have found among many of my study participants. Even if they were not personally exposed to the stresses and deprivations of war, all too many youngsters report having witnessed—and, in some cases, participated in—a disconcertingly high level of violence in their new neighbourhood and school settings. A distinction should be made between what might be called "hard" (physical) violence, and "soft" (psychological or symbolic) violence. While physical violence may be easier to identify, "the workings of psychic and symbolic violence are often more elusive but may be equally devastating in the long run" (Suárez-Orozco and Robben 2000, 1). As I have previously described:

> Encounters with difference, dissonance, and exclusion are counterpoised by a search for new identity, social acceptance and belonging. Gang affiliation is one such effort which, while often associated with transgressive and even violent behaviour, must also be understood as an effort to respond to the many ruptures and transformations of anchors of belonging experienced by young refugees (Ensor 2014, 114).

Although Omaha has had its share of gang violence since the late 1980s, when the Bloods and Crips (two rival Los Angeles-based gangs) arrived to cash in on the emerging crack cocaine market, South Sudanese gangs are a newer phenomenon. By most accounts, the first ones—MJ, a Nuer acronym for "Dog Pussy," and African Pride—started operating in Omaha in 2004. Those that followed—MOB, GBLOCK, 402 (the area code for eastern Nebraska), South Sudan Soldiers, and TripSet—adopted equally colourful names. Some gangs include both Nuer and Dinka members, but ethnic segregation is more common. For instance, the "South Sudan Soldiers," a gang that has established a growing presence in the Omaha area since its founding in 2009, is made up almost exclusively of Nuer youth.

Most of my study participants agree that South Sudanese gangs in Omaha, which have no particular ideology guiding their actions, started not because of politics, drugs, or money, but out of boredom. The bulk of the members are young boys, aged fourteen to seventeen, although a few females reportedly also belong to some of the gangs. Predictably, most of them live in low-income neighbourhoods. Some gang members are believed to have dropped out of school to work so they could send money back to family members in Africa. Others, placed in public schools by their age rather than their typically lower grade level, quit discouraged by their poor performance in class and the derisive attitude of their more schooled classmates. Fights are common and have become more lethal as easily obtainable guns have replaced knives.

"The missing link is the parents," offered an adult South Sudanese male who moved to Omaha in 2003, "Nobody goes after their seventeen-year-old. They just think, 'We know what he's doing, he'll come back later'" (Massara 2010). He believed that lack of proper parental supervision constitutes a large part of the problem. As he admits, "I know a few families whose kids are the top ringleaders of the gang [and] they don't want to admit their kids are in a gang. It's not that they are defending the kids, they're just ignorant of what their kids are doing" (ibid.). His views on parents' responsibility for youngsters' misbehaviour is shared by a mother in her mid-thirties who noted, "In our community, a lot of parents don't know how to discipline their kids without using physical violence; that's what they grew up with" (ibid.).

Ironically, together with Tunisia and Kenya, South Sudan is the third African state to establish full prohibition of corporal punishment for children[6] (Santos 2011). Article 17 of the Transitional Constitution that came into force in 2011 establishes that "Every child has the right…to be free from corporal punishment and cruel and inhuman treatment by any person including parents, school administrations and other institutions." Caning and flogging remain, however, common approaches to child discipline. Furthermore, customary law still prescribes lashings as a suitable punishment for certain offenses committed by children (Ensor 2013b, 156). Proscriptions against the use of physical discipline for children continue to be perceived by many, both in South Sudan and in Omaha, as an ineffective and unjustified intrusion into parental roles. "That's when kids start to get in trouble, because they have no structure and no consequences to their actions," added the young mother (Massara 2010).

While gang-affiliated youngsters constitute only a fragment of the South Sudanese community in Omaha, their adversarial and occasionally violent efforts at self-affirmation have recently given rise to moral panics among local residents. Hardened attitudes towards "immigrants of colour" risk reinforcing patterns of xenophobia, exclusion and stigmatization (Suárez-Orozco 2000, 207). This trend is particularly worrisome for children growing up in immigrant communities for whom "[o]ptimistic hopes for the future are often tempered by pessimism borne of deprivation and disparagement" (ibid. 217).

The Way Forward: New Waves of Displacement and Diasporization

As Van Hear (1998) has posited, displaced groups in exile may go through various phases of re- or de-diasporization, often as a result of changing political circumstances in the homeland. This is particularly the case in conflict or crisis situations, where those abroad may become politically and economically mobilized on behalf of their troubled compatriots. Homeland conditions—and particularly the presence of political instability and conflict—may become important factors that frame the trajectory of diaspora groups, as well as the experiences of differently positioned children and adults within such communities.

Merely 2 years after its 2011 secession from Sudan, newly independent South Sudan plunged into a violent confrontation on 15 December 2013. The resurgence of conflict was triggered by bitter disagreements within the top leadership of the ruling Sudan People's Liberation Movement (SPLM), which splintered the party into several factions. The unabated violence has devastated the lives of millions of South Sudanese, uprooting nearly 2 million children, women and men. Nearly 1.5

---

[6]Also noteworthy, South Sudan ratified the UN Convention of the Rights of the Child on 5th May, 2015, becoming the 195th state to adopt the landmark child rights treaty.

million people have been displaced internally, and another 480,000 have sought refuge in neighbouring countries (OCHA 2014). New diaspora communities are being formed in neighbouring African countries, while more established ones are again mobilizing to respond to the deteriorating local, regional and global conditions.

As a case in point, in early January 2014, a group of South Sudanese diaspora members in Omaha comprising Dinka, Nuer, and other ethnic groups (mainly Equatorians) voiced the need to discuss the on-going conflict in South Sudan. Those assembled denounced the ethnic violence with a unified South Sudanese-American voice. Despite their different ethnic affiliation and the on-going conflict back home, they re-affirmed their renewed commitment to working together through dialogue and mutual assistance. South Sudanese refugees in Omaha have long been involved in a range of activities aimed at promoting the development of their communities, both in the diaspora and in the homeland. Omaha was one of a handful of American cities that hosted voting sites for the referendum on South-Sudan's Independence of 9–15 January 2011. It saw the highest turnout in the United States with over three-thousand ballots cast. Prior to the recent resurgence of violence, some diasporas had chosen to return to their newly independent nation in order to launch small-scale philanthropic projects in and around their home villages, using resources and skills they had acquired in exile. Their actions illustrate the premise that, as circumstances become increasingly disjointed, diaspora members can experience a heightened emotional connection with their homeland. This encourages some to mobilize and increase their political involvement or give financial assistance to relatives or affiliated organizations (Vorrath 2012). Members of the youngest generation, often described as "the future of the nation," are at the frontline of these momentous developments (Ensor 2015, 47).

As the experiences of Chuol, Biel, Aweng, Nyadhial and Riek have illustrated, South Sudanese children are playing a pivotal role in many of the processes taking place in their societies. As is often the case in immigrant communities from war-torn nations where youngsters constitute the majority of the population, young people have played this role in both in their country of origin and their adopted nation. The diasporic identities of current generations of South Sudanese in Omaha are a product of multiple factors. These include historical memories and narratives, fluid and often contested constructions of childhood, shifting inter-generational and gender dynamics, changes in homeland politics, processes of repatriation, new waves of displacement and other global flows. These determinants should be examined alongside identity processes in the host society, including local vernacular discourses and racialized constructions of the African diaspora. Informed by the recent anti-essentialist shift in childhood studies, this chapter argues that children and youth's diasporic identities must always be understood as a product of a particular time and place.

Identity formation and the behaviours of South Sudanese children and youth in Omaha "conjure an image of a disempowered group facing its way to the centre" (Abdullah 2007, 25). Often referred to simply as "diasporas," regardless of their nationality status, their ascribed and self-identified situation of migrancy reflects a

4 South Sudanese Diaspora Children: Contested Notions of Childhood, Uprootedness ... 75

greater concern with social circumstances and cultural allegiances than with legal or geographical considerations. Their narratives at times invoke powerful sentiments of uprootedness and isolation intrinsically connected to exclusionary local constructions of South Sudanese-ness. They also illustrate their struggles to reassess their relationships to one another, and to re-forge cultural notions and expectations of childhood, family and community. The case of South Sudanese diaspora in Omaha thus exemplifies the need for studies of children and migrancy to recognize that the "birth of a community" in exile is not just an event confined to the early years of resettlement. Rather, it is an ongoing process that will continue into the future and will affect younger generations.

References

Abdullah, I. (2007). Youth culture and rebellion: Understanding Sierra Leone's wasted decade. *Critical Arts: South-North Cultural and Media Studies, 16*(2), 19–37.

De Vos, G., & Suárez-Orozco, M. (1990). *Status inequality: The self in culture*. Newbury Park, CA: Sage Press.

Ensor, M. O. (2010). Understanding migrant children: Conceptualizations, approaches and issues. In M. O. Ensor & E. M. Goździak (Eds.), *Children and migration: At the crossroads of resiliency and vulnerability* (pp. 15–36). Basingstoke, UK: Palgrave Macmillan.

Ensor, M. O. (2013a). Youth culture, refugee (re)integration, and diasporic identities in South Sudan. *Postcolonial Text, 8*(3), 1–19.

Ensor, M. O. (2013b). Participation under fire: Dilemmas of reintegration for child soldiers involved in South Sudan's armed conflict. *Global Studies of Childhood Journal, 3*(2), 153–162.

Ensor, M. O. (2014). Crossing borders of geography and self: South Sudanese refugee youth Gangs in Egypt. In S. Spyrou, & M. Christou (Eds.), *Children and borders* (pp. 114–128). London: Palgrave Macmillan.

Ensor, M. O. (2015). Heirs of the world's newest nation: Children as citizens and nation-builders in South Sudan. *Global Studies of Childhood, 5*(1), 47–58.

Gilroy, P. (1993). *The black atlantic: Modernity and double consciousness*. Cambridge, Massachusetts: Harvard University Press.

Hall, S. (2000). Conclusion: The multicultural question. In B. Hesse (Ed.), *Unsettled multiculturalisms: Diasporas, entanglements, transruptions*. London, New York: Zed Books.

Hall, S. (2003). Cultural identity and diaspora. In J. E. Braziel & A. Mannur (Eds.), *Theorizing diaspora*. Malden, Oxford, Victoria: Blackwell Publishing.

Holtzman, J. D. (2000). *Nuer journeys, Nuer lives: Sudanese refugees in Minnesota*. Boston: Allyn & Bacon.

Human Rights Watch, HRW. (1994). Sudan: The lost boys: Child soldiers and unaccompanied boys in Southern Sudan. *Human Rights Watch, 6*(10). Retrieved November 30, 2014 from https://www.hrw.org/sites/default/files/reports/sudan1994.pdf.

Hutchinson, S. (1996). *Nuer dilemmas: Coping with war, money and the state*. Berkeley: University of California Press.

Jok, M. J. (2005). War, changing ethics and the position of youth in South Sudan. In J. Abbink & I. van Kessel (Eds.), *Vanguards or vandals: Youth, politics and conflict in Africa*. Leiden: Brill.

Lim, S. (2009). "Loss of connections is death": Transnational family ties among Sudanese refugee families resettling in the United States. *Journal of Cross-Cultural Psychology, 40*(6), 1028–1040.

Massara, K. (2010). The gangs of Omaha: Sudanese who fled their war-torn country face growing violence in their ranks. Alertnet: Immigration. Retrieved January 10, 2015 from http://www.alternet.org/story/149106/the_gangs_of_omaha%3A_sudanese_who_fled_their_war-torn_country_face_growing_violence_in_their_ranks.

Näre, L. (2013). Migrancy, gender and social class in domestic labour and social care in Italy: An intersectional analysis of demand. *Journal of Ethnic and Migration Studies, 39*(4), 601–623.

Ndhlovu, F. (2009). The limitations of language and nationality as prime markers of African diaspora identities in the state of Victoria. *African Identities, 7*(1), 17–32.

Office for the Coordination of Humanitarian Affairs, OCHA. (2014). South Sudan crisis report. Retrieved November 10, 2014 from http://www.unocha.org/south-sudan/.

Patterson, T., & Kelley, R. (2000). Unfinished migrations: Reflections on the African diaspora and the making of the modern world. *African Studies Review, 43*(1), 11–45.

Poppitt, G., & Frey, R. (2007). Sudanese adolescent refugees: Acculturation and acculturative stress. *Australian Journal of Guidance and Counselling, 17*(2), 160–181.

Santos, P. M. (2011). South Sudan becomes 30th country to prohibit all forms of violence against children. In *Office of the special representative of the secretary-general on violence against children*. Retrieved November 12, 2014 from http://srsg.violenceagainstchildren.org/story/2011-07-29_374.

Skrbiš, Z., Baldassar, L., & Poynting, S. (2007). Introduction—negotiating belonging: Migration and generations. *Journal of Intercultural Studies, 28*(3), 261–269.

Sluzki, C. (1979). Migration and family conflict. *Family Process, 18*(4), 379–390.

Suárez-Orozco, C., Suárez-Orozco, M., & Todorova, I. (2007). *Learning a new land: Immigrant students in American society*. Cambridge, Massachusetts: Harvard University Press.

Suárez-Orozco, C., & Suárez-Orozco, M. (2001). *Children of immigration*. Cambridge, Massachusetts: Harvard University Press.

Suárez-Orozco, C. (2000). Identities under siege: Immigration stress and social mirroring among the children of immigrants. In M. Suárez-Orozco, & A. C. G. M. Robben (Eds.), *Cultures under siege: Collective violence and trauma* (pp. 194–226). Cambridge: Cambridge University Press.

Suárez-Orozco, M., & Robben, A. C. G. M. (2000). Interdisciplinary perspectives on violence and trauma. In M. Suárez-Orozco, & A. C. G. M. Robben (Eds.), *Cultures under siege: Collective violence and trauma* (pp. 1–41). Cambridge: Cambridge University Press.

Tempany, M. (2009). What research tells us about the mental health and psychosocial wellbeing of Sudanese refugees: A literature review. *Transcultural Psychiatry, 46*(2), 300–315.

The Hand Foundation. (2014). The helping hand: The South Sudanese diaspora. Retrieved January 12, 2015 from http://thehandfoundation.org/newsletter/2014/03/helping-hands-the-south-sudanese-diaspora/.

United Nations News Centre. (2015). UN probe says South Sudan attacks 'nadir' of conflict marked by abuses, rights violations. Retrieved January 21, 2016 from http://www.un.org/apps/news/story.asp?NewsID=49759#.Vq5U5vkrKhf.

United States Conference of Catholic Bishops, UCCB. (2016). "Refugee travel loan collection." Retrieved January 21, 2016 from http://www.usccb.org/issues-and-action/human-life-and-dignity/migrants-refugees-and-travelers/refugee-travel-loans-collection.

Van Hear, N. (1998). *New diasporas. The mass exodus, dispersal and regrouping of migrant communities.* London: UCL Press.
Van Hear, N. (2009). The rise of refugee diasporas. *Current History, 108*(717), 180–185.
Vorrath, J. (2012). *Engaging African diasporas for peace: Cornerstones for an emerging EU agenda.* Paris: European Union Institute for Security Studies.

Open Access This chapter is licensed under the terms of the Creative Commons Attribution-NonCommercial 2.5 International License (http://creativecommons.org/licenses/by-nc/2.5/), which permits any noncommercial use, sharing, adaptation, distribution and reproduction in any medium or format, as long as you give appropriate credit to the original author(s) and the source, provide a link to the Creative Commons license and indicate if changes were made.

The images or other third party material in this chapter are included in the book's Creative Commons license, unless indicated otherwise in a credit line to the material. If material is not included in the book's Creative Commons license and your intended use is not permitted by statutory regulation or exceeds the permitted use, you will need to obtain permission directly from the copyright holder.

Part II
Governance

Chapter 5
Lost Between Protective Regimes: Roma in the Norwegian State

Ada I. Engebrigtsen

Introduction

In a recently published book (Karoli 2014), a Norwegian Rom woman who has grown up in Norwegian foster care accused the Norwegian state of ethnic cleansing of the Rom population. She based her accusation on the fact that many Roma children were forcibly taken into custody by the Child Protection Services and raised in Norwegian foster homes, without access to their own language and culture. Although the number of Roma children in Norwegian foster homes is not documented, the allegations caused concern. In this chapter, I discuss the relationship between the Norwegian Rom minority and the State, represented by the Child Protection Services (CPS), as well as the relationship between different, and to some degree, opposing international protective regimes. I see this situation as one expression of a contest between different life-worlds and childhood regimes.

The relationship between Norwegian authorities, represented by the CPS, and the small Rom population in Norway is paradigmatic for three reasons: (1) Norway is a highly developed welfare society with a childhood[1] regime that sets standards for other countries in the world, and the Rom population is very small and vulnerable to political manipulation. We can therefore see how competing discourses about child protection and protection of minorities interact in this context. (2) The growing awareness of the cultural and economic marginalization of Roma in Europe and the political demand that countries integrate their Roma populations also make Norwegian experiences important. (3) Apart from Roma, a growing number of foreign citizens living in Norway, as well as immigrant organizations,

---

[1] In this chapter, "Childhood" with a capital C denotes the ideational aspect of lived childhoods, whereas "childhood" denotes a stage in human life.

A.I. Engebrigtsen (✉)
NOVA, Oslo and Akershus University College, Oslo, Norway
e-mail: ada.i.engebrigtsen@nova.hioa.no

© The Author(s) 2016
M.L. Seeberg and E.M. Goździak (eds.), *Contested Childhoods: Growing up in Migrancy*, IMISCOE Research Series,
DOI 10.1007/978-3-319-44610-3_5

object to what they call "abduction" of their children by Norwegian authorities (CPS).

In this chapter, I argue that Roma children are lost, not only between Norwegian and Roma norms for good parenting and proper Childhood, but between international conventions for the protection of individuals and conventions for the protection of minorities. My main research questions concern the problems of minority children growing up in foster families with different linguistic, cultural, and religious affiliations than the children's birth family and kin. I present the case of Maria and her children to illustrate how the Norwegian child protection regime deals with Norwegian Roma families and children. More specifically, I discuss how individual and collective considerations are weighted against each other when deciding the best interests of Maria's children. What role do local and international laws and conventions play in securing the best interest of the minority child?

I discuss these questions by first examining the case of Maria and her children, a case that has received much attention outside the court. I follow my analysis of this case with the discussion of the Norwegian Childhood Regime, placed within a discourse of "contested childhoods" as the main theoretical framework explored in this volume. I refer here to the discussions in sociology of Childhood as a social construction, to the notion of hegemonic Childhood supported by state institutions, and to the more or less explicit opposition and resistance to this hegemonic Childhood. I then briefly present the historical background of the relationship between the Norwegian state and the Rom population and of Rom childhood. I will then return to a discussion of Maria's case, based on what I see as the dominant Norwegian and international childhood regime and Rom childhood. The conclusion will bring together the different aspects and roles of the two protective regimes and the interests they appear to serve.

The concept of regime employed here denotes the package of rights, duties, norms, practices, and institutions that make up a certain policy. I argue that the Norwegian official concept of childhood defined by its laws, regulations, institutions and practices for the governance of the population is hegemonic in Norway.

Background

My background for raising this discussion is my work and research among Roma populations in Norway and Romania since the late 1970s. From 1978–1985, I was head of one of the kindergartens for Norwegian Roma in Oslo. This kindergarten was one of several institutions set up by the government as a strategy to prepare and motivate Roma families to send their children to school and to participate in adult education programmes. Most Norwegian Roma families sent their children to this kindergarten and many parents stayed with them there for most of the day. The staff, myself included, became quite involved in the lives of these families,

5 Lost Between Protective Regimes: Roma in the Norwegian State

spending time with them outside working hours at parties, weddings, birthdays, and funerals. Even though this experience did not include systematic research, it constitutes valuable background for my later academic research with different Roma groups. In 1996–1997, I carried out fieldwork for my doctoral research in a Rom community in Romania (Engebrigtsen 2007). More recently, I have served as an expert witness for the defence in several lawsuits involving Roma children forcibly placed in foster homes. The case discussed in this chapter is one of these legal cases that I followed closely. It is a typical example of relations between the Roma and the CPS.

Proper Parenting?

Roma children in CPS care are not available to researchers for interviews or observations, and only one Rom child raised by the CPS has spoken publically (Karoli 2014). Consequently, I do not have the details of Maria's actions, nor do I have access to "the children's voices" in this or other cases. The following is a reconstruction of the case based on files from the court case, Maria's accounts and my own participation in meetings with the CPS. All these sources are confidential.

> Maria and her kin group belong to the Norwegian Roma who have lived permanently in Norway since the end of the Second World War. This population includes around 600–700 individuals, bound together by kinship, marriage, a common language, and a way of life. Maria's extended family consists of grandparents and brothers and their wives and children who lived together throughout her childhood. The family travelled a lot for trade and social gatherings all around Europe. Maria and her four siblings only attended school sporadically. Maria was a grown woman when she met and married her husband, a man from another family of Norwegian Roma. These families were not on close terms—no alliance was established between them, although this is normally a central function of Roma marriages. She moved in with her husband's kin, as is the custom among the Roma, and gave birth to three children in three years. In this period, Maria was away from her children for months travelling with her natal family, while her husband and her in-laws took care of the children. Different kinds of fostering, as well as grandparents taking care of grandchildren are widespread among many Roma groups. The Child Protection Services (CPS) were in contact with the family because of reports from neighbours and the police concerning the well-being of Maria's and several other Roma children. The CPS tried in different ways to cooperate with the parents, but without success. When the children were about three to five years old, Maria and several family members were arrested for the criminal offence of fraud. Maria, being only marginally involved, received a short sentence. She was allowed to serve her penalty with her three children in a special institution for single mothers. She was not allowed to receive visitors, but broke the rule several times, arguing that she could not deny the children contact with their family. Because of this breach of terms, she was transferred to a regular woman's prison for the last week of her time, and could not bring the children with her. The Child Protection services took the children into custody without contacting Maria or the children's father. This arrangement was to be temporary until Maria had served her time and settled down. Nevertheless, when

she was released one week later and wanted her children back, the authorities refused to reunite the family. The local CPS office explained the decision, arguing that the children were detrimentally affected by the family's unstable life-style and Maria's deficient mothering. Both parents were suspected of being violent, and the authorities thought they were showing sexualized behaviour, stealing, lying, and not being able to follow rules and regulations. Maria was accused of not being able to provide for her children because she moved from flat to flat, of not protecting her children from instability and conflict, and of having chaotic finances. Both parents were also accused of failing to cooperate with the CPS to better the children's conditions, and of evading control and assistance. Several lawsuits, appeals, and new lawsuits followed. The CPS eventually wanted to permanently remove the children from their parents. It accused the parents of: an unstable and unprotected lifestyle, violent behaviour by the father, possible sexual abuse, and the suspicion that Maria still lived with him.[2] Maria was seen as an immature mother with poor caring abilities. CPS considered her to have weak bonds with her children because she had left them with her mother in-law on several occasions. There was no suspicion of drug abuse and Maria was not found guilty of violence. After a verdict in the lower court, the three children were placed in different foster homes in different parts of Norway. Their whereabouts were kept secret from the family. No family members were considered as suitable foster parents and no steps were taken to assist Maria in her home at this stage, despite this being a condition in the Child Protection Law. The court upheld the care order.

During the first year in which the care order was in operation, Maria was allowed to see her children, but she was not allowed to speak to them in Romanes, only in Norwegian. The authorities believed that if the family spoke Romanes, Maria might make plans to abduct her children. After several complaints from her lawyer, the family was permitted to converse in their native language. However, the visits did not continue for much longer. CPS stopped Maria's visits citing anxiety exhibited by the children before and after their mother's visits. Since this decision, Maria has been engaged in one task: to get her children back and to become a "proper" mother. The children have not seen their parents or family for the last three years.

As I am writing this in 2016, the children are between 9–12 years old. According to Maria, the last time she saw them they were ashamed of speaking their mother tongue and told Maria they have forgotten it. They show many symptoms of self-hatred as "sigøyner" ("gypsy") and blame their misfortune on the fact that they were born Roma and hence are bad.

It is estimated that an undocumented number, around 30–40 Roma children of different ages, have been forcibly separated from their families and kin. They are all living in Norwegian families, generally at secret addresses, separated from siblings and often without contact with their family, kin, and friends. Most Roma in Norway live in the capital, but these children are placed all over the country, usually far away from Oslo. Thus, they are not only separated from their parents, siblings, kin, and socio-cultural environment, but they lose the possibility to speak and develop their mother tongue, Romanes, and thus the prospect of re-connecting with their

---

[2]Roma children are often suspected of being victims of sexual abuse in cases where by Child Protection Services are involved. Roma children are often seen by Norwegians to be "unnaturally" sexually provocative, showing sexualized language and comportment. Among Roma, children are regarded as non-sexual beings and sexual games between children are not problematic while expressions of adult sexuality are strongly tabooed.

families and communities as adults. Before I return to a more detailed analysis of Maria's case, I will discuss some characteristics of the idealized Norwegian Childhood and present the historical relationship between the Norwegian Roma and the government.

Pastoral Power and Child Rescue

In his influential and widely discussed book *Centuries of Childhood*, Aries' (1996) main argument is that childhood as we know it is a cultural construct that varies according to time, place, and contexts. Childhood is also always governed by political regimes, both national and, increasingly, global (Wells 2009). Wells discusses the impact of international and national protective regimes for children, such as The UN Declaration of Human Rights and the UN Convention on the Rights of the Child. Her argument is that childhood regimes in many parts of the world are becoming increasingly universalized, in spite of the great global variety of Childhoods and children's lives. Wells also discusses the history of what she terms "child saving" or "rescuing" (Wells 2009, 26) which became particularly important in the nineteenth century as urbanization and child poverty became more visible than before, and the fear of juvenile criminality grew among the middle classes. Poverty was seen as an individual problem concerning particular groups of people and their moral character. Saving children often meant rescuing them from immoral and deficient parents and families: "In fact, 'child savers' collapsed together… poverty, disease, their families, their neighbourhoods and immorality" (Wells 2009, 28). Wells shows how the child rescue paradigm of the nineteenth century was challenged by the child rights paradigm of the twentieth century with the UN Convention on the Rights of the Child. She argues, however, that the child rescue paradigm is still alive and well in political approaches to childhood and children.

Foucault introduced the term "pastoral power" to analyze genealogies of modern governance (Golder 2007). Pastoral power is derived from the religious narrative of Jesus as the shepherd (pastor) of his flock. Foucault notes that pastoral power is a fundamentally beneficiary power, as the duty of the pastor is to save his flock from harm. Finally, it is an individualizing power as it is the individual sheep that is its object, together with the whole flock as individuals (Golder 2007). Foucault seems to mean that modern state power is derived from this kind of Christian image of power and governance. Pastoral power, when exercised by state institutions is the kind of "power through care" that parents have over their children, and according to Foucault the kind of power that governments increasingly exert over their subjects. Because the pastor, if necessary, must sacrifice himself for the salvation of his flock, the pastor and his flock (subjects) become closely interdependent. This interdependence explains the development of self-governance, where the pastor's subjects

86   A.I. Engebrigtsen

internalize his true, good intentions (Golder 2007). Thus, norms, values, and practices are internalized and experienced as "inner" and self-evident. In Whites' (1998, 267) words: "Foucault's exegesis of the relationship between language, power and knowledge has illuminated the particularly pervasive role played by welfare professionals in the regulation of subjects." The problem with governance through care and self-control is, of course, that it is difficult to oppose and criticize.

The modern Scandinavian welfare state with its childhood regimes may be seen as an expression of pastoral power that disguises the political idea and strategy behind seemingly natural phenomenon such as childhood. The agenda behind the governance of the assimilation and integration programmes for minorities in the 19th century focused on the coercive rescue of children from bad environments. This governance strategy has now changed to more pastoral projects based on the idea of the child's best interests and the need to lead families along appropriate paths. However, in either approach the coercive power of the state is always present.

Before discussing the confrontation between the Norwegian childhood regime and the Roma, I will look at the academic discussion of the Norwegian hegemonic childhood regime, the normative basis for state intervention in families.

Growing up Norwegian—State, Class and Childhood: the Hegemonic Childhood Regime

In the Norwegian welfare discourse, the future sustainability of the welfare state is increasingly regarded as dependant on the well-being of the family and the cognitive and emotional capacity of children (Esping-Andersen 2002). Children's lives have changed rather drastically the last fifty years due to several factors including a strong increase in families' purchasing power, intended political changes in gender relations, and the last thirty years' influx of immigrants from all parts of the world. Scholars have described Norwegian childhood as increasingly modelled on middle class life courses and norms (Stefansen 2011; Gullestad 1996; Leira 2004). Norwegian childhood is managed through institutions such as primary health care, kindergartens, schools, sports clubs, parent education, TV programmes, and housing politics among others. These institutions benefit the middle class and are supported by middle class values and ambitions. Social researchers see children's role in the family now foremost as emotional, confirming the intimacy of family bonds (Aries 1996; Gullestad 1996; Stefansen 2011). Gender equality politics advocate both parents as wage-earners and as child carers, guiding their children from being totally dependent objects towards a life more and more independent from parents and family where they become active subjects and agents in their own right able to search for their "true self" (Kjørholt 2008; Nilsen 2008). In spite of the fact that more control is exerted over the Norwegian child by parents and by state institutions than any time in history, independence and individuality is strongly valued (Boli-Bennet and Meyer 1978). Ideas about children and childhood in Norway are, of course, more complex and diverse than the hegemonic Childhood that governs state regimes, but the government's regime for a proper childhood still concerns all families in Norway.

To most middle-class families, the resulting Norwegian childhood regime is experienced as natural and self-evident, not as an imposed political project. However, precisely because it is a cultural and political product, this Childhood is not self-evident to all inhabitants of Norway. Many Norwegian-born parents have lived under different childhood regimes than their children. Class and minority position, ethnicity and gender intersect in different ways and may represent different material and symbolic environments than middle-class positions do. Many people have not been subject to the Norwegian variants of pastoral power, have not attended the main institutions of the Norwegian childhood regime, or live different lives. This is the situation of most migrant and some minority populations, who may contest and even resist the hegemonic idea of childhood covertly or openly. This conflict often has its most dramatic expression in the encounter between families and the CPS.

Some Notes on the History of Governance of Minorities in Norway

Contemporary Norwegian Roma are descendants of groups that travelled in Norway between the late 1860s and the late 1920s. During the 1920s, all Roma families left the country. Lidén and Engebrigtsen (2010) attributes this exodus to restrictive assimilation policies aimed at different groups of Norwegian Travellers (*Tater, Romani, Splint*)[3] as well as the indigenous population of the Saami. The assimilationist regime began in the late 1800s and lasted until the late 1970s. Traveller children were the main targets of these assimilation measures, legitimized by the government's determination to solve the "Traveller problem." Families were rounded up, often with no legal basis, and given the choice of either being sent to disciplinary camps or having their children placed in Norwegian foster homes or orphanages (Hvinden 2000; Pettersen 2005). When the authorities signalled interest in including the Rom population in this assimilatory project, all Roma left the country.

When, in 1934, the same Roma with Norwegian birth certificates and passports tried to enter the country to seek protection from the rising persecution in Germany. They were denied entry, and sent back to Germany where the majority died in concentration camps. In the 1950s, the surviving "Norwegian Roma" returned to Norway and applied for citizenship based on their own or their parents Norwegian

---

[3]Norwegian ethnonyms.

passports and birth certificates. After several years and several lawsuits, they were granted citizenship. More families followed. In the late 1960s, there were about three extended Roma families, some 60 individuals, living in Norway.

Following a request from a prominent Rom "king," the municipality of Oslo started to plan a comprehensive programme. The *Rehabilitation of the Norwegian Gypsies* was launched in 1972, and lasted until around 1990 (Engebrigtsen and Lidén 2010). The new programme represented a break from earlier policies of forced assimilation. Children and youth were important targets in the new programme as well, and their best interest was determined to be a settled life, working parents with fixed salaries, and access to education. The programme aimed at integrating Roma families into the Norwegian labour market, educational system, permanent settlement, and family planning. After around twenty years with meagre results, the programme was shut down. Evaluation reports explained the failure of the program citing the government's lack of understanding of the lives and interests of the Roma and their resistance to this kind of change (Hjemdal 1982; Hervik 1999; Engebrigtsen 2007; Engebrigtsen and Lidén 2010; Lidén and Engebrigtsen 2010). The programme did, however, influence the social organization and life of the Rom population in Norway in important ways.

Overall, most families had gained economically from the programme, but not in the ways the authorities had intended. It seems that the welfare benefits given to individuals over the age of eighteen undermined the traditional authority of Roma elders and fostered an independence that, for many, resulted in social marginalization. Dependency on welfare prevented several families from long journeys for economic purposes, and many families abandoned or reduced their itinerant lifestyle. Some families continued their old businesses, primarily as itinerary vendors in "Persian" carpets,[4] but as this business was technically illegal,[5] they still officially lived on welfare benefits. More and more children did attend school, but the majority only did so for limited periods, many leaving school to travel with their families. Thus, they were not adequately prepared for the labour market, causing their parents to believe that school was not worth the effort. Some families became "addicted" to social welfare and stopped generating income in other ways; they became permanently poor. The contact between Roma youth and non-Roma youth in poor neighbourhoods with many social problems increased and drug-abuse became a problem. Mobile families managed better, both economically and socially. Research in Romania indicates that Roma groups that maintain their nomadic life style are better off socially and economically than semi-assimilated settled Roma (Voiculescu 2004). This also seems to be the case among the Norwegian Roma.

In 2006, the Norwegian State Church and the Norwegian Government extended an official apology to the Norwegian Roma for their deportation to Nazi Germany in 1934.

---

[4]This was an illegal, but tolerated activity (Hjemdal 1982).

[5]Ambulant trade was against the law.

Growing up Roma—from Autonomy to Dependency?

The Norwegian Roma make up what could be termed a parallel society in Norway. They are organized in extended families that are related through kinship or inter-marriage with the eldest male or couple of each family as leaders. Several families travel abroad for business during spring, summer, and autumn. The Rom community in Norway is closely knit, characterized by limited social contact with non-Roma, and fraught with internal conflicts. The core of the Rom moral code is concerned with separation between Roma and non-Roma in terms of purity of language, body, and society. This cosmology strengthens a deeply felt mistrust towards the non-Rom society that children learn from infancy. The Norwegian Roma have their own Pentecostal Church and their moral values are maintained through their religious practice. Last, but not least, the complicated balance between personal autonomy and collective responsibility means that members of the Rom community may follow their own will and interests within the limits of Roma values and the common good of the community (Mirga 1992). This self-segregation must be interpreted as a way of surviving centuries of state persecution, exclusion, discrimination, and abuse in most parts of Europe (Rosvoll 2013; Engebrigtsen and Lidén 2010; Achim 2004; Mirga 1992).

Roma children grow up in an almost exclusively Rom social environment (Lidén and Engebrigtsen 2010; Engebrigtsen and Lidén 2010). They learn from infancy that being Rom is different than being non-Rom, and that protection and morality is achieved by adhering to Roma norms. Ideally, they grow up in large extended families with many caregivers, siblings and cousins. Children lead a life quite similar to the adults. They are around their parents, aunts, and uncles all day participating in whatever is going on. This is not so different from the life of children in France in the Middle Ages (Aries 1996). They are much indulged as infants and toddlers, and trusted to fend for themselves as young children. They sleep when they are tired and eat when they are hungry. In spring, summer, and fall, extended families move into caravans and travel all over Scandinavia and Europe for religious meetings, business, and to meet kin. The Rom child is seen as an unfinished adult with a will of their own that is respected and opens space for negotiation between children and adults. Adult life starts with marriage, often arranged, and binds boys and girls together and to their kin from an early age. Mothers train their daughters for whatever chores they have. Boys learn the occupation of their fathers and male relatives. Assertiveness, self-expression, and courage are valued characteristics in children. Elders encourage children to challenge adults, especially non-Roma. Thus, non-Roma generally characterized Roma children as "wild" and undisciplined (Engebrigtsen 2007; Engebrigtsen and Lidén 2010; Lidén and Engebrigtsen 2010). However, the conceptualization of childhood has changed among Norwegian Roma. The Roma are neither unaware nor un-receptive to the Norwegian childhood regime. Since the 1970s and 1980s, fertility rates have decreased from approximately six or seven, to three or four children. Other changes followed: smoking where children are present is no longer accepted; many children attend kindergarten; and most children do attend school more or less regularly.

In summary, the Rom childhood regime is based on dependency on family and kin, and is not socialized by Norwegian state institutions. A Rom child is expected to express individuality and assertiveness and is allowed much personal autonomy even at a very young age. A Rom child is expected to adhere to Roma cultural values, which include honouring Roma elders, showing loyalty to their own kin-group, and stressing difference and separation from mainstream society. A Rom child thus grows up with a strong identification with his kin and ethnic group and a strong sense of being Rom and being different from non-Roma people.

The reality is, however, more complex. Several families are entirely dependent on social benefits and are stuck in one place, mostly in Oslo, often in poor and deprived areas with little social support. Several young parents are addicted to prescription medication, narcotics, or alcohol, and some young parents live more or less separated from their extended kin because of their own or their parents' substance abuse. These children may experience neglect and abuse, but family members may be reluctant to offer assistance for fear of destroying the strong ethos of autonomy and self-determination lauded by the Roma (Stewart 1997; Engebrigtsen 2007). Even abused children may have strong bonds to their sisters and brothers, cousins, uncles, aunts and grandparents and other relatives. Many do not speak other languages than Romanes until late childhood and know little about other ways of living.

The Child Protection Services—Individualization and Legislation

The Child Protection Services form one of many instruments of the Norwegian Government's childhood regime. Their mission is: *To make sure that children and youth living under conditions that can harm their health and development, receive the proper help and care at the right moment—to contribute to the development of good and safe living conditions for children and youth* (Moufack 2010, 12). The Norwegian CPS was established in 1896 when a new law, the Guardianship Act (*Vergemålsloven*), was passed.[6] Since then the child welfare system has evolved along with other state welfare institutions (White Paper No. 40 2001–2002, On the protection of children and youth). The goal of CPS is to provide a wide range of services from economic support to poor families through relief measures targeting children and families to coercive steps such as forced foster care.

---

[6]This law defined the public administration of the means belonging to a person declared a minor according to the law.

Developmental psychology and attachment theory are the founding models of child welfare in Norway as elsewhere, where the intimate bond between a mother and a child, nowadays increasingly also a father and a child, is given crucial importance in child development. Although psychological models as a basis for legalization have been deconstructed and challenged internationally (White 1998), these critical stances do not contest the firmly established development model in child welfare. White notes, "...a clear preference can be detected for locating the causation of 'abnormal' development in inadequate or deficient parenting, rather than in biology, culture or chance" (White 1998, 271). She argues that while biological pre-programming is accepted as a valid explanation for normal development, it is rejected as explanation for deviant behaviour. Child-care professionals show instead a preference for a discourse where parents are culpable, and she notes: "Thus, under the influence of this particular form of developmentalism, the child's body becomes the repository for, and the measure of, 'good enough parenting'" (1998, 271). I will return to this issue when analysing Maria's case.

As discussed in the previous section, Norwegian childhood has become increasingly governed by national and global legislation (Reynaert et al. 2009). In 1991, Norway ratified the UN Convention on the Rights of the Child (CRC). A year later, in 1992, the Law on Child Protection Services[7] was passed. In 2003, the CRC was incorporated into Norwegian law and into the Universal Declaration of Human Rights (UDHR). That means that the CRC became Norwegian law and may overrule other regulations in other jurisdictions if they are contradictory. These laws were developed and established to protect children from harmful authorities and environments, counteract the negative results of families in difficult life situations, protect children from parents with problematic child rearing practices, and support families with children with behavioural problems. CPS interventions usually result from both external concerns and families seeking support. Local and international laws and conventions oblige the CPS to make sure that the best interest of the child prevails in all contexts.

However, children's lives are dependent on their families' class position, economic situation, ethnicity, history, health condition, and not least whether they grow up in towns or on farms and whether they are boys or girls. Is this multiculturalism understood and acknowledged in the work of CPS professionals? By analysing seventeen court cases in Norway that resulted in children from immigrant backgrounds being placed in care in foster homes, Hofman (2010) found that although the child's cultural background (ethnicity, religion) played a role in the decisions for placing children in public care, cultural aspects were not taken into consideration at all in the choice of foster homes. Although Roma children have grown up mostly in Norway, they have grown up in a segregated Rom environment with little contact with mainstream Norwegian society. A Norwegian foster home will probably represent an even greater break from their cultural background, than it will for many immigrant children.

---

[7]The law on public Child Care was passed in 1953.

The Framework Convention for the Protection of National Minorities—Liberation or Control Through Care?

In 1999, Norway passed the Council of Europe's *Framework Convention for the Protection of National Minorities*. This convention states that national minorities shall be protected from discrimination and shall be granted the ability to keep and develop their language, religion, and culture. With this convention, Rom childhood in Norway is not only protected as an individual experience, but as collective way of life, and with it, the individuals' right to belong to the Rom collective and to maintain and develop cultural traits such as language, religion, and culture.

The Roma willingly accepted the status as "national minority." However, the framework convention appears to have become a mixed blessing for the Rom population. Designating the Roma as a national minority, the Council of Europe expected that they would successfully "integrate" into the mainstream society in their respective countries. The authorities' ability to register, control, and monitor this minority in order to assure their wellbeing and future inclusion into the welfare state, is increasingly managed by referring to "the best interest of the child," in accordance with national and international legislation such as the Convention for the Rights of the Child. This renewed engagement of the State with Roma families means an increased pressure towards what they see as assimilation. Roma in Norway experience education in Norwegian language, norms, and ways of life as a threat to their language, cosmology, and society (see among others Voiculescu 2011). As the Convention for the Protection of National Minorities, unlike the Convention for the Rights of the Child (CRC), is not incorporated into Norwegian law, its protective function is limited and in practice, it is subordinate to the CRC.

The Universalized Political Regime and Norwegian Child Protection Services

Scholars have criticized the development of international and national regimes of childhood, for their technicalization and decontextualization (Reynaert et al. 2009) of childhood, for their defamiliarization (Therborn 1993) and for their education-alization, or biased preoccupation with school education (Reynaert et al. 2009, 529). The critics tie this model of the childhood regime to the development of liberal politics in Europe focused on the individual, autonomous, and choosing subject. International convention regimes are based on the ideas of a general child, freed from class, ethnicity, gender, and poverty. This autonomous child's rights are in conflict with the rights of the parents to foster a child, and are at the same time strongly focused on institutionalized education, both private and public (Reynaert et al. 2009, 529).

However, in spite of its universalizing scope, The UN Convention on the Rights of the Child is meant to be culturally sensitive, to be conscious of the diversity it represents and thus to protect families from state power when that is necessary. In combination, the Childcare law, the Convention on the Rights of the Child and the Convention for the Protection of National Minorities, should guarantee the protection of the best interest of the child, even for minority children.

In spite of the international conventions' stress on the necessity to "take diversity into consideration," the Norwegian version of Childhood has become more universalized and streamlined through these globalized processes, and different childhoods have increasingly been treated with suspicion in this process (Wells 2009). Like Europe in general, Norway is increasingly multi-ethnic. An increasing part of the Norwegian population has grown up elsewhere with different languages, norms, values and life trajectories and corresponding experiences. Their childhoods, more or less compatible with the Norwegian norm, are not part of the Norwegian concept of Childhood except as challenges and deficits (Boddy 2013). This assumed challenge of diversity has led to the development of parent education programmes for foreigners, based on Norwegian middle-class values and streamlined by "international and culturally neutral scientific methods for 'good parenting'" (see for instance Øyby 2007). Practitioners and politicians do not regard these models and programmes as politically and ideologically shaped, by global or national cultural norms. They are not seen as parallel to other child-rearing practices, but as inherently better and better suited to improve the quality of life for children, and as such they are seen to represent both progress and the realization of children's human rights (Wells 2009, 179). This may explain why cultural differences are often neither understood nor taken into consideration when choosing foster homes for minority children (Hofman 2010). This is the case in spite of the overwhelming evidence from research on children and children's worlds, and research on class differences in early childhood, showing that child-rearing practices are embedded in cultural worlds and value-systems and are difficult to learn outside these in some sort of value-neutral way (James and Prout 1997; James et al. 1998; Wells 2015). Although Roma children have grown up mostly in Norway, they have grown up in a parallel society of Roma, with other cultural norms and practices, generally with no or little school attendance, and with a mother tongue other than Norwegian.

Perceptions, Dilemmas, and Ambiguity Dealing with Roma Families

Maria: Poor Mothering

Maria's parenting defied Norwegian childhood in important ways. She left her children with her husband and close relatives for long periods while travelling with her natal family. Her children grew up dependent and attached to a group of kin, rather than to their parents alone. Her marriage appeared to be unstable. When she eventually moved away to live with her children, she moved from flat to flat because she had difficulty paying the rent. When the CPS tried to contact her to establish cooperation for the good of the children, she moved or did not keep the appointments. She did send her children to school, but too late according to Norwegian law. The school reported that the children had difficulties adapting to the classroom norms and teachers described them as wild and uncontrollable. The headmaster of the special institution where Maria served her penalty also experienced her children as anti-social, and Maria was accused of breaking the rules she promised to adhere to when she was admitted.

Maria's behaviour is not pathological from a Rom point of view. She had a much narrower network of supportive kin than is the norm among Roma women, because of problems between her natal family and her in-laws. In general, she behaved very much in line with general Rom way of life, where economic instability, repeated change of residence, leaving children with relatives, and not protecting children from family conflicts is the norm rather than the exception. Maria herself has only sporadically attended school, and she knew little about the laws and regulations that govern primary education. Many Roma regard formal schooling as an assimilatory strategy (Engebrigtsen 2007; Engebrigtsen and Lidén 2010; Voiculescu 2011) and evading school has been, and for some families still is, a way to resist assimilation.

This case is only one of several cases that confronted the CPS with difficult dilemmas. The fact that neither Maria nor her husband were wage earners, but were receiving welfare, like the majority of the Norwegian Roma, was another concern to the CPS, together with the fact that Maria and her in-laws had criminal records. Finally, the CPS found indications that the father had been violent towards some of the children and that there was a suspicion of sexual abuse. Maria's behaviour was consequently interpreted as an expression of "poor ability to care for her children," because she was not able to protect her children in a proper way. Rom child rearing traditions and family life patterns, the "normality" of Roma children, or any other aspects of their cultural background seem not to have been taken into consideration. Neither was her special situation, giving birth to three children in three years, discussed as a burden that could overstretch her mothering abilities.

How were the CPS to interpret this way of life and how could they secure the children's rights without "rescuing" them from their parents and environment? How could they have balanced securing the rights of the children as individuals in accordance with Norwegian and international law, while also considering their right to grow up in their natal ethnic group and develop their ethnic identity and language? The Norwegian CPS has difficulty reconciling these considerations for cultural awareness with the approach and the tools they have at their disposal today.

Transferring a child from a Rom environment to a Norwegian foster home implies a total transformation of that child's life-world and identity. As already discussed, the Roma children are socialized in opposition to the Norwegian life-world. For these children to manage this transformation and to attach to new parents, they need to deny their "Rom-ness," their biological parents, and their entire background. The Roma are a stigmatized population in Norway, as they are all over Europe, and Roma children will always be reminded of their ancestry. There is a considerable likelihood that Roma children in Norwegian custody develop self-hate and insecure identities (Høgmo 1986; Eide and Aanesen 2008). Regardless of the quality of the foster family, they will most probably have been exposed to the majority's pejorative view of the Roma. To handle this stigma without internalizing it, the individual depends on an affirmative social group that will support them. Roma children in Norwegian foster care are without the social protection of an affirmative Rom community and will most probably internalize the stigma attached to them and develop insecurity and a negative identity. What will happen when these children are no longer under CPS-care? Will they contact and try to re-unite with their families? Will they be accepted? Will they be accepted by and attach to the majority society, or will they linger between these conflicting societies without finding their place? What has been gained by removing the children from their families if they grow up without the personal security they need to handle a difficult life?

Lost Between Protective Regimes?

Children need protection from neglect, abuse, and violence from their caretakers, the environment, and from the general public, but not least from government agencies. The development of national and international laws and conventions have highlighted the lives and conditions of children and secured a better life for children in many parts of the world. But, as Wells, following Foucault (2009), points out, universalized children or "the best interest of the child" is increasingly an instrument for a state's political goals. This was the case in the Afghanistan war, where girls' education was an important argument for intervention. It is also the case in the implementation of national integration programmes for the inclusion of minorities and immigrants, where arguments based on the best interest of the child predominate. As White (1998) argues, the best interest of the child has been moulded on psychological theories that are reified and legalized by being incorporated into the judicial field and presented as self-evident. In spite of good intentions, state intervention can also be abusive and harmful to children and their caretakers. The transfer of Roma children to Norwegian foster homes can be regarded as a process of forced assimilation that can be analyzed as symbolic violence (Bourdieu 1986) with a very indecisive result. Placing minority children in Norwegian foster homes can also be regarded as state discrimination. While Norwegian children are placed in Norwegian foster homes, where their national culture, traditions, faith and language are known and can be developed, Roma children are placed in families that do not resemble their native families. They lose not only their parents, but their entire life world, their ethnic group, and their mother tongue. Thus ideas of the child as a free-floating individual that can be uprooted and replanted without concern for her cultural, social and linguistic context prevails.

But are there no ways to reconcile the child as an individual and as a collective member in CPS service? There are several options. Foster parents can be actively sought in Roma communities both in Norway and in other countries. The Roma are a transnational population with kin all over Europe. Of course, this solution implies new problems. Instead of placing Roma children in foster families with strong expectations of intimate attachment to new parents, one should also develop small orphanages, modelled on SOS Children's Villages[8] where siblings can live together and keep in touch with their family and kin. Most importantly, Roma children in CPS custody in whatever model need support and assistance to be able to maintain contact and communication with their ethnic group, develop their language, intellectual abilities, identity, and sense of belonging. If and when foster children wish to reconnect in some way with their family and kin, the chance of not fitting in or of being rejected may thus be minimized.

The aim of this chapter has been to highlight how protective regimes may be contradictory, and, in the case of Roma families, how conventions and laws to protect the individual child overrule protective conventions that are intended to protect minorities from state discrimination. The notion of the universal, individual, right holding child—the child as agent—is the basis of legislation on children. Therefore, the notion of the child in context, the social child, is overruled. The UN Convention and the best interest of the child may thus support state abuse against Roma children, by separating them not only from their parents, but also from their entire social and cultural world.

References

Achim, V. (2004). *The Roma in Romanian history*. Budapest and New York: Central European University Press.

Aries, P. (1996). *Centuries of childhood*. London: PIMLICO.

Boddy, J. (2013). Ethic tensions in research with children across cultures, within countries. In H. Fossheim (Ed.), *Cross-cultural child research: Ethical issues*. Norwegian National Research Ethics Committees: Oslo.

Boli-Bennet, J., & Meyer, J. (1978). The ideology of childhood and the state: Rules distinguishing children in national constitutions, 1870–1970. *American Sociological Review, 43*(7), 797–812.

Bourdieu, P. (1986). *Outline of a theory of practice. Cambridge series in social anthropology*. Cambridge: Cambridge University Press.

Eide, B., & Aanesen, E. (2008). *Nasjonens barn*. Oslo: Conflux Forlag.

---

[8]An international NGO developing and running orphanages as villages based on a family model where children grow up in "social families" with a "mother" "siblings" and sometimes a "father." Co-operation with the biological family is sought after (http://www.soschildrensvillages.org.uk/).

5 Lost Between Protective Regimes: Roma in the Norwegian State 97

Engebrigtsen, A. I. (2007). *Exploring gypsiness: Power, exchabge and interdependence in a Transylvanian village*. New York, Oxford: Berghahn Books.

Engebrigtsen, A. I., & Lidén, H. (2010). Å finne sin plass som minoritet—Rombefolkningen i Norge i dag. In B. Lund, A. Bonnevie, B. Moen, & B. Bolme (Eds.), *Nasjonale minoriteter i det flerkulturelle Norge*. Tapir Forlag: Oslo.

Esping-Andersen, G. (2002). A child centred social investment strategy. In G. Esping-Andersen (Ed.), *Why we need a new welfare state*. Oxford: Oxford University Press.

Golder, B. (2007). Foucault and the genealogy of pastoral power. *Radical Philosophy Review, 10* (2), 157–176.

Foucault, M. (2009). Governmentality. In G. Burcell, C. Gordon & P. MIller (Eds.), *The Foucault Effect: Studies in Governmentality*. Chicago: University of Chicago Press.

Gullestad, M. (1996). From obedience to negotiation: Dilemmas in the transmission of values between the generations in Norway. *Journal of the Royal Anthropological Institute, 2*(1), 25–42.

Hervik, P. (1999). *Den Generende Forskellighet—Danske svar på den stigende multikulturalisme*. København: Hans Reitzel.

Hjemdal, O. K. (1982). *Evaluering av arbeidet med sigøynerne*. Oslo: Sosialdepartementet.

Hofman, S. (2010). Hensyn til kultur og barnets beste—en undersøkelse av 17 barnevernssaker om omsorgsovertakelse og plassering av minoritetsbarn. In *Kvinnerettslig skriftserie*. Oslo: Avdeling for kvinnerett, barnerett, likestillings—og diskrimineringsrett (KVIBALD) Universitetet i Oslo.

Høgmo, A. (1986). Det tredje alternativ. Barns læring av identitetsforvaltning i samiske områder preget av identitetsskifte. *Tidsskrift for samfunnsforskning, 27*, 395–416.

Hvinden, B. (2000). *Romanifolket og det norske samfunnet*. Bergen: Fagbokforlaget.

James, A., & Prout, A. (Eds.). (1997). *Constructing and reconstructing childhood: Contemporary Issues in the sociological study of childhood*. London, Washington: Falmer Press.

James, A., Jenks, C., & Prout, A. (1998). *Theorizing childhood*. Cambridge: Polity Press.

Karoli, S. (2014). *Norske sigøynerbarn-Etnisk rensing og barnerov?*. Forlag: Marxist.

Kjørholt, T. (2008). Children as new citizens. In A. James & A. L. James (Eds.), *European childhood: Cultures, politics and childhoods in Europe*. New York: Palmgrave Macmillan.

Leira, A. (2004). Omsorgsstaten og familien. In A. L. Ellingsæter & A. Leira (Eds.), *Velferdsstaten og familien: Utfordringer og dilemmaer*. Gyldendal norske forlag A/S Akademisk: Oslo.

Lidén, H., & Engebrigtsen, A. I. (2010). De norske Roma og deres historie. In B. Lund, A. Bonnevie, B. Moen, & B. Bolme (Eds.), *Nasjonale minoriteter i det flerkulturelle Norge*. Tapir Forlag: Oslo.

Mirga, A. (1992). Roma territorial behaviour and state policy: The case of the socialist countries of East Europe. In M. J. Casimir & A. R. Casimir (Eds.), *Mobility and territoriality: Social and spatial boundaries among foragers, fishers, pastoralists and peripatetics*. Oxford: Berg.

Moufack, M. F. (2010). *Et sensitivt barnevern. Mastergrad*. Trondheim: NTNU.

Nilsen, R. D. (2008). Children in nature: Cultural ideas and social practices in Norway. In J. Allison (Ed.), *European childhoods: Culture, politics and childhoods in Norway*. New York: Palgrave Macmillan.

Øyby, A. L. M. (2007). *Er somalisk og norsk kultur som olje og vand? Somaliske mødres tilværelse i Norge—et studie om socializering i et fremmedkulturelt samfund*, Sosialantropologisk institutt of Oslo, Oslo.

Pettersen, K. S. (2005). *Mangfold, makt og motstand*. Oslo: NOVA, Norwegian Social Research.

Reynaert, D., Bouverne-de-Bie, A., & Vandervelde, A. (2009). A review of children's rights literature since the adoption of the United Nations convention rights of the child. *Childhood, 16*, 518–534.

Rosvoll, M. (2013). Antisiganisme. *Materialisten, 1*(2), 7–39.

Stefansen, K. (2011). *Foreldreskap i småbarnsfamilien: Klassekultur og sosial reproduksjon*. Oslo: NOVA Norwegian Social Research.

Stewart, M. (1997). *The time of the gypsies*. Colorado: Westview Press.

Therborn, G. (1993). The politics of childhood: The rights of children in modern times. In F. G. Castles (Ed.), *Families of nations: Patterns of public policy in Western democracies*. Aldershot and Vermont: Dartmouth Publishing Company.

Voiculescu, C. (2004). Temporary migration of Transylvanian Roma to Hungary. In *Proceedings of the International Seminar on New Patterns of Labour Migration in Central and Eastern Europe, Cluj Napoca, Romania, 15–19 July 2004*.

Voiculescu, C. (2011). To whom God speaks: Struggles for authority through religious reflexivity and performativity within a gypsy pentecostal church. *Sociological Research Online, 17*(2), 10. doi:10.5153/SRO.2600.

Wells, K. (2009). *Childhood in a global perspective*. Cambridge: Polity Press.

Wells, K. (2015). *Childhood in a global perspective* (2nd ed.). Cambridge: Polity Press.

White, S. (1998). Interdiscursivity and child welfare: The ascent and durability of psycho-legalism. *The Sociological Review, 46*(2), 264–292.

White Paper No. 40 (2001–2002). *On the protection of children and youth*.

Open Access This chapter is licensed under the terms of the Creative Commons Attribution-NonCommercial 2.5 International License (http://creativecommons.org/licenses/by-nc/2.5/), which permits any noncommercial use, sharing, adaptation, distribution and reproduction in any medium or format, as long as you give appropriate credit to the original author(s) and the source, provide a link to the Creative Commons license and indicate if changes were made.

The images or other third party material in this chapter are included in the book's Creative Commons license, unless indicated otherwise in a credit line to the material. If material is not included in the book's Creative Commons license and your intended use is not permitted by statutory regulation or exceeds the permitted use, you will need to obtain permission directly from the copyright holder.

Chapter 6
When Policy Meets Practice: A Study of Ethnic Community-Based Organizations for Children and Youth

Marianne Takle and Guro Ødegård

Ethnic Community-Based Organizations

> Immigrant youth are rootless. They do not know whether they belong to Norwegian society or if they are a part of something else. This is also my experience. Where do I belong? I find it useful to bring the best from both cultures: maintain roots, acquire resources and integrate into the Norwegian society.

This is a quote from a leader of an ethnic community-based organization for children and youth in Norway. He is a young man who came to Norway as a child from Kurdistan, and has lived most of his life in his adopted country. When asked why it was useful to establish special ethnic community-based organizations for children and youth in Norway, he answered that these kids are struggling with the question of belonging and identity. His answer is typical. Many ethnic community leaders working with immigrant youth share his opinion. They bemoan the fact that many of their members seem to forget their cultural heritage. In turn, they encourage cultural and social integration among their members within the organizations, and emphasize simultaneously that this will lead to integration into mainstream Norwegian society.

The Norwegian government has funded several ethnic community-based organizations for children and youth. The leader quoted above represents one of eight such organizations that received support in 2013. The members of these organizations have cultural or ethnic bonds to Sri Lanka, Turkey, Vietnam and Azerbaijan, and two organizations have members from different regions in Kurdistan. While some members are themselves immigrants, others were born in Norway to immigrant parents. The Norwegian state categorizes all of them as children and youth of immigrant background. This classification is congruent with Norwegian citizenship legislation, which considers children born in Norway to

---

M. Takle (✉) · G. Ødegård
NOVA, Oslo and Akershus University College, Oslo, Norway
e-mail: marianne.takle@nova.hioa.no

© The Author(s) 2016
M.L. Seeberg and E.M. Goździak (eds.), *Contested Childhoods: Growing up in Migrancy*, IMISCOE Research Series,
DOI 10.1007/978-3-319-44610-3_6

immigrant parents citizens of their ancestral homelands. Children of immigrant parents can apply for Norwegian citizenship, but they must give up their former citizenship, as Norway does not recognize dual citizenship (Takle 2006). This legislation makes it problematic for children born in Norway to escape the migrancy framework the state puts them into. In this chapter, we apply the concept of migrancy as defined in the introduction to this book. We regard migrancy as a socially constructed category, which does not solely reflect the condition of being a migrant, as it is attributed beyond those who have migrated. It is not a place, but a social space (see the introduction to this book written by Seeberg and Goździak).

The migrancy framework is reinforced by the government's funding to ethnic community-based organizations for children and youth. This funding developed within the context of the relationships between civil society (including voluntary organizations), the government and the welfare state in Norway. In Norway, Sweden, Finland, and Denmark there have been interactions between popular movements, civil society, and the state to create and sustain what has been termed *the Nordic welfare state model* (Kuhnle and Selle 1992). In all Nordic countries, voluntary organizations often have a broad membership base. Participation in voluntary work is generally seen as an integral part of being a member of an organization and organizations are democratically structured (Trähgårdh and Vamstad 2009; Wollebæk and Sivesind 2010). The state's support to ethnic community-based organizations for children and youth is meant to strengthen their civic engagement and political participation in the larger society.

In this chapter, we examine how eight ethnic community-based organizations, which received funding from the state, identify themselves and develop their practice within the framework of the Norwegian tradition of voluntary organization. Our main thesis is that ethnic community-based organizations work to maintain their members' cultural heritage, and may at times contest the Norwegian understanding of voluntary organizations as a stepping-stone to individual participation in the larger society.

We have interviewed eight leaders or representatives of seven of the state-supported organizations. Two of the leaders were born in Norway to immigrant parents, four immigrated when they were between the age of twelve and fourteen years, and one came to Norway at the age of 23. The youth trace their roots to Kurdistan, Vietnam, Azerbaijan, Sri Lanka, and Turkey. In our analyses of these interviews, we find it useful to distinguish between two aspects. First, we examine how these organizations adapt to the category "children and youth of an immigrant background," and how the state defines special schemes for ethnic community-based organizations. We analyze whether they accept or contest the migrancy framework within which they, and their organizations, are placed by the Norwegian state. Secondly, we examine whether these organizations' identities and practices are in line with the government's aim of defining and supporting them as democratic communities. We analyze whether the government and the organizations have diverging goals of establishing special ethnic community-based voluntary organizations for children and youth.

Moreover, we discuss how the concept of political opportunity structures is developed in academic literature (Jacobs and Tillie 2004; Koopmans et al. 2005; Morales and Giugni 2011) and apply this to youth organizations in the Nordic context. Moreover, we make analytical distinctions between the cultural, social, civic and political dimensions of integration (Eriksen 2010). Although the production of cultural meaning, social interactions, civic engagement and political participation often overlap in practice, these analytical distinctions are useful to overcome a one-sided focus on cultural integration. By using these distinctions, we can examine and compare the similarities and differences in how the Norwegian government and the ethnic CBOs combine these dimensions of integration and thereby contribute to analyses of identity, belonging, and civic and political participation.

Several studies show that young people who have immigrated as children or are born to immigrant parents have different challenges and forms of belonging than their parents and grandparents (Crul and Mollenkopf 2012; Wessendorf 2013; Ødegård et al. 2014). There is, however, lack of knowledge about how these young people organize themselves in migrant organizations. Our study aims to contribute to this debate by analysing ethnic community-based organizations' practices. We examine how they work to encourage members to take part in activities in their ethnic community and in the larger society.

The chapter is divided into five sections. The introduction is followed by a section that examines how government funding for voluntary youth organizations can be understood within the Nordic context. The third part discusses both our contribution to the on-going academic debate on ethnic community-based organizations and the cultural, social, civic and political dimensions of integration. The fourth section covers empirical analysis of the organizations' practice, which we examine in relation to the cultural, social, civic and political dimensions of integration. The chapter concludes that CBOs challenge the government's understanding of integration as processes taking place within nation state boundaries.

Youth Organizations in the Nordic Context

The concept of the political opportunity structure was developed within the framework of studies of social movements and subsequently adapted to studies of migration (Koopmans and Statham 2000). Examples of such adaptation are the studies conducted by Koopmans et al. (2005) on how the combination of citizenship regimes and cultural group rights affect immigrants' collective actions in several European countries. Studies of political opportunity structures argue that institutions that are created in the receiving countries for immigrants influence the way in which immigrants organize themselves and participate in the larger society through collective action such as immigrant organizations (Odmalm 2004; Togeby 2004; Predelli 2008).

Several scholars have, in the social capital tradition of Putnam (2000), focused on what role ethnic organizations play in immigrants' civic and political participation (Fennema and Tillie 2001; Jacobs and Tillie 2004). Studies from several European cities find that immigrants' membership in ethnic organizations has a significant bearing on political participation, but also reveals variations between different ethnic groups and different forms of political participation (Jacobs and Tillie 2004; Tillie 2004; Berger et al. 2004; Bay et al. 2010).

More recent studies from several European cities combine these two approaches through analyses of how different compositions of political opportunity structures, organizational membership, and individual factors influence immigrants' political participation (Morales and Giugni 2011). Studies conducted within this analytical framework show that membership in ethnic organizations leads to increased political participation if combined with an open political opportunity structure in the form of multiple group rights (Morales and Pilati 2011, 110; Myrberg and Rogstad 2011, 194; D'Angelo 2015).

These European studies show that both membership in immigrant organizations and the political opportunity structure of the organizations affect the political participation of immigrants and their children. This research, however, does not examine which conditions within the immigrant organizations lead to the members participating in the majority society's civic and political activities. Taking these findings, which are mostly based on quantitative studies, as the point of departure gives rise to a need to conduct a qualitative study of what the immigrant organizations do to promote civic engagement and political participation among members.

Nordic research shows an increasing connection between the state's support of civil society institutions and greater involvement of civil society organizations to promote integration of ethnic minority groups into majority society (Pyykkonen 2007; Bengtsson 2010; Kugelberg 2011; Agergaard and Michelsen la Cour 2012). In Norway, two national institutions register voluntary organizations for youth. One is *Fordelingsutvalget*, the Distributive Committee, which is an administrative body under the Ministry of Children, Equality and Social Inclusion. The committee's main task is to distribute grants to Norwegian voluntary children and youth organizations. In order to receive financial support, the state requires that the youth organizations are both membership-based and have an internal democratic structure. These requirements can be understood within the framework of central characteristics of the voluntary sector in the Nordic countries.

The other national institution is the Norwegian Children and Youth Council, *Landsrådet for Norges barne- og ungdomsorganizasjoner* (LNU). LNU is an umbrella organization for approximately ninety non-governmental organizations for all children and youth in Norway. This includes a variety of organizations, such as religious, political, cultural and leisure organizations. LNU is an independent and democratic organization, which both represents the member organizations' common interest in relation to political authorities and offers different types of services (such as seminars, meetings, international networking etc.) for its member organizations.

LNU—as a body for youth organizations' interests—can be understood as integrated in the wider Nordic tradition of voluntary organization. As mentioned above, central characteristics of this tradition is that voluntary organizations often have a broad membership base, participation in voluntary work is generally seen as an integral part of being a member of an organization and organizations are democratically structured (Trähgårdh and Vamstad 2009; Wollebæk and Sivesind 2010). The normative ideal is that organizations should be democratically organized in such a way that their actions reflect their members' preferences (Lorentzen 2004, 31). Groups are seen as a collective of individuals, and democratic procedures within groups give all members an opportunity to participate. Participation in organizations socializes each individual member into democratic values and gives them training in practical democracy.

The Nordic tradition of voluntary organizations is also characterized as a people's movement model, and in the Norwegian context, people's movements have brought broad groups from all over the country into the public domain since the latter half of the 19th century (Østerud et al. 2003). Historically, the aim has been to create political weight and legitimacy through mass membership, built on a broad social mobilization. The Norwegian emphasis on democracy can partly be explained by the fact that civil organizations were established in the same period as national independence. Nineteenth century mainstream popular movements followed the same organizational structure as the political parties. They have been characterized by a hierarchical organization, where local organizations are linked together in regional and national organizations (Østerud et al. 2003). People's movements provided local interest in the political centre, and in many cases acted as counter-cultures to the majority culture.

In line with the Nordic tradition, hierarchical and rule-based organizations are established outside the state administration. They function as an alternative political channel, and a form of political influence outside the party system and the election channel (Rokkan 1966). The voluntary organizations function as a parallel bureaucratic structure, but there are also huge overlapping zones between voluntary organizations and state administration.

Voluntary organizations are crucial to Norwegian democratic culture and identity (Lorentzen 2004). The idea is that voluntary organizations can be places where members learn democratic values in practice—both civic and political. They are socialized in democratic decision-making procedures even when the organizations do not aim to have political influence, but are rather engaged in civic, cultural and social activities. Hence, within the Nordic tradition, the distinction between civic and political engagement often becomes blurred. Both types of engagements imply relations between individuals or groups and public institutions. This can include civic engagement in public institutions and political participation such as voting in elections or running for elected office.

Although scholars find that there has been a gradual transition in the Norwegian voluntary sector away from the people's movement model towards philanthropy, they simultaneously conclude that as a normative ideal, the membership-based, democratic, and hierarchical model of voluntary organizations has vitality (Wollebæk and Sivesind 2010; Folkestad et al. 2015).

Studies from the Nordic countries show that central elements of the Nordic tradition of organizing the voluntary sector are applied to ethnic community-based organizations (Borevi 2004; Pyykkonen 2007; Predelli 2008; Hagelund and Loga 2009; Bay et al. 2010; Ødegård 2010; Kugelberg 2011; Myrberg and Rogstad 2011; Takle 2014). When we place the ethnic community-based organizations for children and youth in our study in the wider context of the Nordic tradition of civil society, we recognize these central characteristics. The government formulates the democratic ideal by referring explicitly to this tradition:

> Meanwhile, the government is concerned that the voluntary organizations, including immigrant organizations, follow democratic principles. By allocating support to organizations it has traditionally been emphasized that the organizations must have a democratically elected leadership and an elected board. This also applies to immigrant organizations (White Paper No. 39 2006–2007, 62).

It thus appears that the policy is based on the belief that identities are important, but that identities linked to other ethnic or national groups shall not influence majority institutions. Analysing White papers from the early 2000s, Gressgård (2005) finds a general recognition of cultural differences, but in practice these policies are tied to the individual. The Norwegian government's respect for immigrants and their descendants' culture as groups is limited to some areas and rather instrumental. The government sees the ethnic and national groups as places for cultural and social integration in small communities. The idea is that such integration among equals will lead to increased participation in the wider society:

> Immigrant organizations can function as a stepping stone for contact with other inhabitants and participation in other arenas, and in this way strengthen immigrants' belonging to the larger society (White Paper No. 6 2012–2013, 126).

In accordance with the Nordic tradition of voluntary organization, ethnic community-based organizations engaged in cultural and social activities can be places where members learn democratic values in practice. The government's rationale for seeing the CBOs as a stepping-stone to wider civic and political engagement is the belief in this Nordic tradition where the voluntary organizations are expected to contribute to democratic education (White Paper No. 6 2012–2013, 123). There is an ambiguity in Norwegian government policy in this field: The aim of supporting ethnic community-based organizations is not to strengthen the group as such, but rather to use the organizations as an arena to nudge individual children and youth towards civic and political participation in the Norwegian mainstream society. According to Berkaak (2012) the Norwegian policy is both ambiguous and vague, and when this policy is gradually implemented it might lead to measures that counteract each other in practice.

The Concept of Integration

There is an on-going academic debate on whether ethnic community-based organizations lead to integration of their members in the host society or to increased segregation among minorities (Jacobs and Tillie 2004; Portes et al. 2007; Yurdakul 2009; Bay et al. 2010; Glick Schiller 2010; *Faist* 2010; Morales and Pilati 2011). Several studies show that most ethnic CBOs are both preserving the cultural heritage of their country of origin and facilitating migrants' integration into the country of settlement (Amelina and Faist 2008, 2012; Handy and Greenspan 2009; Glick Schiller 2010). This can be contrasted with countries with a long history of immigration such as Canada (Bauder 2011). In the Norwegian context Ødegård et al. (2014) show that ethnic community-based organizations and networks have different purposes for different groups. For newcomers, the organizations play a crucial role as an arena for social contact between different waves of immigrants. The organizations also operate as a forum for disseminating essential information about rights, eligibility for welfare and access to education and childcare. The organizations serve as meeting places for young people who position themselves in relation to dual identities, and for those struggling with balancing cultural practices rooted in the country of origin and the country of settlement. For children born and raised in Norway, these networks also serve as an arena to learn their heritage language and traditional cultural expressions. Finally, ethnic community-based organizations contribute to the political mobilization of networks of immigrants in a Norwegian context (see also Bjørklund and Bergh 2013; Takle 2014).

Refuting the assumption that ethnic community-based organizations are a hindrance to successful immigrant integration in their countries of settlement, studies have shown that ethnic CBO's transnational activity and their members' integration in their settlement society are not at odds with each other (Amelina and Faist 2008; Horst et al. 2010). Amelina and Faist (2008) conclude in their study of Turkish organizations in Germany that religious, economic, and political organizations in Germany combine their transnational ties with German integration pressure, but in various ways. Such findings are of special relevance for Norwegian ethnic CBOs for youth as members of the organizations included in this study have lived most or all of their lives in Norway.

The Cultural, Social and Civic/Political Dimensions of Integration

Inspired by Eriksen (2010, 69–109), we define the cultural, social, civic and political dimensions of integration in the following way: (1) The cultural dimension of integration refers to understandings of implicit and explicit communication, and this requires common language, codes, and symbols. These are often based on common historical experiences. (2) The social dimension of integration refers to persons, network and feelings of belonging. This implies interactions between friends and colleagues, and is often based on face-to-face contact. (3) Both the civic and the political dimensions of integration refer to individuals' relations to the system such as bureaucratic and democratic institutions. They mainly imply relations between individuals or groups and public institutions. Such relations can both include civic engagement in public institutions and political participation such as voting in elections or running for election. Although the production of cultural meaning and social interaction mostly overlap in practice, we can imagine situations where individuals understand the world in a similar way, and understand each other, without having any interactions. This is often the case within abstract national frameworks (Anderson 1991).

It is, however, crucial to distinguish between different levels of integration. Integration in the larger mainstream society refers to the relationship between individuals, or groups, and public institutions. This is an abstract relationship, which also has cultural aspects (Takle 2014). In contrast, membership in an ethnic community-based group refers to small-scale integration, in which people meet each other face-to-face. Both are forms of formal belonging, which stand in contrast with informal networks and close friends.

The civic and political dimension of integration refers to the macro level, such as public institutions and their stability and reproduction. These are public institutions such as police, hospitals, schools and public administration. The social dimension of integration can both take place within public institutions and at the micro level through kinship groups and friends. While the civic and political dimension of integration refers to how public institutions work, the social dimension refers to the characteristics of personal interactions within such institutions. There can also be distrustful relations in cases where public institutions such as the police and public administration do not work. In contrast, public institutions might function in situations where there are weak social networks and a lack of feelings of belonging. Moreover, if the social networks and feelings of belonging are only related to separate groups and there are no common institutions that mediate between personal networks and groups, the society becomes fragmented. The outcome might result in lack of trust in abstract systems (Eriksen 2010).

The three dimensions may take various forms in relation to the feeling of belonging of an ethnic community-based group and of the larger society. Young people can be integrated in the country they live in through friends, school, work, and in relation to politics and public administration. Simultaneously, their cultural and social dimensions of integration can be bound to ethnic communities. Moreover, ethnic community-based groups are often oriented towards their members' countries of origin and tie their identity to these homelands. Although the organizations' members do not necessarily travel between countries, the organizations might structure their cultural, social, civic and political dimensions of integration in multiple nation-state contexts (Amelina and Faist 2008). Transnational ties might be reflected in how ethnic community-based organizations aim to pursue the identity of their members' country of origin within their country of settlement, and thereby challenge an idea of integration as processes taking place within nation-state boundaries.

Eight Ethnic Community-Based Organizations for Children and Youth

There are several local ethnic CBOs for youth in Norway. This study covers all eight ethnic CBOs for children and youth that received funding from the Norwegian state in 2013. To receive such funding, the organization must have a minimum of 100 paying members below the age of 26, and they must have local branches in two municipalities in Norway. Just to compare: regular youth organizations—with no recruitment limitations such as ethnic community-based organizations (for example leisure- and political organizations)—need 700 paying members below the age of 26, and local branches in five municipalities.

We have selected well-established organizations that are relatively robust and provide activities for large groups of youth. Students' and sports organizations are not included in this support scheme, and are therefore excluded from our analysis. None of the ethnic CBOs that receive this funding works to promote religion. Moreover, the selected organizations are formally independent from their parent organizations.[1]

The selected organizations reported mainly to have members from one ethnic community. The organizations represent children and youth tracing their roots to Kurdistan, Vietnam, Azerbaijan, Sri Lanka, and Turkey. These countries do not, however, reflect the countries of origin of most immigrants in Norway. In 2014, there were 663,110 immigrants in Norway, and 126,075 children of two immigrant parents born in Norway. Around 12 % of the population are immigrants, and around 2 % are children of immigrants. While the largest national groups of immigrants come from Poland, Sweden, and Lithuania, the largest national groups of Norwegian-born children of immigrant parents come from Pakistan, Somalia, and Iraq (SSB 2014). We can only speculate about the reasons for the divergence between the ethnic community-based organizations for children and youth that receive funding, and the largest immigrant groups. All ethnic CBOs can apply, and most of those who apply receive funding. While there are no formal restrictions preventing various groups from applying, there might be informal reasons not to apply. We have, however, concentrated on the eight organizations that received government support in 2013.

---

[1]Children- and youth organizations must be defined as self-governed associations to receive funding. Accordingly, the government requires that they have an internal democratic structure which ensures the members right to express themselves and be heard through formal annual meetings. The rights for individual members are regulated by the organization's statutes. Decisions made in an organization's formal meetings, cannot be overruled by any other organizations.

The methodology is based on document analysis and interviews. We have studied public documents that give criteria for funding to children and youth organizations with members from various regions in Norway. We have visited the organizations' webpages and their profiles on Facebook, and we have studied their statutes. Moreover, we have conducted interviews with leaders of seven organizations. We approached the leaders by sending emails and text messages. Several of the leaders do not live in Oslo. None of them were employed by the organization they lead; all were fully engaged in work or studies. Their contribution as leaders was voluntary and they performed their duties in their spare time. Four interviews were conducted in the organizations' offices, while the remaining three were conducted at our research institute. These were semi-structured interviews; we followed an interview guide where questions and topics we wanted to cover were recorded. We started each interview by asking personal questions about the leaders' motivation for using their spare time to work for the organization. We then followed up with questions related to the organizations' aim, main activities, and the members' engagement. Each interview was concluded with a question about the organizations' future. While we used a common interview guide for each conversation, follow-up questions were also discussed when appropriate. While one researcher asked the questions, the other took notes.

The Organizations' Practice

The question examined in this section is how the ethnic community-based organizations for children and youth combine cultural and social activities in ethnic CBOs with civic and political integration in the mainstream society. As mentioned in the introduction, we both examine how these organizations adapt to the migrancy framework they are put in by the state, and how they define the aim of establishing special ethnic CBOs for children and youth.

We have to bear in mind that these are relatively small organizations without any full-time employees. Four of them have accountants in part-time positions, but volunteers carry out the daily work. While the registered members are below the age of 26, some organizations also have supporting members above this age. The largest organization has 1,969 Tamil members who have parents who immigrated to Norway from Sri Lanka, or were born to immigrant parents. The organization has fourteen local branches, and is also the oldest organization, founded in 1992. Two organizations have a total of 327 and 379 members. These are immigrants from Vietnam or children of Vietnamese immigrants. Although these have organized activities over several years, they have only received funding for the last few years. One organization, founded in 2006, has members originating in Azerbaijan. This organization has 209 members, and two local branches. These organizations mainly arrange language courses and cultural activities to maintain the cultural heritage from their ancestral country.

There are four small organizations with fewer than 209 members. Two of these are Kurdish organizations, which are linked to mother organizations in Kurdistan—one in Koye and one in East-Kurdistan. Furthermore, there are two organizations for youth of Turkish origin. One was founded in 2001 and aims to promote cultural, academic, and social activities. For several years, this organization served as an important channel for youth to reach the attention of political authorities in Norway. In 2014, the organization dissolved when the founder quit her unpaid job as General Secretary in the organization. In 2005, the other organization for youth of Turkish origin was founded (Centre for Multicultural Youth). All members speak Turkish and focus on arranging social and cultural activities. All organizations are non-profit, non-religious and non-political voluntary organizations, in the sense that they do not support a specific political party, neither in Norway nor in Turkey.

The leaders of the organizations are resourceful individuals, who have crucial influence on the organizations' ideas and practice. They describe how they are integrated in the larger society in relation to cultural, social, and political dimensions. All leaders have higher education. They have all been active in voluntary work since they were children. Currently, they each devote the bulk of their voluntary efforts to the organization they are leading.

Migrancy Framework

While six leaders had immigrated to Norway and two were born in Norway to immigrant parents, all informants emphasized how their parents' migration histories define their own cultural heritage. They all referred to strong relationships with their parents. All leaders emphasized that it is important that the members' parents have knowledge of the organizations' social network and cultural activities. This makes it easier for the youth to participate in the organizations. Nevertheless, the organizations have diverging approaches to intergenerational relations. Four leaders explained that parents encourage their children to participate in the activities of the organizations because they want their children to maintain their ethnic identity. Parents feel that the organizations are safe spaces for their children. However, four other leaders emphasized that parents should not attend activities organized by the group. One of them even emphasized that the establishment of a self-governed youth organization was in part a rebellion against sceptical expressions in the immigrant society regarding the organization's non-religious profile and that it included all young people of diverging cultural, religious or ethnic family background.

All leaders called themselves immigrant children and youth, or children and youth from an immigrant background. None of them made distinctions between persons who have immigrated and Norwegian-born children with immigrant parents. We did not, however, ask whether they have applied for Norwegian citizenship, as we were mainly interested in the organizations. As we have seen, the Norwegian citizenship policy forms the legal basis for the migrancy framework, in which the state situates the children and youth. The migrancy framework is reinforced by the special support schemes for ethnic CBOs. Altogether, the definitions and use of these categories are crucial for how the children and youth understand their position in the Norwegian society.

One way of understanding why the leaders never questioned the migrancy framework they were placed into might be that they adapt to the funding schemes. No one criticized these schemes. The existence of a special funding system for ethnic community-based organizations is encouraging children and youth to organize themselves as ethnic communities and establish such organizations. The organizations' adaptation to the migrancy framework might also be a question of selection. Those persons who have strong connections to their ethnic community and immigration histories might be more prone to apply for such funding. Although all leaders told us that their ideas and activities are based on their own experiences, they also emphasized how their parents' migration histories define their own cultural heritage. The question is how this understanding defines the organizations' identity and practice, and whether the organizations maintain their members' lives in migrancy.

Cultural Maintenance

The point of departure for the organizations' ideas and practices is that their members are culturally and socially integrated in Norwegian society. They know the Norwegian language, codes, and symbols. Moreover, they have personal interactions and networks within the framework of public institutions at school and at work.

In contrast, the cultural and social dimensions of integration within their ethnic community are weak, and according to the leader quoted in the introduction, this makes immigrant youth and children of immigrant parents rootless. All organizations emphasized that it is crucial that the youth do not forget "their own culture." Four leaders emphasized that young people seem to forget their language and cultural heritage. One leader emphasized that they cannot lose these forms of belonging:

> We have tried to get as many youth as possible together so that they do not forget their background and culture. We have seen that when they come to Norway they forget their background. We want the youth to bring with them their own culture and simultaneously learn the Norwegian culture.

The leaders' central argument is that it is not possible to choose between these two forms of belonging. They do not perceive this as a question of either/or but rather of both. Their aim is to develop robust hyphenated identities. All leaders argued that their members' challenges are related to how they combine both forms of belonging, as one leader put it:

We wish every individual to mix two cultures. This is difficult for the first generation of immigrants, while the second generation have Norwegian education and live with such a mix. The third generation is mainly Norwegian.

The leaders aim to use the organizations as a mean to build young peoples' identity, and one leader said:

We must build identities where we combine two cultures so that each young individual can be independent in various situations. This will strengthen the youth as individuals and give them more possibilities.

All leaders emphasized explicitly, as we have seen in different words, that the building of identities is a way to broaden the young peoples' cultural repertoire. Two leaders referred to the problematic age between thirteen and eighteen, and how young people tend to form their identity during this developmental period. Both of them referred to their own experiences and how important it was for them to meet young people with a similar cultural heritage.

The organizations' practices follow similar patterns of activities. All organizations offer language courses to their members. Four leaders indicated that their members attend Norwegian schools and have mastered the Norwegian language, but have limited knowledge of their heritage languages and need to learn them in order to be able to communicate with community members and understand their culture of origin. This focus on the cultural dimension of integration within the ethnic community is reflected in the organizations' main activities: cultural pursuits such as dancing, music festivals, and sport activities.

Social Network for People with the Same Cultural Heritage

The organizations also arrange social activities for their members, such as barbecues, trips to country cottages, and mountain walking. These activities aim to offer places where people with heritage from the same country can get together and integrate socially. One of the leaders articulated this goal as follows:

I have a personal motive with this work. I can see what they are struggling with. We can get the youth off the streets; get them socially together, and encourage them to study and to integrate more. I was the first generation of youth from our group. When I came to the university, I did not know what to study. I have gone through a lot, and I have learned much. I have seen many young people with the same problems as I had. I can help them.

His own experiences are crucial for how the organization combines various forms of social activities. Another leader linked his personal motive to voluntary work as a duty:

I see it as a duty to participate in voluntary work. Several people have been helping me. Without them, I would not have been the person I am now.

They described how their organizations are dependent on their work and engagement. One of the leaders referred to how the social network is an intrinsic part of his work:

> Much of the organization's operations are dependent on me. To take over after me would imply a huge responsibility and also a great pressure. I know the work, and I deliver work of high quality. I know everyone, and people know who I am.

While informal social networks are crucial for all leaders, the formal organizations offer an arena where the leaders can get in contact with and encourage youth to maintain their ethnic identity and foster participation in the larger society. All leaders described their organizations as places where young people can meet and recognize the value of knowing other people who navigate between two cultures. Most leaders referred to how this awareness can lead to increased self-confidence, and one of them argued:

> If you do not have an identity you cannot behave as an independent individual. You must be able to combine in relation to what you want, and how you want to organize your everyday life. All this is dependent on who you want to be, and that decides what parts of the culture you take with you.

The goal of several organizations is to build social networks based on various combinations of membership in an ethnic community-based group and civic and political participation in the larger society. This will, according to the leaders, give the young people a broad cultural competence. As one of the leader said:

> If young people want to succeed, they have to know themselves. Young people are standing in the middle of two cultures. There are negative parts of both cultures, but we must take with us the positive parts. It is extremely useful to have knowledge of two cultures. I use this at work every day.

Civic and Political Engagement

Most organizations arrange seminars where they inform their members about the Norwegian education system and about how the political system works. These are efforts to promote the civic and political dimension of integration in the larger society, and are often combined with social activities. As several leaders said, to encourage members to participate in different events, the organizations must combine information about public institutions with fun and appropriate activities. Nevertheless, most of the leaders emphasized their members' knowledge about democratic procedures. Four leaders highlighted internal democratic structures in the organizations and how the group of leaders changes every second or third year, after national meetings. Three of the leaders were central in the establishment of the organizations, and they have been leading the organizations since then. They did not refer to internal democratic elections, but to receive funding they also must follow democratic procedures.

Most organizations arrange seminars where they inform about the history and political situation in the country they or their parents emigrated from. The aim is that members should have knowledge about the political conflicts in their ancestral countries and thereby the reason why they have emigrated to Norway. Although this is related to the political system in these countries, none of the organizations state that they work with political issues. Three leaders emphasized, however, that their organization's existence is political. These three organizations have members with bonds to Kurdistan and Sri Lanka. All three organizations' practices are related to teaching young people languages, cultural, and historical traditions, which political regimes around Kurdistan and Sri Lanka aim to eliminate. These are cultural traditions which are political because they are perceived as a threat to political regimes. This type of political conflict is a part of these CBOs members' daily life and define these groups' understanding of themselves. One leader says that:

In our enemies' opinion we will always be political, this is a part of our existence.

All organizations are transnational in the sense that they aim to maintain the language and culture of the countries of origin and combine this with civic and political participation in the Norwegian society. However, the organizations are mainly dedicated to improving their members living conditions in Norway. Although they function as bridge between cultures, only one organization defines itself as a bridge between two countries. All organizations have some loose cooperation with sister organizations in the Nordic countries and most leaders aim to increase this cooperation. One organization has close relations to a mother organization in Kurdistan, and members of this organization travel between these countries. Another organization has applied for funding from Norwegian authorities to be able to send some of their members to their ancestral homelands. Three organizations have sent funding to other countries, while one organization has received funding from another country to promote this country's culture in Norway. While this indicates that the ethnic community-based organizations for children and youth have a modest interest in civic and political integration, they fulfil the government's formal requirements to get funding. They do not have to be politically active to fulfil the government's aim to increase democratic participation.

Cultural Heritage Preservation and Democratic Participation

This study shows how the Norwegian policy on ethnic CBOs for children and youth meets practice. The political opportunity structures show that the government has an ambiguous policy. The aim in supporting these organizations is not to strengthen their ethnic community-based identity, but rather to encourage cultural and social activities. The organizations are seen as places where members learn democratic values in practice and thus function as a stepping-stone to individual democratic participation in the larger society. This confirms how previous studies have argued that Norwegian policy is based on vague and ambiguous policy and when this policy is gradually implemented—after several years with immigration—it will lead to measures that counteract each other in practice (Berkaak 2012).

Both the government and the ethnic CBOs for children and youth perceive the organizations as an arena for cultural and social activities among young immigrants or Norwegian-born children of immigrants. Both assume that the organizations can help their members to combine membership in an ethnic community-based group with participation in the larger Norwegian society. They differ, however, in how the organizations should carry out this dual mission.

While the organizations' ideas and activities are based on their members' own experiences, the leaders also emphasized how their parents' migration histories are crucial for their members' cultural heritage. They did not contest being defined and supported in relation to their own, and their parents', immigration history. This can be interpreted as an instrumental adaptation to the Norwegian government's funding system. However, some seem to have internalized the migrancy status inscribed on them. They, thereby, not only maintain the state's migrancy framework, but also consolidate young people's lives in migrancy.

However, they refuse to perceive the activities in the organizations as only a step on their way to individual participation in the larger society. In contrast, the ethnic community-based organizations define their main goal as encouraging young people to maintain the cultural heritage and socialize with people who have similar immigration histories. The organizations emphasize that immigrant youth or children of immigrants seem to forget their common immigration roots and culture. They also forget their language, codes and symbols. The organizations' aim is to maintain their cultural heritage as a way of strengthening their members' identity as Norwegians with cultural heritage from another countries or regions.

In this way, the Norwegian policy on ethnic CBOs for children and youth meets practice. The government's political opportunity structures define an ambiguous policy and leaves it open for children and youth to determine the content. When the organizations' cultural and social dimensions of integration are defined in relation to their membership in an ethnic community, it is crucial that these languages, codes, symbols and social network are transnational. The civic and political dimension of integration is based on the cultural and social dimension, and become visible in their transnational networks. By combining two cultures and two kinds of social networks in relation to two countries, the ethnic CBOs for children and youth work to broaden their members' cultural repertoires and thereby shape new hybrid and transnational identities that also include an identity as political actors. This challenges the Norwegian government's idea of perceiving ethnic CBOs as stepping-stones to individual participation in the Norwegian society.

References

Agergaard, S., & Michelsen la Cour, A. (2012). Governing integration through sports. *Nordic Journal of Migration Research, 2*(1), 26–34.

Anderson, B. (1991). *Imagined communities. Reflections on the origin and spread of nationalism.* London, New York: Verso.

Amelina, A., & Faist, T. (2008). Turkish migrant associations in Germany: Between integration pressure and transnational linkages. *Revue européenne des migrations internationales, 24*(2), 91–120.

Amelina, A., & Faist, T. (2012). De-naturalization the national in research methodologies: Key concepts of transnational studies in migration. *Ethnic and Racial Studies, 35*(10), 1707–1724.

Bauder, H. (2011). *Immigration dialectic: Imagining community, economy and nation.* Toronto: University of Toronto Press.

Bay, A. H., Hagelund, A., & Finseraas, H. (2010). Civil society and political integration of immigrants in Norway. In B. Bengtsson, P. Strömblad, & A. H. Bay (Eds.), *Diversity, inclusion and citizenship in scandinavia* (pp. 295–323). Newcastle upon Tyne: Cambridge Scholars Publishing.

Bengtsson, B. (2010). Political opportunity structure and ethnic organization: How political, what opportunities, which structures? In B. Bengtsson, P. Strömblad, & A. H. Bay (Eds.), *Diversity, inclusion and citizenship in Scandinavia* (pp. 241–269). Newcastle upon Tyne: Cambridge Scholars Publishing.

Berger, M., et al. (2004). Political integration by a detour? Ethnic communities and social capital of migrants in Berlin. *Journal of Ethnic and Migration Studies, 30*(3), 491–507.

Berkaak, O. A. (2012). De andres mange ansikter—Mangfold i tanker, ord og gjerninger. *Norsk antropologisk tidsskrift, 23*(1), 66–76.

Bjørklund, T. & Bergh, J. (2013). *Minoritetsbefolkningens møte med det politiske Norge. Partivalg, valgdeltakelse, representasjon.* Oslo: Cappelen Damm Akademisk.

Borevi, K. (2004). Den svenske diskursen om staten, integrationen och föreningslivet. In B. Bengtsson (Ed.), *Föreningsliv, makt och integration.* (pp. 31–65). Rapport från Integrationspolitiska maktutredningens forskningsprogram. Rapport 49.

Crul, M., & Mollenkopf, J. (2012). *The changing face of world cities. Young adult children of immigrants in Europe and the United States.* New York: Russel Sage Foundation.

D'Angelo, A. (2015). Migrant organizations: Embodied community capital. In L. Ryan, U. Erel, & A. D'Angelo (Eds.), *Migrant capital. Networks, identities and strategies* (pp. 83–101). London: Palgrave Macmillan.

Eriksen, T. H. (2010). *Samfunn.* Oslo: Universitetsforlaget.

Faist, T. (2010). Diaspora and transnationalism: What kind of dance partners? In R. Bauböck, & T. Faist (Eds.), *Diaspora and transnationalism. concepts, theories and methods* (pp. 9–35). Amsterdam: Amsterdam University Press.

Fennema, M., & Tillie, J. (2001). Civic community, political participation and political trust of ethnic groups. *Connections, 24*(1), 26–41.

Folkestad, B., et al. (2015). Frivillig innsats i Noreg 1998–2014. Kva kjenneteikner dei frivillig og kva har endra seg? Oslo: Senter for forskning på sivilsamfunn og frivillig sektor.

Glick Schiller, N. (2010). Long distance nationalism and peripatetic patriots. In B. Riccio & C. Brambilla (Eds.), *Transnational migration, cosmopolitanism and dis-located borders* (pp. 27–53). Luglio: Guaraldi.

Gressgård, R. (2005). Hva mener regjeringen med flerkulturelt mangfold? *Nytt Norsk Tidsskrift, 22* (1), 72–79.

Hagelund A. & Loga J. (2009). *Frivillighet, innvandring, integrasjon. En kunnskapsoversikt.* ISF Report 1.

Handy, F., & Greenspan, I. (2009). Immigrant volunteering: A stepping stone to integration? *Nonprofit and Voluntary Sector Quarterly, 38*(6), 956–982.

Horst, C., Carling, J., & Ezzati, R. (2010). *Immigration to Norway from Bangaldesh, Brazil, Egypt, India. Morocco and Ukraine. PRIO Paper.* Oslo: Peace Research Institute Oslo.

Jacobs, D., & Tillie, J. (2004). Introduction: Social capital and political integration of migrants. *Journal of Ethnic and Migration Studies, 30*(3), 419–427.

Kuhnle, S & Selle, P (1992). Government and voluntary organizations: A relational perspective. In S. Kuhnle & P. Selle (Eds.), *Government and voluntary organizations*, Aldershot, Hampshire, England: Avebury, Ashgate Publishing.

Kugelberg, C. (2011). Integration policy and ethnic minority associations. In C. Shore, et al. (Eds.), *Policy worlds. anthropology and analysis of contemporary power* (pp. 264–282). New York: Berghahn Books.

Koopmans, R., & Statham, P. (2000). Migration and ethnic relations as a field of political contention: An opportunity structure approach. In R. Koopmans & P. Statham (Eds.), *Challenging immigration and ethnic relations politics: Comparative European perspectives* (pp. 13–17). Oxford: Oxford University Press.

Koopmans, R., et al. (2005). *Contested citizenship: Immigration and ethnic relations politics in Europe.* Minnesota: Minnesota University Press.

Lorentzen, H. (2004). *Fellesskapets fundament—sivilsamfunnet og individualismen.* Oslo: Pax.

Morales, L. & Giugni, M. (2011). *Social capital, political participation and migration in Europe: Making Multicultural democracy work?* Basingstoke: Palgrave.

Morales, L., & Pilati, K. (2011). The role of social capital in migrants' engagement in local politics in European cities. In L. Morales & M. Giugni (Eds.), *Social capital, political participation and migration in Europe: Making multicultural democracy work?* (pp. 87–115). Basingstoke: Palgrave.

Myrberg, G., & Rogstad, J. (2011). Patterns of participation: engagement among ethnic minorities and the native population in Oslo and Stockholm. In L. Morales & M. Giugni (Eds.), *Social capital, political participation and migration in Europe: Making multicultural democracy work?* (pp. 172–198). Basingstoke: Palgrave.

Odmalm, P. (2004). Civil society, migrant organizations and political parties: Theoretical linkages and applications to the Swedish context. *Journal of Ethnic and Migration Studies, 30*(3), 471–489.

Ødegård, G. (2010). Foreningsliv i et flerkulturelt lokalsamfunn. En studie om integrasjon og sosial kapital, *ISF Rapport* 6, Oslo.

Ødegård, G., et al. (2014). *Fellesskap og forskjellighet. Integrasjon og nettverksbygging i flerkulturelle lokalsamfunn.* Oslo: Abstrakt forlag.

Østerud, Ø., et al. (2003). *Makten og demokratiet. En sluttbok fra Makt- og demokratiutredningen.* Oslo: Gyldendal.

Predelli, L. N. (2008). Political and cultural ethnic mobilization: The role of immigrant associations in Norway. *Journal of Ethnic and Migration Studies., 34*(6), 935–954.

Putnam, R. D. (2000). *Bowling alone: The collapse and revival of American community.* New York: Simon & Schuster.

Portes, et al. (2007). Immigrant transnational organizations and development: A comparative study. *International Migration Review, 41*(1), 242–281.

Pyykkonen, M. (2007). Integrating governmentality: Administrative expectations for immigrant associations in Finland. *Alternatives, 32*(1), 197–224.

Rokkan, S. (1966). Norway: Numerical democracy and corporate pluralism. In R. A. Dahl (Ed.), *Political oppositions in western democracies.* New Haven: Yale University Press.

SSB. (2014). Statistisk sentralbyrå. Statistics Norway. Retrieved March 3, 2015 from http://ssb.no/innvbef/.

Takle, M. (2006). Statsborgerskapsdebatt i Norge og Tyskland. *Internasjonal Politikk, 64*(2), 199–213.

Takle, M. (2014). Immigrant organizations as schools of bureaucracy. *Ethnicities, 15*(1), 92–111.

Tillie, J. (2004). Social capital of organizations and their members: Explaining the political integration of immigrants in Amsterdam. *Journal of Ethnic and Migration Studies, 30*(3), 529–541.

Togeby, L. (2004). It depends… How organizational participation affects political participation and social trust among second-generation immigrants in Denmark. *Journal of Ethnic and Migration Studies, 30*(3), 509–528.

Trähgårdh, L., & Vamstad, J. (2009). *Att ge eller att beskattas. Avdragsrätt för gåvor till ideell verksamhet i Sverige och andra länder.* Stockholm: Tankesmedjan för det civila samhället.

Wessendorf, S. (2013). *Second-generation transnationalism and roots migration.* London: Ashgate.

White Paper No. 39. (2006–2007). Norwegian Ministry of Culture.

White paper No. 6. (2012–2013). Ministry of Children, Equality and Social Inclusion.

Wollebæk, D. & Sivesind, K. H. (2010). Fra folkebevegelse til filantropi? Frivillig innsats i Norge 1997–2009. Oslo: *ISF Report* 3.

Yurdakul, G. (2009). *From guest workers into muslims: The transformation of Turkish immigrant associations in Germany.* Newcastle, UK: Cambridge Scholars Press.

Open Access This chapter is licensed under the terms of the Creative Commons Attribution-NonCommercial 2.5 International License (http://creativecommons.org/licenses/by-nc/2.5/), which permits any noncommercial use, sharing, adaptation, distribution and reproduction in any medium or format, as long as you give appropriate credit to the original author(s) and the source, provide a link to the Creative Commons license and indicate if changes were made.

The images or other third party material in this chapter are included in the book's Creative Commons license, unless indicated otherwise in a credit line to the material. If material is not included in the book's Creative Commons license and your intended use is not permitted by statutory regulation or exceeds the permitted use, you will need to obtain permission directly from the copyright holder.

Part III
Identities

Chapter 7
Identity Development Among Youth of Vietnamese Descent in the Czech Republic

Andrea Svobodová and Eva Janská

Identity and belonging of immigrant children and children of immigrants are important topics in the current debates about migration and integration. In these debates, immigrant youth and children of immigrants are often presented as either a problem group "stuck between two cultures" or as "culture brokers" who translate and transmit the host society's culture to their parents (Fog Olwig 2013). Based on empirical research conducted between 2012 and 2014, this paper discusses dynamics of identity formation among children of Vietnamese descent in the Czech Republic from their own point of view. With 57,000 Vietnamese residing in the Czech Republic, Vietnamese are the third largest immigrant community in the country. Children and youth (up to 26 years of age) of Vietnamese immigrants— both those born in Vietnam and those born in the Czech Republic—represent approximately 40 % of this population (Kušniráková 2014). Despite these numbers, there has been remarkably little research on the topic of Vietnamese children and youth in the Czech Republic up to now. Existing studies focused mostly on integration in educational settings (Janská 2006; Drbohlav et al. 2007; Janská et al. 2011; Kostelecká et al. 2013).

A critical question that often accompanies this research relates to the identity label these children use: Do they call themselves Vietnamese or Czech? Or does their identify fall somewhere in-between these labels? The latter may be indicated by the term "banana child," invented by the Vietnamese children themselves, which points to the person being "yellow" on the outside but "white" inside. However, our chapter contests the necessity of this identification in the migration context and brings a new perspective to the Czech research environment by focusing more on the process through which the children of Vietnamese immigrants construct a sense of self (Somerville 2008), than on the "identity outcomes."

A. Svobodová (✉) · E. Janská
GEOMIGRACE, Charles University, Prague, Czech Republic
e-mail: plackova.andrea@seznam.cz

© The Author(s) 2016
M.L. Seeberg and E.M. Goździak (eds.), *Contested Childhoods: Growing up in Migrancy*, IMISCOE Research Series,
DOI 10.1007/978-3-319-44610-3_7

It is commonly assumed that there are differences between the identity perceptions and identification processes of first generation immigrants and their children. To begin with, these "migrant children" are not migrants, although the term "second-generation migrants" is widely used. Some of them have been born in the Czech Republic or came to live here at a very early age, with little if any recollection of their previous homes. They have gone through the Czech school system, mastered the language, often form very steady friendships with Czech peers, and are more or less integrated into the mainstream population. That is why some believe that, unlike for their parents, ethnicity should no longer be of great importance to them (Gordon 1964). But if it is not ethnicity, then what is it that shapes the identity perception of these children?

According to Crul and Schneider, the most important driving forces behind most of the actions of immigrant children and children of immigrants are age, gender, educational levels, and other "common" factors, not the fact that they are children of immigrants (Crul and Schneider 2010; Portés and Rumbaut 2001). We agree with Crul and Schneider that the role of ethnic and migration background has been exaggerated in the study of immigrants and their offspring in the past years, especially when it comes to questions of immigrants´ integration (Crul and Schneider 2010). But at the same time we also believe that migrant background and the culture of their parents play a very important role in the lives and identity formation of these children (Min 2002; Kibria 2002).[1]

The fact that these children are growing up in a social space we call "migrancy" means that they have to face different challenges in their lives than their peers from the majority society. To put it simply, we all reflect upon our identity sometimes (Jenkins 2004) and adolescence is a hard time for almost everyone, but in the case of immigrant children and children of immigrants, there are issues that make it at least more complicated, if not harder (Huang 1994; Chow 1999, 20).

This chapter aims at a broader understanding of how the identities of these children are formed by adopting the "growing up in migrancy" concept which views "migrancy" not only as a social space, in which children are growing up (even when they are not migrants, but because their parents or even grandparents once were), but also as a social category, which has the same impact on these children and young people as, for example, social class or gender (Näre 2013). We look at how these young people contest identities for themselves while trying to come to terms with the fact that they are growing up "in migrancy" and "between two cultures."

---

[1]Min says that: "despite the tendency among Asian American scholars to downplay their importance, primordial ties, especially their parents' home country and its culture are of a great significance for the second generation."

Vietnamese in the Czech Republic

Vietnamese migration to the Czech Republic has a long tradition. Diplomatic relations between Vietnam and the former Czechoslovakia were established in the early 1950s when Czechoslovakia provided temporary refuge to Vietnamese war orphans. Subsequent waves of Vietnamese migrants came to Czechoslovakia on the basis of reciprocal agreements. In the 1970 and 1980s, bilateral agreements on scientific and technological cooperation brought apprentices, workers, and exchange students to be trained in the textile, engineering, and paper industries. The aim of the Vietnamese government was to bring back a qualified labour force from the ČSSR to war-torn Vietnam to assist in its renewal. Between 1979 and 1985, when Czechoslovakia had a shortage of local labour, a large influx of labour migrants from Vietnam came to the country.

A temporary rupture in Czech-Vietnamese relations occurred after 1989, when the transformation of the Czech economy forced many Vietnamese to return home. After treaties for the professional training of Vietnamese citizens in the Czech Republic and mutual employment were renewed in 1994, some Vietnamese began returning to the Czech Republic. The 1990s were therefore a time when people typically made use of earlier contacts and knowledge of the Czech environment. These people were followed by their relatives and friends as well as by people who came to the country with the assistance of intermediaries or through recruitment agencies. From 2006, the number Vietnamese migrants working on the basis of regular employment contracts has increased significantly. Most of these Vietnamese migrants are factory workers. The main reason for this was a legal adjustment in 2004 that allowed intermediary agencies to hire foreign workers (Janská 2006).

Vietnamese who settled in the Czech Republic after the fall of communism often drew on community networks to launch their careers in business, especially in retail. Initially, Vietnamese immigrants clustered in the country's border regions and mainly sold textiles, electronics, and groceries. From this period comes the common stereotype of a Vietnamese migrant as a "stall-keeper." Recently Vietnamese businesses have been moving out of the market into retail space and extending into more varied branches (Martínková 2008; Hofírek and Nekorjak 2009). Vietnamese have opened nail salons, dry-cleaners, and small restaurants offering authentic Vietnamese food. They are also working as translators, in social care, and some have set up successful medium scale companies (Martínková 2008; Pechová 2007). As the children of these migrants started to attend Czech schools a new stereotype emerged. This time it was the more positive stereotype of a "model minority," which suggests that all Vietnamese are overachievers and perfect students. In the following section, we show that the labels describing Vietnamese as stall-keepers or a model minority are insufficient, and that the reality is much more complex and the experiences and identities of young Vietnamese are much more diverse.

Stories as Entrance to Personal Identity

This chapter is based on analysis of fourteen "life-stories" (Atkinson 2002) conducted among young people of Vietnamese descent. The interviews were conducted by Andrea Svobodová between 2012 and 2014 in different parts of the Czech Republic. In the interviews, the young people produced narratives about their lives from their own perspective. By paying attention to the thematic content and structure of their life stories, it was possible to understand the meaning that they are giving to their lives (Kacen 2002). In selecting the respondents, two criteria have been taken into account. First was age, which was limited to 16–29.[2] Second was the place of birth. Here the respondents were either born in the Czech Republic or born in Vietnam, but lived in the Czech Republic from an early age (before the age of twelve). We choose to include both these groups since they share many linguistic, cultural, and developmental experiences (Zhou 1997). The interviews were further limited to young people whose parents are described in the literature as "old settlers" (Brouček 2003). Today, these people represent an economically successful and well-integrated group of Vietnamese migrants in the Czech Republic (Kušniráková et al. 2013). In order to protect their anonymity while retaining the human element evoked by proper names, we have given all the research participants Vietnamese pseudonyms with no connection to their real names.

The Stable Point of Identity Development

Adolescence, a turbulent time for most young people, is also a time of reflection on and formation of identity (Jenkins 2004). Research indicates that in the case of immigrant children and children of immigrants, identity issues are more complex (Huang 1994; Chow 1999; Portés and Rumbaut 2001; Kibria 2002; Min 2002). Young people who participated in this study are not an exception. Most of them have, at one point in time or another, asked themselves: where do I belong? Am I more Vietnamese or more Czech? Even if some of them cannot answer these questions, it is incorrect to say that they are "stuck somewhere between two cultures." As the presented research shows, the period of struggle to identify with the culture of their parents or the culture of the country where they grew up is just one of the stages in their lives where their feelings and opinions about themselves evolve and change over time.

The understanding of identity as something socially constructed, fluid, and changeable in time and space corresponds with the constructivist perspective on identity development (Berger and Luckmann 1999). This perspective is very often presented in opposition to the essentialist perspective, which perceives identity as

---

[2]This stage of life described by Lee and Zhou as an overlapping stage between childhood and adulthood is marked by exploring and forming of one's identity (Ericsson 2068).

something fixed, biologically given, omnipresent and ahistorical, waiting to be discovered. By paying closer attention to these concepts, we can see that both perspectives understand identity as something unstable and developing over time. The difference is that from the essentialists' point of view this unstable process reaches a stable point (often during the transition phase from adolescence to adulthood) (Erikson 1974), while from the postmodernist view this can never be the case (Bauman 2001). The question is: what then is the search for identity about if there is no stable ground that we can build on Brubaker and Cooper (2000); Jenkins (2004) and Huang (1994) both present an interesting answer to this question. Jenkins says that the inclination of human nature to categorize the world and make it more reachable and graspable is something that naturally derives from how human minds work. From his point of view, the "omnipresent and natural" part of identity is not the identity itself but the search for it (Jenkins 2004). To Huang (1994), identity combines change and consistency. The stable, persistent part of identity "resides in the identity salience hierarchy," and the process of choosing an identity, which is most appropriate to the given situation, is at the basis of coherent ethnic identity (Huang 1994, 48).

The Dynamic Nature of Migrant Children's Identities: Negotiating Ethnic Identity Between Highly Polarized Expectations

The main focus of the presented study was not on ethnic identity, but on identity as such. That is why no direct questions about ethnicity were posed to the research participants in the first part of the interview. This resulted in a production of narratives which were different in many aspects. However, questions of ethnicity, culture, and ethnic identity struggles were always present, and proved to be very important in the lives of the interviewed children and young people. What also became clear from these narratives was the situational and dynamic character of ethnic identity, which developed and changed over time.

In her qualitative study of ethnic identity among second-generation Asian Americans, Hung Cam Thai shows that as they grew up, her research participants were marked by feelings of marginalization, and that during childhood and adolescence they often experienced feelings of not belonging to either their "old" or "new" social worlds. On reaching adulthood, these feelings often changed as they started to be more interested in their cultural heritage. As they accepted their ethnic and racial identities, they became more confident about themselves and more proud of their ethnic and racial backgrounds (Thai 2002). Although we believe that identity development stages do not capture all the facets and the dynamic nature of the ethnic identity of every individual child, we think they are useful because they show how ethnic identity continually changes and grows. These stages should also not necessarily be viewed as lineal because young people often revert back and forth between them (Phinney 1989). The results of the presented research conducted among the children of Vietnamese descent show many similarities with the Asian Americans studied by Thai, although there are also some differences.

From "Blessed Unconsciousness" to Rejecting the Ethnicity Which is Different from the Mainstream

In order to examine how ethnic identity changed over time, we want to present the case of Lin. Lin is a 27 year old woman who was born in the Czech Republic, left for Vietnam, and came back again at the age of ten.[3] Lin, like most of the other study participants, grew up in a place where there were not many other Vietnamese, or if there were, they did not live in visible ethnic communities. She went to schools with predominantly Czech pupils, made Czech friends and sometimes spent more time with her Czech nanny than with her own parents.[4] Searching through her childhood memories, she reconstructs four different stages that marked changes in her perception of how she thought about herself and her ethnicity. As first she mentions the stage of early childhood "when the child isn't aware of any differences or doesn't care about them, she/he knows that she/he is less strong and (there are reasons) why the children bully him/her, but he/she doesn't realize that it is because of his/her nationality," she said.

This period of "blessed unconsciousness" ended in early puberty (between thirteen and fifteen years of age), when she started to realize that there was something "different" about her and began asking herself questions like "So who are you going to be? Are you going to be Vietnamese or Czech? Do you want to be different or not?" Lin experienced the pressure to conform to the majority in this stage of life (Min 2002) very strongly. She tried to "be and act like others," "to be Czech." To a certain degree, this effort to fit in was also accompanied by her rejection of the parental culture and ethnicity, which was perceived as different from the mainstream, even inappropriate in some cases (Min 2002). Lin's parents, like the parents of most of the other respondents, were described by her as strict, conservative, hardworking, overprotective, too concerned with her school achievements and future, and sometimes not very empathetic. They expected Lin to honour certain traditional Vietnamese values: respect the elderly, be polite, put family first, fulfil her family obligations, be industrious, and strive for self-cultivation and improvement. Lin thought of these attitudes and values as culturally bounded, connected with the Vietnamese way of living, and different from the more "individualistic" Czech lifestyle which she was exposed to on a daily basis. The result was her contestation of her parents' ideas, which she saw as old-fashioned and limiting her freedom. Her growing-up was therefore marked by

---

[3]We choose this example because of the great self-reflectivity in Lin´s story which allows us to see how this young girl interprets her feelings and behaviour from her perspective.

[4]The phenomenon of nannies, which is widely spread among the Vietnamese living in the Czech Republic, has been studied by Adéle Souralová (Souralová 2013).

conflicts with her parents over dating, going out in the evening, or staying overnight at friends' homes, which is something acceptable in the Czech society but not approved of in Vietnamese families.

"Ethnic Revival": The Renewed Interest in the Parents' Ethnicity and Culture and the Change of Social Circle

Later we see Lin maturing and starting to view her parents and their culture from a different perspective, which makes her question her identity again.

> Then comes the period, around the age of sixteen, seventeen, when you start to turn back to that culture, you say to yourself that you aren't Czech at all, because you have completely different problems that your classmates couldn't understand, you are being raised differently. Now you want to go back to that core, why it is that way, why your parents are raising you that way, why they have these opinions. At the age of thirteen you might say to yourself, they are stupid, but at the age of eighteen you want to understand why they do what they do.

In this period of her life, she "decided to be Vietnamese" and started to immerse herself in the Vietnamese language and culture wanting to find out more about her "roots." Her choice was influenced not only by the renewed interest in her "roots," but also by the pressure from her parents. From what she is saying, we can surmise that she saw her ethnicity as something not voluntary: "I chose this because I thought that it is right, that it should be like that. I look Vietnamese, I have Vietnamese parents, and I am comfortable with Vietnamese culture. I started to be really interested in all this," she said. At this time, she also started creating new friendships and strengthening old relationships with her friends of Vietnamese descent.[5] The reason for this was not "ethnicity," but rather shared experiences of growing up. Czech kids usually did not understand why she could not go dancing at the age of sixteen like anybody else or why she had to help her parents in their shop on weekends, but in the eyes of the Vietnamese friends, this was something quite normal and did not need to be explained.

Contesting the Dual Reference Frame of Identity and Belonging and Embarrassment of Both Cultures

Learning more about the culture of her parents helped Lin to become more confident. However, her identity development did not end at the stage of "ethnic revival." In her story there is a fourth stage, which she describes as a stage of

---

[5]This is a phenomenon which we refer to as "changing of the social circle" occurs not only in the narratives of most the other research participants, but which has been observed also in the case of Asian American youth (Min 2002; Kibria 2002).

broader options and independence, which came at the time when she left her parents' home and went to study at the University in Prague. She describes it as follows:

> When I went to study at the University, when I broke away from my family, started to live alone and to meet other people, at that time I said to myself, "Look there are also other options, you don't have to be only Czech or only Vietnamese." I can choose what I want to, but I have to be able to work with it, and to fight for it. So I started to mix it up more, which caused more and more troubles at home, but I am not small any more, having to put up with it. I am not dependent any more, financially nor psychologically. And this now suits me the best, that I am stronger and more independent.

As we can see, the stage of so-called "ethnic revival" was only a stage in her life when she needed to further process the problems connected with her ethnic origin. Once these were resolved, she did not wish to see her Vietnamese friends more often than her Czech friends, and she wants to embrace both cultures without feeling the need to choose between them. Lin's narrative clearly shows that: "contrary to widespread folk and political ideas about identities, belonging is never confined to just one category" and that "It is also not necessarily put in either/or terms" (Crul et al. 2012, 290). On the contrary, people can have multiple identities, from which they can more or less freely and selectively use and combine according to the situation (Min 2002; Bauman 2001; Hall 1996; Huang 1994; Eriksen 2002).

The same could be said about most of the other children and young people who participated in the research. Some of them were very rebellious, but even these rebellious kids never went so far as to reject completely the traditions that their parents tried to pass on to them. They did not put the "collectivistic" and "individualistic" values against each other, but rather next to each other by constructing their identity around the idea that they are special, because of the privilege of seeing life from different angles. They definitely cannot be seen as "just" cultural brokers who only translate the culture of the migrant country to their parents. They should rather be seen as active members of the society who consciously create a culture of their own (Hirschfeld 2002).

These findings bring us to the theoretical background of the study and the question if there is a stable part of identity development that can be reached. The narrative of Lin, along with the narratives of other research participants which evolved in the same way, suggest that the "stable part" of their identity perception is in the way they are selecting among different identities according to the situation, which for them presented a stable conceptual framework. (Huang 1994, 48).

Partner Choice and Family Expectations

The great weight of parental expectations was one of the most prominent themes in the story told by Lin. Most of the other interviewed children and young adults spoke extensively about how their parents' views on how they should be and behave influenced them and sometimes made their lives difficult. One of the situations when young people are expected "to negotiate differences between their parents' cultural preferences and their own" is the choice of a romantic partner (Crul et al. 2012). Among the research participants, this process of negotiation varied with the individual. There were those with a Czech partner who had to overcome many obstacles and disapproving reactions of their parents, but the majority did not encounter these problems, simply because they chose to date or to marry a co-ethnic. Some of them acknowledged that they respected—consciously or unconsciously—their parents' wishes and preferences. Lin is a case in point. She said that her parents never told her not to marry a European man: "Like they told me to marry whomever I wanted, but in the end, they would probably be quite surprised if I would bring a European home," she says.

The situation of choosing a partner does not always have to be seen as a struggle between the expectations of the children and the parents. Sky, a girl who was born in Vietnam but has lived in the Czech Republic from the age of 5, made her statement clearly. From her point of view, it is not so important whether her spouse be Vietnamese or Czech ("race doesn't matter"). What really matters is culture, mentality, and common experiences of growing up, which represent important factors behind the "success" of any relationship and this she absolutely will not undervalue. From this point of view, Sky is not going to marry somebody only because of her parents' wishes, but will make her choice taking into account all the important aspects of "her" personal situation:

> I am always saying that I wouldn't mind having a Czech boyfriend, but it would have to be somebody who is going to be interested in the Vietnamese culture, who for example is going to learn Vietnamese and who will know about Vietnamese culture, because if he knows the language then he will be able to communicate with my parents, even though they both speak good Czech. But through studying the language one learns how to understand the mentality of that nationality and that is very important, because if it wasn't like that then I would understand him because I grew up here and I know how it goes, but it wouldn't work in the opposite direction, and I think to have a good relationship you need to have mutual understanding from both sides.

Another interesting perspective on co-ethnic partner choice was provided by two young women, Jana and Phuong, both aged twenty-one and both born and raised in the Czech Republic. After some negative experiences at school, both concluded that Czech boys did not find them attractive. This feeling led them to a decision that it would be better to look for a partner among the young people of Vietnamese descent. From their point of view, they were not pushed by their parents but rather by the circumstances, such as their negative experiences with Czech boys.

That Is Not Who I Am: Contesting One's Identity Against Generally-Held Stereotypes

For children of Vietnamese migrants in the Czech Republic, growing up in "migrancy" does not only mean that they have to cope with different kinds of expectations from their parents and majority society. Growing up in "migrancy" also means that they have to cope with prejudice and racism. While contesting the ascribed identities in an environment full of prejudice, many of the research participants tried to distance themselves from the group of what they called "new wave" Vietnamese migrants who have come to the Czech Republic in the past ten years (Pechová 2007; Kušniráková et al. 2013) by drawing on stereotypes used in the media. The stereotypes describe this group of Vietnamese as uneducated peasants, drug dealers and criminals. This strategy of so-called "disidentification" which is described by Goffman in *Stigma* (1986) does not have to be applied in direct contact with a person who shows some aggressive behaviour, for example by making racist comments. On the contrary, the research findings show that this urge to defend oneself is something almost omnipresent in one's mind. Here we can find parallels between the cohort in our study and the second generation African Americans studied by Mary Waters in the United States. These young people also did not want to be identified with the society's negative portrayals of "poor blacks" and while trying to differentiate themselves from them, they also built on stereotypes of lower-class African Americans, such as lack of discipline and work ethic (Waters 1994). Due to the fact that recent migrants to the Czech Republic are supposed to be from poorer economic backgrounds (Kušniráková 2014; Pechová 2007), the reason that they wanted to distance themselves from this group of immigrants could, as Kibria says, "be based not only on their aversion to 'foreignness' but also on their own class identification" (Kibria 2002, 91).

Other stereotypes that the research participants built on while distancing themselves from other Vietnamese were those that in their view represented the classical "conservative and less developed" Vietnamese society. For example, while talking about the choice of partners the so-called "Vietnamese traditional role" of the spouse was viewed as something that did not suit them. While most of the female research participants preferred to date Vietnamese men born or raised in Czech Republic rather than Czechs, they all agreed that they would definitely choose a Czech above a man born and raised in Vietnam. In their eyes, these men were too traditional and would probably not be able to cope with their "Westernized" manners. As Sky says:

> There is just something I wanted to add, that when we choose partners, we need to have these European Vietnamese, actually if I can say it like that, we are this "one-and-half" generation, we have this Czech and Vietnamese mentality combined, but if someone was purely Vietnamese, without this Czech experience, then we couldn't get along, because we are more emancipated and liberal in some opinions. And maybe some Vietnamese guy, would not get over it, if I can say it like that.

The very experience of growing up in migrancy makes a big difference. From their recollections of Vietnam and in the way the research participants reflect upon their visits of their ancestral country, we can see that life and people there are viewed as different and distant from them and their lives in the Czech Republic. Linda explained the reason why she is happier to live in the Czech Republic rather than in Vietnam as follows:

> I am happy that I grew up here in the Czech Republic, rather than in Vietnam. Because I see it in the case of my nieces living there. For example, my uncle makes a lot of money in Vietnam and there you are either very poor or very rich. And my uncles, they all have lot of money and they have children of my age, who use drugs and these kinds of things, because that is something that is like very trendy there, very European, so going to parties, drinking and those kinds of things.

Another stereotype that the research participants build on while constructing their identity is the one which presents Vietnamese in the Czech Republic as "closed, incommunicative and segregated" (Brouček 2003, 4, 26). During his narrative Viet Van, a young man of 21, born in the Czech Republic, stressed that his family is not a "classical Vietnamese" family. Instead, he described his parents as open and communicative, which he illustrated by saying that his father often goes to pubs with his Czech neighbours.

> My father, usually after work, visits local pubs with his colleagues, he isn't that kind of type, like it is said that Vietnamese are reserved. My father absolutely isn't like that, he, you know, he just lives a Czech life here. He goes with them to the pub, chats, sometimes he even doesn't come home for dinner.

The model minority stereotype (Kibria 2002; Waters 2001) paints all Vietnamese children as super-smart overachievers. Research participants challenged this stereotype by emphasizing that they are not such intellectual types. Study participants also contested the presumption that they had strict Vietnamese parents, because they did not want to be seen as obedient people without any free will. As we can see, the question of "who we are" is often closely related to the question of "who we are not." The desire to positively evaluate one's self has led the research participants to the construction of cognitive boundaries that differentiate those who are similar to them from those who are different (Rosenberg and Kaplan 1982). What we also understood from the narratives of the research respondents is that they did not gain an understanding of themselves only by stressing differences and distancing themselves from others, but rather through interaction with "different" or "same" others (Jenkins 1997). Positive identification and disidentification were happening at the same time (Jenkins 1997). For example, when they were trying to distance themselves from a group of Vietnamese whom they saw as "more conservative," while at the same time identifying themselves with those of Vietnamese descent who were more like them, better educated and more "Westernized."

Symbolic Ethnicity and Race

Another important question that should be discussed when talking about ethnic identity is the question of whether ethnicity is a matter of choice and how it is connected to race. According to Gans (1979), ethnicity in time becomes optional and people who keep ties with their ethnic identities are making this choice voluntarily because they can gain something positive from it. But Gans formulated his theory of "symbolic ethnicity" in reaction to the so-called "ethnic revival" among the third generation "immigrants" in the U.S. and the group he was referring to were "White" (non-racialized) immigrants. The same counts for Richard Alba, who suggests a great deal of choice in the case of ethnicity (Alba 1990). On the other hand, authors, who studied "non-White" (racialized) minorities in the U.S. (Waters 1990, Kibria 2002), present a completely different picture when talking about symbolic or voluntary ethnic identity. In the case of Asians, Nazli Kibria argues that "a part of their ethnicity is not optional and they cannot, in the perception of others, unlike white ethnics who practice symbolic ethnicity, slip in and out of 'being ethnic'" (Kibria 2002, 101).

For most of the study participants, ethnicity was not always a matter of choice. Some of them said that this was because even if they would try to "slip out" of being "ethnic," others would not let them because they would always see them as different or foreign. This presumption of foreignness in the eyes of others does not always have to be articulated directly to be truly felt. For example, compliments paid to the research participants by other people about their perfect knowledge of the Czech language, or the estimation that they should be "experts" on the topic of Vietnamese culture aroused awkward feelings among these young people, putting their identities in question. On the other hand, not everybody experienced ethnicity as something involuntary. For example, Karel, who dated a Czech girl and had almost only Czech friends, said that he had never experienced the feeling of being different. "It is true," he said, "that in the beginning, when people don't know me yet, they ask about my origin." To him, however, this was something natural and normal, which did not constrain him in claiming the identity of his choice. "Of course I know I look different, but, you know, I actually never think about it," he said. As we have seen earlier in this chapter, race was also not a prominent issue in the case of making friends or choosing a suitable partner. What really mattered with this decision were culture, mentality, and common experiences of growing up in migrancy. Although some societal issues and involuntary ascriptions associated with racialized or non-white identities (Waters 1994) were felt by some of the interviewed children and young adults, the question of race did not constitute a major concern for them.

It Is Not All About Ethnicity: Contesting the Ethnic Majority–Minority Framework

We have shown that the question of ethnicity plays an important role in the ways the interviewed youth perceive and construct their identities. However, there are other equally or even more important factors, common to all young adults irrespective of their origin, that in the eyes of the research participants shaped them into who they are. First love (reciprocated or not), first "serious" relationships, friends, physical distinctions or defects (congenital or caused by injuries), or even travel experiences, experiences of living abroad, and hobbies that turned to passions all had a big influence on the lives of the study participants and their identities. Furthermore, the turbulent relationships with their parents should not only be seen as something connected solely to struggles caused by cultural gaps, but as something that normally occurs in the relationship between child and parent, irrespective of ethnic background. One of the themes that appear through Karel's narrative is that of his first serious relationship. His love for this Czech girl and the things that he learned from her, as he put it, introduced him to a radically different perspective and led him to re-evaluate his outlook on life and ideas about himself. Marek (twenty-seven), who came to Czech Republic at the age of nine, also mentions how his love for a girl while he was in primary school presented the main "motivator" behind almost all his actions.

> In the case of forming my own "me," I fell in love with a girl, I was into her from the age of nine and it took me more than three years to keep lying to myself about that I was not good enough, like I was telling myself that I am not sportive enough, smart enough and so on. This actually kept me going, kept me motivated in perfecting myself. Every time she declined my "offers," I was partially sad, partially pissed off and because she turned me down thirty-five times in all, I at that time realized that you cannot get everything even if you really try hard. Because that was what I was thinking before, before I met this girl. So she really influenced me and I changed in the way that I wasn´t that ambitious, choleric guy anymore but became more relaxed.

Ethnicity clearly is not always that important and there are many situations when it does not matter at all (Crul and Schneider 2010; Eriksen 2002). In order to define themselves, people can choose from different identities and statuses, according to the social situation (Huang 1994). Even when it is relevant, ethnicity is not always the most relevant factor (Eriksen 2002). From this point of view, the idea that migrant or ethnic minority children and youth are essentially "different" from the "other" majority kids becomes irrelevant.

Conclusions

This chapter has touched on some aspects of identity perception and formation among young adults of Vietnamese ancestry living in the Czech Republic. The purpose was to show how these young people create an identity for themselves while growing up in "migrancy." We were particularly interested in the question of whether these children and young people face identity struggles more often, or in different ways, than children who are not growing up in immigrant families, as well as what role ethnicity, culture, and migrancy play in their identity construction. Contrary to the general assumption that ethnic identities in the second and following generations become less salient (Hall 1996), ethnicity turned out to be very important for the youth in our study. On the other hand, it was also obvious that not all their actions and views were motivated by their families' migration experiences and/or ethnic heritage. We can therefore conclude that their identities derive from both ethnic and non-ethnic identifications (Huang 1994), within the social space of migrancy.

Although we, as researchers, regard identities as socially constructed, the research participants did not always share this view. On the contrary, ethnicity was very often seen and presented as given by nature, as we, for example, could see when the research participants ascribed some character traits of their parents or even themselves to the fact that they were Vietnamese. We do not wish to suggest that identity and ethnicity are something primordial and fixed in an objective kind of way, but rather to support Clifford Geertz (1973, 255–310), who says that it is often seen and experienced as such by the members of the ethnic communities themselves.

Through capturing the fluid and dynamic nature of ethnic identity perception in the life stories of the research participants, we also wanted to challenge the dominant Western notions of a fixed and stable nature of childhood and youth. Here we especially contested the assumption of cultural essentialism that constructs children of migrants as trapped between two cultures by demonstrating that the interviewed youth did not feel comfortable with the idea that they should choose between the identity of their parents and the identity of the majority. According to the way they see themselves, the idea of multiple ethnic identities, from which they can freely and selectively choose according to the situation, makes much more sense. From this point of view, the inner struggle that these young people went (or were still going) through was not a consequence of the inability to choose one "culture" above the other, but rather a result of the societal pressure put on them by their parents and by members of the majority population that they should do so.

Acknowledgments The presented research was funded by a financial grant project from the Charles University Foundation, GA UK, no. 685812/2012 "Migrant descendants in Czech Republic—Integration, Identity and Belonging."

References

Alba, R. D. (1990). *Ethnic identity: The transformation of white America*. New Haven, London: Yale University Press.

Atkinson, R. (2002). The life story interview. In: J. F. Gubrium & J. H. Holstein (Eds.), *Handbook of interview research. Context and method* (pp. 121–141). New York: Sage Publishing.

Bauman, Z. (2001). Identity in the globalizing world. *Social Anthropology, 9*, 121–129.

Berger, P. L., & Luckmann, T. (1999). *Sociální konstrukce reality*. Praha: Centrum pro studium demokracie a kultury.

Brouček, S. (2003). *Aktuální problémy adaptace vietnamského etnika v ČR*. Praha: Etnologický ústav AV ČR.

Brubaker, R., & Cooper, F. (2000). Beyond ethnicity. *Theory and Society, 33*(1), 31–64.

Chow, C. S. (1999). *Leaving deep waters*. New York: Penguin Books.

Crul, M., & Schneider, J. (2010). Comparative integration context theory: Participation and belonging in new diverse European cities. *Ethnic and Racial Studies, 33*(7), 1249–1268.

Crul, M., Schneider, J., & Lelie, F. (Eds.). (2012). *The European second generation. Does the integration context matter? IMISCOE research*. Amsterdam: Amsterdam University Press.

Drbohlav, D., Dzúrová, D., Černík, J. (2007). Integrace cizinců, žáků základních a středních škol, do české společnosti: příklad Prahy. [původní článek]. In *Geografie, Sborník* (Vols. 112, No.2, pp. 161–184).

Eriksen, T.H. (2002). *Ethnicity and nationalism: Anthropological perspectives* (2nd edn.). London: Pluto Press

Erikson, E. (1974). *Identity: youth and crisis*. New York: Norton.

Fog Olwig, K. (2013). Migration and care: Intimately related aspects of Caribbean family and kinship. In L. Baldassar & L. Merla (Eds.), *Transnational families, migration and the circulation of care: Understanding mobility and absence in family life* (Vol. 29, pp. 133–148). Routledge Research in Transnationalism.

Gans, H. J. (1979). Symbolic ethnicity: the future of ethnic groups and cultures in America. *Ethnic and Racial Studies, 2*(3), 1–20.

Geertz, C. (1973). The integrative revolution: Primordial sentiments and civic politics in the new states. In C. Geertz (Ed.), *The interpretation of cultures. Selected essays* (pp. 255–310). New York: Basic Books, Inc. Publishers.

Goffman, E. (1986). *Stigma*. New York: Touchstone.

Hall, S. (1996). Introduction: Who needs 'identity'? In S. Hall & P. Du Gay (Eds.), *Questions of cultural identity*. London: Sage Publications.

Hirschfeld, L. (2002). Why don't anthropologists like children? *American Anthropology, 104*(2), 611–627.

Hofírek, O., & Nekorjak, M. (2009). Vietnamští imigranti v českých velkoměstech—integrace přistěhovalců z Vietnamu. In M. Rákoczyová & R. Trbola (Eds.), *Sociální integrace přistěhovalců v České republice*. Praha: Slon.

Huang, J. N. (1994). An integrative view of identity formation: a model for Asian Americans. In E. P. Salett & D. R. N. M. C. I. Koslow (Eds.), *Race, ethnicity and self-identity in multicultural perspective*. Washington, DC: National MultiCultural Institute.

Janská, E. (2006). Druhá generace cizinců v Praze: příklad dětí z mateřských školek a jejich rodičů. *Geografie-Sborník České geografické společnosti, 111*(2), 198–214.

Janská, E., Průšvicová, A., & Čermák, Z. (2011). Possibilities for researching the integration of Vietnamese children in Czechia: The example of Prague-Kunratice elementary school (Možnosti výzkumu integrace dětí Vietnamců v Česku: Příklad základní školy Praha-Kunratice.). *Geografie, 116*(4), 480–496.

Jenkins, R. (1997). *Rethinking ethnicity. Arguments and explorations*. London: Sage Publications.

Jenkins, R. (2004). *Social identity*. London: Sage Publications.

Kacen, L. (2002). Supercodes reflected in titles battered women accord to their life stories. *International Journal of Qualitative Methods, 1*(1), 2–21.

136 A. Svobodová and E. Janská

Kibria, N. (1993). *Family tightrope: The changing lives of Vietnamese Americans*. New Jersey: Princeton University Press.

Kibria, N. (2002). *Becoming Asian American. Second generation Chinese and Korean American identities*. Baltimore: The Johnson University Press.

Kostelecká, Y., Kostelecký, T., Kohnová, J., Pokorná, K., Vojtíšková, K., & Šimon, M. (2013). *Žáci cizinci v základních školách: Fakta, analýza, diagnostika*. Karlovy, Praha: Pedagogická fakulta Univerzity.

Kušniráková, T. (2014). *Vietnamci v Česku a ve světě- migrační a adaptační tendence*. Slon: Praha.

Kušniráková, T., Plačková, A., & Tran Vu, V. A. (2013). Vnitřní diferenciace Vietnamců-pro potřeby analýzy segregace cizinců z třetích zemí. Výzkumná zpráva—rozšířená verze, Ministerstvo pro místní rozvoj, Praha.

Martínková, Š. (2008). Sociabilita vietnamského etnika v Praze, In Uherek Z.,Korecká Z., Pojarová T. et al., *Cizinecké komunity z antropologické perspektivy, vybrané případy významných imigračních skupin v České republice*. Praha: Etnologický ústav AVČR, 167–210.

Min, P. G. (2002). *The second generation—ethnic identity among Asian Americans*. Walnut Creek: AlltaMira Press.

Näre, L. (2013). Migrancy, gender and social class in domestic labour and social care in Italy: An intersectional analysis of demand. *Journal of Ethnic and Migration Studies, 39*(4), 601–623.

Pechová, E. (2007). *Migrace z Vietnamu do české republiky v kontextu problematiky obchodu s lidmy a vykořisťováním*. Praha: La Strada a MV.

Phinney, J. S. (1989). Stages of ethnic identity development in minority group adolescents. *The Journal of Early Adolescence, 9*(1–2), 34–49.

Portés, A., & Rumbaut, R. G. (2001). *Legacies: The story of the immigrant second generation*. Oakland: University of California Press.

Rosenberg, M., & Kaplan H. A. (1982). *Social psychology of the self concept*. Arlington Heights, IL: Harlan Davidson.

Somerville, K. (2008). Transnational belonging among second generation youth: Identity in a globalizing world. *Journal of Social Science, Special, 10*, 23–33.

Souralová, A. (2013). Children of Vietnamese parents brought up by Czech nannies: Reconstructing and redefining family ties. In *Gender and migration: Critical issues and policy implications* (pp. 48–56). London: London centre for social studies.

Thai, H. C. (2002). Formation of ethnic identity among second-generation Vietnamese Americans. In P. G. Min (Ed.), *The second generation—ethnic identity among Asian Americans* (pp. 53–85). Walnut Creek: AlltaMira Press.

Waters, M. C. (1990). *Ethnic options: Choosing ethnic identities in America*. California: University of California Press.

Waters, M. C. (1994). Ethnic and racial identities of second generation black immigrants in New York city. *International Migration Review, 28*(4), 795–820.

Waters, M. C. (2001). *Black identities: West Indian immigrant dream and American realities*. Cambridge, Massachusetts: Harvard University Press.

Zhou, M. (1997). Growing up American: The challenge confronting immigrant children and children of immigrants. *Annual Review of Sociology, 23*, 69–95.

Open Access This chapter is licensed under the terms of the Creative Commons Attribution-NonCommercial 2.5 International License (http://creativecommons.org/licenses/by-nc/2.5/), which permits any noncommercial use, sharing, adaptation, distribution and reproduction in any medium or format, as long as you give appropriate credit to the original author(s) and the source, provide a link to the Creative Commons license and indicate if changes were made.

The images or other third party material in this chapter are included in the book's Creative Commons license, unless indicated otherwise in a credit line to the material. If material is not included in the book's Creative Commons license and your intended use is not permitted by statutory regulation or exceeds the permitted use, you will need to obtain permission directly from the copyright holder.

Chapter 8
Mixed Parentage: Negotiating Identity in Denmark

Helene Bang Appel and Rashmi Singla

> There are many who ask where I come from, though I can see myself that I'm half Japanese… Now I live in Denmark, so I think personally that I am Danish. But anyway as such, I like better the thought that I am Japanese. I think it is more interesting and different (Naja, 16 years).

"Mixed" Children—An Overlooked Category

When we consider how globalization today leads to more marriages across national and ethnic borders, it is a paradox that such families are hardly mentioned in academic research and literature in Scandinavia (Torngren 2011). Such "mixed" marriages and children challenge notions of "us" and "others," as they represent a mixing of persons with different ethnic backgrounds (Williams 2004, 2010; Edwards et al. 2012). Small and King-O'Riain (2014) highlight an increasing political, public, and intellectual interest in themes related to "mixedness." The most common designation imposed on mixed race people of all ancestries is the inference that they are fragmented beings (Mengel 2001, as cited in Ifekwunigwe 2004, 9). People of "mixed" parentage may also contend with old conceptualizations of mixed people as somehow less than a whole person. They are also "seen as culturally weak and confused individuals with a troubled mind" (Ifekwunigwe 2004).

In this chapter, we examine the situation of children of mixed parentage in Denmark with particular attention to notions of identity and belonging, with a point of departure in the Danish context and the phenomenon of mixedness.

H. Bang Appel (✉)
Metropolitan University College, Copenhagen, Denmark
e-mail: helenehee@live.dk

R. Singla
Roskilde University, Roskilde, Denmark

© The Author(s) 2016
M.L. Seeberg and E.M. Goździak (eds.), *Contested Childhoods: Growing up in Migrancy*, IMISCOE Research Series,
DOI 10.1007/978-3-319-44610-3_8

Our work is driven by three central questions: What are the children's own lived experiences in the temporal context of historical and contemporary understandings of mixedness? How do they define themselves? Do they contest the old notion of the "troubled mind" and show a way towards other paradigms? In Denmark, out of a current population of 5.66 million, 8.9 percent are immigrants and a further 2.8 percent are the descendants of immigrants[1] (Statistics Denmark 2015, 2016). As of 2015, there were 94,587 couples where one spouse was of Danish origin and the other an immigrant or a descendant of immigrants. According to Bille (2011), there are 39,354 families with children where one parent is Danish and the other parent is an immigrant or a descendant. The number of children of mixed parentage increased from 74,731 in 2007 to 85,773 in 2010—a rise of 15 percent in 4 years according to specially acquired data from Denmark Statistics. In Denmark, these children are categorized broadly as "Danes" (see the above footnote). In Norway, another Scandinavian country, there is also no specific category for children of mixed parentage: Children of one Norwegian and one immigrant parent must be categorized either as children from an immigrant background or as Norwegian children (Backe-Hansen et al. 2014). Such mainstream categorizations do vary from one country to another in different time periods.

However, countries with diverse populations—resulting from increased immigration and demographic changes—such as the United States or United Kingdom—have established a category of persons with a "multiracial" identity. That points to an important shift in thinking about race and ethnicity in these countries. In the U. S., people of mixed parentage were included as a separate group in the 2000 Census and seven million people chose this option. In the 2010 U.S. Census, approximately 9 million individuals, or 2.9 percent of the total population, self-identified as mixed. The current growth rate of biracial families is three times faster than that of the rest of the population (Pew Research Center 2015). Similarly, Aspinall and Song (2013) note that the mixed race population is the fastest growing segment of the British population and numbered 1.25 million in the 2011 Census.

Numbers and statistical categories do not tell us how these children negotiate their identity or relate to their parents' values and life. The children's experiences merit attention in their own right, and also provide useful insights into fundamental aspects of Danish society and transnational connections that might otherwise remain unnoticed. In this chapter, we focus on how children and young people describe themselves, form social networks, and express their subjective experiences of mixedness and transnational relations.

---

[1]The definition of "descendants" is as follows: descendants are born in Denmark. Neither of their parents are Danish citizens nor were they born in Denmark. When one or both Denmark-born parents become Danish citizens, their children will not be classified as descendants. If both Denmark-born parents keep their foreign citizenship, their children will be classified as "descendants." Persons of Danish origin are persons—regardless of birthplace—who have at least one parent who is both a Danish national and born in Denmark (Statistics Denmark 2016, our translation).

Consequently, we believe that this study can serve as an entry point into a discourse about race—the socially constructed focus on the biological features including phenotypes such as skin colour and facial features that is a controversial topic in Denmark. Here we agree with Nader (2001, 614), who argues "If the biological category of race is without meaning, the social category of race is determining life chances." The dominating Danish discourse about ethnic homogeneity hinders the ability to address everyday life paradoxes related to such chances (Jenkins 2011). In this light, historical attitudes towards mixedness, intimate relationships, and parenting across ethnic boundaries are an overlooked theme. How race has been tabooed through history impacts current understandings of racialization in the case of children of mixed parentage. This shapes the exclusion/inclusion dynamics faced by the participants in our study.

In the 1960s and 1970s, many labour migrants from Turkey, Yugoslavia and Pakistan arrived in Denmark. Some formed intimate relationships with Danish women, leading to children of mixed parentage who were visibly different. These relationships and families tend to be understood in terms that derive from earlier times of "racial mixing," i.e. the history of slavery and colonialism. Larsen (2008) states that Denmark used about 100,000 black African slaves during the 17th until the 19th century—a fact hardly mentioned in mainstream Danish history. In Europe during the period of colonization and slavery, an image of the "other" as inferior and belonging to "another race" was formed. The relationship to the "other" (including Danes who traced their family back to slaves) is complex and problematic. This silenced part of Danish history reflects traditional restrictions on practices of racial mixing, where marriage across racial borders and children of mixed parentage would be stigmatized and sanctioned.

As we have seen, despite the increasing number of "mixed" children, the Danish state tends to ignore these children as a specific category in contrast to the UK and the U.S., where there are "mixed categories of identity" that reflect their colonial past and slavery and immigration history respectively. Consequently, in the UK, there is more openness and acknowledgement of being mixed in the past decades especially since 2000 (Tizard and Phoenix 2002).

In Denmark, people of mixed parentage are still invisible in the general statistics and their strengths and needs are not discussed in sectors such as educational and psychosocial services. It is certainly intriguing to think of this growing part of the population who are portrayed as "white" Danes while their mixedness officially ignored, yet—as we shall see—it is highly relevant to their lives and experiences within Danish society.

Mixedness—An Ambiguous Term

To examine how children of mixed parentage construct identity and a sense of belonging in everyday life, our use of the term mixedness needs to be understood. The term itself appears to presuppose the existence of "pure" marriages and children. Therefore, we view the very category "mixed" as potentially problematic despite its use by researchers such as Aspinall and Song (2013) and Edwards et al. (2012). However, we have chosen to use it because our study shows that it is a socially relevant category, like the term "race" (see Nader 2001, above).

For the purposes of this study, we define children of mixed parentage and people of mixed descent as immediately descended from two racialized discrete and socially identifiable groups. These groups are socially constructed, implying culturally distinct practices and hierarchical positions (Olumide 2002; King-O'Riain 2014). These understandings can be contested by different stakeholders. "Being mixed" or "fifty-fifty" are the self-descriptive terms used by our research participants. One of the challenges of socio-psychological research is to link the abstract theory and the lived experiences of the participants. In the following section, three historical phases of mixedness are delineated, showing how mixed parentage has been conceptualized within a broad Euro-American context (Ifekwunigwe 2004).

From the 17th to the 19th century, mixed persons were considered culturally weak and genetically confused individuals, mainly due to—now discredited—evolutionary myths. Accordingly, people of different races were prevented from mixing through segregation and legal sanctions (Ifekwunigwe 2004). In the 20th century, these views have been challenged and legal restrictions were removed. A number of authors, some of whom themselves identify with mixed race, argue for the recognition of more complex and changeable identities (Ifekwunigwe 2004; Root 1996; Tizard and Phoenix 2002). They reject the now obsolete, but surprisingly persistent notion that people with mixed backgrounds are weak and have ambiguous feelings of identity (Olumide 2002). Currently, new myths appear: Mixed people may be considered to possess a stronger genetic profile, be more beautiful, healthier, and more intelligent than "mono-racial" people. These views arise from the older implicit premise that they are somewhat different from "mono-racial" people (Edwards et al. 2012). This premise is in turn challenged by new studies which indicate the diverse ways in which mixed people feel about how they are perceived (Ali 2012; Aspinall and Song 2013).

Through our empirical research we seek to establish how children of mixed parentage position themselves and construct identities in everyday life (Bang 2010). In the following, we present our methodology, theoretical framework and analysis of identity construction among children of mixed parentage in contestation with ideas of apparent purity and homogeneity.

Researching Mixed Children's Own Perspectives

The first author conducted ten qualitative interviews, and the ongoing project was discussed by both authors (Bang 2010). The qualitative method involving a phenomenological approach gives us a deeper understanding of identity construction processes (Golafshani 2003, 600), as it is ultimately an effort to understand the meaning of human action or human experience in general (Conklin 2007, 276). We

8 Mixed Parentage: Negotiating Identity in Denmark 143

Table 8.1 Participants

Pseudonym	Age	Gender	Background		Locality
			Mother	Father	
Naja	16	Female	Japanese	Danish	Copenhagen
Alex	11	Male	Indian	Danish	Copenhagen
Marek	18	Male	Indian	Danish	Elsinore
Mona	16	Female	Indian	Danish	Elsinore
Lærke	11	Female	Thai	Danish	Copenhagen
Nicola	11	Female	Thai	Danish	Copenhagen
Maiken	14	Female	Japanese	Danish	Copenhagen
Mia	14	Female	Philippine	Danish	Copenhagen
Ashvin	16	Male	Danish	Indian	Copenhagen
Henrik Christer	17	Male	Vietnamese	Danish	Elsinore

focused on children aged 11–18 years old and young people from Asian-Danish backgrounds—one Asian and one Danish parent—in order to focus on a narrow group of research participants based on both authors' Asian background. This age group was chosen as children and adolescents in this developmental period are able to communicate more explicitly than in earlier phases. Also, this age range marks an important transition period from childhood to adulthood, where psychological processes such as identification and autonomy are especially salient.

The participants were very open and positive. The primary language was Danish, mixed with some English. They had volunteered to participate in the research, which they found interesting. They were contacted through relevant networks and all participants were located around the municipality of Copenhagen and a nearby town in relatively ethnically heterogeneous areas. Table 8.1 introduces all the participants in main demographic terms:

Theoretical Framework

We combine a post-structural approach, a first person perspective on people's feelings, and theory about negotiating mixed identity with transnationalism. This is advantageous as it reduces the risk of reductionism (Køppe 2008, 15–17; Verkuyten 2005, 17). Holding the position that identity is socially established and negotiated, we also consider it important to gain an understanding of an individual's personal feelings or reflections on topics about belonging and occupying a mixed position (Verkuyten 2005, 3). Within the broad theoretical framework of this book, how these children and young people relate to migrancy as a social space is an empirical question. In our case, perhaps "partial migrancy" is a better term as one parent is native and the other parent is a "migrant."

Our theoretical understanding adds nuances to the concept of growing up in migrancy. Elsewhere in this book, writers emphasize that an increasing number and proportion of the world's children are growing up in this space when they themselves are not migrants but their parents or even grandparents once were. In our study, only one parent is a migrant. Furthermore, the first chapter of this book elaborates that migrancy is inscribed on certain bodies by the larger society in general and legislative practices in particular. As we shall see, for some of the mixed children and young people, their appearance and responses to how they look are paramount.

We simultaneously look at how the environment affects each child, and how they choose and reflect on their own surroundings. Our eclectic approach allows us to look at identity from different perspectives.

The mixed identity theory, developed by Maria Root (1996), a pioneer researcher in the field, also inspires the construction of our framework. According to Root, there are three major strategies of negotiating identity, which may overlap:

- The first strategy describes how a child can bridge borders by having feet in both camps and respecting multiple perspectives simultaneously. The child can practice situational ethnicity and race by foregrounding or backgrounding different aspects of identity in different contexts.
- The second strategy highlights how a child can choose to belong to only one group.
- The third strategy outlines how a child of mixed parentage decisively goes beyond any borders and categories when having to describe or define himself or herself.

The subject is shaped according to the discourses he or she is taking part in (Rasmussen 2007, 349; Chow 2006, 202). This is important when we look at children and their experiences of alterity in society. Thus identity is constructed through communication and interaction with other people. Identity or self-narrative can be seen as a product of time and history, which perpetually changes according to certain beliefs and values. Identity construction is partly shaped in accordance with which discourse the person is taking part in.

The post-structural discourse allows for new ways of existing in the world. The child can construct a powerful self which reformulates outdated notions of identity (Hall 1992, 281; Honneth 2004, 463–464, 474). We acknowledge that although the individual is subjected to means of regulation and elimination within the discourse, the human being still has the possibility of constructing a powerful self. Thus, we want to avoid reducing the children to just reflections of social positions and consider their identities as more than a result of social structures and discourse (Verkuyten 2005, 22).

Our Understanding of the Children's Narratives

In this section, we present the children's own personal voices on how they view life in different domains. We have chosen to focus on four specific themes, which are based on close reading and analysis of their narratives. Our inquiry is centred on

8 Mixed Parentage: Negotiating Identity in Denmark

self-descriptions, friends in school, festival and leisure time, and transnational ties. Our focus is directed towards different kinds of identity formation patterns among the children and how they negotiate identity in various settings.

Self-descriptions

Some participants define themselves as "half-half"—for instance Danish-Asian, such as the participants Lærke and Naja. In this way, they define themselves as a mixture of their Danish and Asian descent. Thai-Danish Lærke states:

> Well, I guess I am Danish, but in a way I am also Thai because my mother is from Thailand, but I was born in Denmark, and when you are born in Denmark, you are Danish (…) Sometimes I don't know if I am a Dane or if I am half-Danish or half-Thai. There are a lot of people who don't think, well, if their mother or father is from Denmark, and the other parent from another country, then they just say that they are half-Danish and half-American or something like that.

It is evident that identity negotiations are constructed and influenced by different social contexts, such as family compositions, the influence of the non-native parent, transnational relations, friends and teachers in school and media coverage. Family composition seems to have an impact upon Japanese-Danish Naja and how she views herself. She presents herself in a way which can be analyzed as indeterminable (Aspinall and Song 2013) or ethnically ambiguous (E.A.), a term used by Ann Phoenix in Singla (2015, xii).

> There are many who ask where I come from, though I can see myself that I'm half Japanese… Now I live in Denmark, so I think personally that I am Danish. But anyway as such I like the thought that I am Japanese. I think it is more interesting and different.

On the other hand, Vietnamese-Danish Henrik Christer goes beyond any categorization and simply regards himself a multi-cultural person perceived as a world citizen and a cosmopolitan, combining French/Vietnamese and Danish aspects.

> I think it is wrong to be either or, well not wrong, but I like the idea of being a mixture and having different perspectives on different cultures and nationalities. I have studied French in primary school and high school, and I don't understand anything, but I like the culture, and I feel the French way of being appeals to me. However, other times, I also like to sit in a vest with a beer in my hand and watch football (laughing) and eat potatoes. In a way, I see myself very, well not multi-cultural, but maybe a little multi-cultural, I try to be like that.

In different ways, most participants described so far in our research relate to both cultures and claim their mixedness. Still, one participant—Mona—mainly identifies herself with being Danish—not mixed. She considers herself Danish above all. She lives in an upper middle class, predominantly Danish neighbourhood and describes her identity like this:

> Well, I guess I am Danish, since I have grown up here. Even though I have a mother who comes from another country, I am still surrounded by my friends who influence me a lot,

and they are all Danes. Besides, this is what I am most comfortable with, and I don't think I would ever say that I was Indian. I do not know what it means, or how it is, because I have not really been in India so often, and I do not know what the country has to offer...

However, Mona defines herself in contradictory ways. For instance, she describes having a hybrid identity in terms of having different perspectives. She describes how the practice of evening prayer ritual, which she has learned from her Hindu Indian mother, is important to her:

I say my prayers in the evening, which is not so normal for Danes. I lie down in my bed and say the prayer, which my mother has taught me... My father doesn't have faith in any religion, so no Christianity.

The children's narratives show us that most of them negotiate identity by positioning themselves between both cultures when having to describe themselves to others. They express that they have roots in both groups and identify themselves with more than one culture, which gives a broader perspective on life. Some negotiate identity by mixing categories and claiming their mixed Danish-Asian heritage. However, one participant simply claims himself as a world citizen and thereby ignores any categories or need to place himself between two cultures. Another participant considers herself only Danish and plays down having a mixed heritage. Her self-narrative is contradictory, as she considers herself Indian in more private contexts. It seems that the dominant discourse in society is powerful; who does not want to fit into the Danish community? Moreover, it shows that the hidden race discourse is alive. Overall, most participants express having a mixed position, but Danish society has apparently not created a category that allows individuals to express such a mixed identity.

Social Networks

Another important focus in our research is context. To what extent does context influence who the children identify with? When they are among friends in their everyday life, do they then feel Danish or Asian or something completely different? In the following quote, Naja expresses how she identifies herself with her Asian heritage among her Japanese friends and emphasizes culinary commonality with them. On the other hand, she identifies as Danish during other common activities, such as dancing.

Then you have something in common with the Asian friends like food and culture (...) particularly food. Then we talk about, well, we eat a lot of rice and stuff, the Danes eat more potatoes, and then we cook together sometimes (pause). Well, a lot of my Danish friends, they don't like sushi, which is strange because I am so used to it...When I spend time with my Asian friends, then I just feel more Asian... I guess that is what we have in common, we are Asians (...) I dance with two of my Danish friends, so we have that in common, dancing and stuff.

8 Mixed Parentage: Negotiating Identity in Denmark   147

Another participant, Henrik Christer, expresses very clearly this notion of having a changeable identity among his friends, but, in contrast to Naja, he declares that he feels more Asian among his Danish friends in his everyday life. This is the case when he has to explain in detail a specific Vietnamese cultural tradition like the Asian New Year:

> Sometimes I feel more Asian when they ask about traditions that are normal for me (...) for instance, the Asian New Year, and then they ask if I also celebrate the Danish New Year and stuff. Then they want to know how I celebrate the Asian New Year. I think there is a difference in terms of who you are with–when you are with some friends who are more Danish than you, then you might feel more Asian, then the feeling is kind of amplified, I guess, but it isn't something I have investigated further, really (laughs).

Some narratives show us that a few participants only identify themselves with their Danish friends in school. This notion emphasizing common activity—participant in leisure time and being part of a "girl band"—is expressed by siblings Marek and Mona respectively:

> Well, again it is limited how much I spend time with these people. Most of my time is spent with my classmates. Of course I know some of the others; I just don't spend time with people with another ethnic background, only Danes. I don't know why. I don't know if it is an unconscious choice. Well, I guess that is just how it is.Well, I think the girls from the drum majorettes have shaped me into becoming the person I am today. I started when I was only 8 (years old), it was new and you have in a way developed in relation to this environment...Yes, I guess all of them are Danes.

When we look at how the children negotiate identity among their friends, the participants express how identity is a situational construction. Some participants foreground or background their Asian identity according to which context and friends they are among. One participant foregrounds his Asian identity among his Danish friends, while another participant foregrounds her Asian identity when she is among her Asian friends. This shows that identity is changeable and complex, as one given situation can amplify either feelings of belonging or alienation. Only a few do not relate to different groups, which can be seen as yet another example of wanting to be included into the dominant group and not having an in-between identity. As seen before, the dominant discourse is powerful, as the fear of being othered is always present. One participant experiences this among his friends when they ask questions about his Vietnamese culture.

Subjective Experiences of Being Mixed

When we questioned the children about negative and positive aspects of being mixed, the answers indicate awareness at different levels. For eleven-year-old Indian Danish Alex, there are symbolic disappointments related to the fact that his mother has lived under different climatic conditions and avoids participation in Danish winter activities. At the same time, he points to the positive metaphoric "spice" in his everyday life through his mother's Indian culinary practices (Chaudhary 2007):

> ... my mother doesn't like cold weather and in the winter, she wouldn't go and play with snowballs with my father and me, she just wouldn't join us. It is irritating, because I really want her to join us. The advantage is that I don't have to eat just meat and potatoes all the time. My mother likes to make shish kebab, it is also meat but it is delicious.

For Naja, the advantage of having a Japanese mother are linguistic and broader geographical experiences through travel to Japan:

> My mother, she rarely speaks Japanese, and we just had a Japanese cousin visiting us.... I can't speak but understand when she asks us to brush our teeth... some Japanese. We had three weeks vacation in Japan, met my mother's relatives. Japan is really different, I miss it. Japanese are so polite... It is really good service in the shops.

Mona, on the other hand, perceives herself as Danish, yet she is able to describe the advantages of being mixed as follows:

> I think it is more interesting as you can try different things from two different cultures and find out how they are. You just don't have one culture, it can be boring... It is great that when I come to India, I have a belonging to the country as compared to being only Danish and not knowing about other things. In your presentations... in school you can draw on two cultures, you can add perspectives and that is smart.

In terms of leisure time, most participants combine different aspects of the Danish and Asian cultures, such as religion, traditions and food habits, which show that they identify themselves with their mixed heritage. One example is Marek, who declares that he celebrates Christmas and Easter, but also Indian festivals. Moreover, he expresses how he relates to Indian religion:

> I think I am a Hindu. I guess I am a mixture of my father and mother from not really believing in anything and yet believing in Hinduism (...). I have some prayers that I say sometimes, but I don't say the Lord's Prayer, I don't, so I will define myself as being a Hindu.

When asked to describe themselves and their experiences of discrimination, the replies were rather evasive entailing subjective negation from some participants. Naja positioned her "Japanese" category as not subject to discrimination, unlike "others" with the explicit phenotype "black" as the ones who were discriminated.

> Racism... no not all. I think also, not many people have anything against Japanese. I think if you are Black, then people have many prejudices ...in my school, there are such persons [with prejudices].

Alex, on the other hand, does not identify himself with having an Indian phenotype, implying the ethnic ambiguity mentioned earlier.

> ... When people look at me, they don't think: 'He is Indian'. People think I am Norwegian or Swedish.

Similarly, Mona also answers that she has not experienced discrimination because others cannot immediately tell she is of mixed-race background due to her

8 Mixed Parentage: Negotiating Identity in Denmark

light skin colour. She points out that her brother Marek has a darker skin colour. Their narratives indirectly underpin the salience of physical appearance, especially skin colour in relation to discriminatory experiences, where light skin colour is privileged (Meszaros 2013).

> No, because I don't look so Indian, so people don't think about it, especially as compared to my brother, he looks more Indian than me.

In contrast to the above three narratives of negation of personal discriminatory experiences related to phenotypes, Marek recollected one episode seven years back, in which he was perceived as Indian—not a mixed person—and told to return to his home country. The emotions of rejection paint a vivid story. Living in a predominantly white neighbourhood, with just one mixed Vietnamese-Danish friend, the comment was highly hurtful for him.

> I think perhaps, it was once in the leisure time club, when I was young. I think I came to blows with one person… Liv, a Danish girl. I think I was in 5th class, where she said that I should go back to my home country, because she said that I was Indian… Go back to your home country, well, where to take home, my homeland? I am home. I think that's the only time.

Asked further about his reaction, he replied:

> I think I was sad, actually. But yes, it went on and then she apologized also a week later. I didn't talk to my parents about it, it was once, it was not so important.

Reflecting on the issue of discrimination, Marek mentioned a current episode about naming "Racist of the year" in school. Despite claims of humour, he judged it as mean and patronizing, especially considering the stigmatization implied especially for his Turkish class mates.

> There is some discrimination. There was the title—racist of the year, they said it was for fun. I could not just see the fun in it, because then I looked at my Turk classmates and… they did not feel amused.

Thai-Danish Nicola experienced being bullied in the school through ethnic slur "Chinese" because of her phenotype:

> … the whole school is filled with immigrants and of course there are also some Danes, but there is probably a majority of immigrants, some always bully others. For example, now I am called Chinese, I have nothing against Chinese, but I'm not so happy to be called Chinese.

Nicola emphasizes that she is bullied often and how she responds either by overlooking the episode or questioning the persons perpetrating the discriminatory behaviour:

> … so I ignore them because I do not really want to discuss with them. But then, if they are of my own age or class I can ask them why must you call me that?

Japanese-Danish Maiken talks positively about her Asian heritage when she spends time with friends or is approached by other people. Maiken considers herself lucky to tan faster and at the same time points to the disadvantage of standing out:

Well, it is not negative because the advantages are that you tan faster. I know a blonde Danish friend who gets totally red in her face. Still, it can be annoying at times, for instance, if you have your picture taken, and you stand among blonde girls who have totally white skin. Then you just stand there and look very yellow (laughs).

Even though Maiken laughs and uses humour and considers herself lucky, she comments that other people subject her to the "gaze"—i.e. subjected to being a visible object—due to her Asian appearance. Philippine-Danish Mia also feels that her Asian looks can have an impact on how she is treated. She narrates her experiences of discrimination by her handball coach:

Well, during a match, I have to sit on the bench and if someone with another ethnic background joins the team, he is discriminating against them as well.... I have told some of my friends about it and then just laughed (...) Besides, I think team handball is boring because I cannot really play when my coach doesn't want me to (...).

She convincingly demonstrates how the exclusion of herself and others is contingent on their ethnic minority background.

These narratives demonstrate a nuanced understanding of mixedness in this context of partial migrancy among the participants. They are able to perceive a range of positive aspects such as spices in food, double festival celebrations, linguistic plurality, broader cultural horizon, and belonging to another country, which will be discussed in the next section. One participant appreciates her mixed background, as she considers just one culture "boring." The narratives also bring out negative aspects of being mixed as they experience racism related to phenotype: comments on skin colour or other visible features or the "gaze" that separates them from their Scandinavian classmates. They express in different ways how racial discrimination and othering causes hurt. The hidden race discourse exists. It is remarkable that none of the children discuss their different looks among friends or family, although they are aware that they look more "Indian" or more "Japanese" than others. Their silence about these experiences among their family and peers reflects the historical silencing of these issues and missing reflection of these salient themes with the "significant others" (Mead 1934). Finally, this confirms how difficult it is to negotiate oneself out of the margins if society ascribes a marginal position to you. The racial hierarchy exists and mixed children are subjected to it in different ways. Other studies also report that mixed persons have been subjected to racial slurs or felt annoyed by people's assumptions about their mixed-race background (Ali 2012). At the same time, there is a positive possibility of close relations in other contexts such as the migrant parent's country of origin leading to broader awareness and horizons.

Transnational Relations

In relation to the "migrant" parent's country of origin, our research shows that some participants view their stay in Asia as just another aspect of their daily life. Indian

8 Mixed Parentage: Negotiating Identity in Denmark

Danish Ashvin views his father's country, India, as a familiar place, where he spends time with his cousins, yet foreign regarding the Indian cuisine:

> It is very different. Well, the food is different, which I have to adjust to, because they like it very spicy...if it gets too spicy, it is annoying to eat it. Apart from being in India during my holidays, I guess it is the biggest difference compared to being in Denmark. Instead of being with friends and playing football, I spend my time with my cousins in India and play cricket, so in a way it is the same. The culture is different, but you just adjust to it, and then it is just another part of your everyday life.

However, he also expresses the contradictions he feels when he identifies himself with multiple cultures, for instance, when it comes to different communication norms entailing respectful politeness towards the older generation in India (Chaudhary 2007):

> Well, I like it in India (pause). I feel different because I don't have the same manners like the Indians. That is normal when I live my life in Denmark which is very different. I don't know how to explain it, but I feel kind of different from them, but I still like to be there. My family lives there, and I know them well, and I know who they are. I feel different, definitely, but it isn't something I feel bad about. I really haven't thought of it before.

Although most participants are perceived as identifying with their Asian background, Maiken is the only one who actually wants to live in Asia, based on some academic awareness and interest opportunities in Japan:

> I would very much like to study at the university in Japan, but I don't know if I would live there, but I would like to try it out maybe a year or two because it sounds very exciting and challenging and stuff like that.

Mona, however, seems to feel uncomfortable when she visits India:

> ...there is a lot of pollution, and I really don't like the poor people, but of course I like to see my family. Then there are lots of cheap things to buy...but it gets too much for me when I stay there for a longer period of time. It smells badly (unclear), and you have to run across the streets, something I am unfamiliar with in Denmark where everything is more structured and clean (laughs).

Mona appreciates the Indian family ties, yet she feels uncomfortable being in India because of structural conditions—such as poverty and environmental pollution—and she thus perceives her mother's country of origin in predominantly negative terms.

Most participants in our research describe having roots in both groups and holding different perspectives when they visit Asia. One participant expresses how he simultaneously feels at home and foreign in India, and seems to describe a situational identity which changes according to context. Another participant faces the dilemma of combining different cultural lifestyles, which can be seen as a way of navigating and adjusting successfully in different settings no matter what. However, one participant identifies primarily with the Danish system, implying a "one camp belonging," yet perceiving the transnational family ties positively. These narratives do document active transnational ties in different ways and reflect the partial migrancy especially relations and awareness of migrant parent country of origin.

Emerging Strategies and Paradigm

Practices of childhood in different social fields and negotiation of identity are far from trivial. Our findings show how many paradoxical ways of negotiating identity exist in everyday life among children of mixed parentage. The participants negotiate identity by combining various approaches, such as "having both feet in both camps" and practicing situational ethnicity, choosing only one group or simply going beyond any categories in various contexts. Some reject describing themselves with a limited category. They seem to require a new category of their own that expresses having an in-between "mixed" status. They contest the current categories and challenge this limited way of thinking, which hardly reflects real life. One participant stands out, as he simply declares himself a multi-cultural cosmopolitan and rejects narrow labels. Even the participant who declares herself to be Danish indicates a simultaneously positive awareness of multiple belongings. Our data shows that the participants overall construct their identity based on different negotiating strategies in everyday life (Root 1996).

Our theoretical understanding takes into consideration the context and the realities of society which shape the identity of the child and enables us to show how interaction with parents, peers, siblings, and community are important factors in shaping an individual's life. Along with examining the context, the theory places human existence in a specific historical time and space; the child can construct changeable identities while adjusting to a specific social environment.

The three strategies mentioned in the theoretical framework bring into focus the changeable aspects of different contexts, as identity is understood as a constantly changing phenomenon throughout life. Such a multi-dimensional model gives an opportunity to have more memberships and multiple identities with different groups (Root 1992, 6; Spickard 1992, 22). In fact, today a child of mixed parentage can choose to embrace some or all aspects of his identity, although within societal constraints (Spickard 1992, 21–22). In this way, social ambiguity and fluid identities are seen as possible ways of viewing oneself as defined and united.

The participants' narratives demonstrate that you can belong to multiple cultures. They see it as a strength and advantage, despite clear disadvantages. This notion challenges the simplified perception of belonging to just one group, a contrast to the historical perception of mixedness as pathologized (described in the beginning of the chapter). In fact, the children's self-narratives and identities are much more dynamic, having their own complex nature. Although most of the participants are proud of their mixed origin, they also report having suffered from discrimination and bullying. There is a big gap between how they see themselves and how the world views them due to continued ignoring of mixedness at the societal level. As there is no policy focus on the impact of mixedness in the educational and social institutions in Denmark, children of mixed parentage are, should the need arise, also deprived of relevant psychosocial services and counselling, adapted to their experiences of "mixedness" (Singla and Holm 2012; Singla 2015). Their experiences of growing up in the social space of partial migrancy should be included in such services.

Along with expressing a feeling of belonging to more cultures, the children's narratives challenge the old stigmatizing idea of being confused and troubled individuals, who should be pitied. A new paradigm slowly seems to be emerging in the field of mixedness studies, while the old one still exists. Children's own voices and narratives contest this outdated perception, as they claim a powerful, interesting and proud identity by expressing various positions. McKenzie (2012) is in line with this notion: the voices of white mothers with children of mixed parentage in Nottingham show how they are proud of their children's mixed and hybrid identities and interchangeable cultures, although these are simultaneously stigmatized by others. This study challenges other studies, which still pinpoint problematic aspects of mixedness (Barn et al. 1999; Twine 2010). Thus, a new paradigm is developing that argues against problematic discourses that focus on troubled and confused minds. However, at times they are ignored, stigmatized and discriminated against by Danish society.

Furthermore, when the children were asked about discrimination, their answers were evasive. Several of the children had experienced prejudice in their everyday life. Such discriminatory behaviour affects the mental health—not only of the child —but also of the person who discriminates (Cohrs and Kessler 2012). The hidden race discourse from mainstream society exists and some of the children express what it feels like to be excluded in everyday life situations.

Methodologically, it requires a very safe setting to reveal such experiences, which we, to some extent, must have managed, as they all seem to confide in us. Suki Ali (2012) has studied mixed children, mixed race politics, and senses of solidarity among mixed race people in Britain, arguing that no child should be raised as a mixed child without being able to discuss being mixed. In our study, not even one participant talked openly with their families or "significant others" about looking different than their peers or some family members. The silence is striking. Although the participants are proud of their mixed background, they have ambiguous and negative feelings when required to discuss their Asian looks: Physical appearances matter. The links between history and the present day are fascinating, significant and disturbing. A study about Danish-Japanese young people in Denmark (Nielsen et al. 2016) also entails that that their identity is affected by mixedness in different ways, though the theme should receive more attention so that young people can embrace the gift of being mixed with all the advantages and disadvantages that come along with it.

Nevertheless, identity can be regarded as a construction and a changeable phenomenon, which indeed reveals itself as very context-dependent in our study. At the same time, the process of negotiating identity should be seen in interplay with society's restrictions and ideology. In order to avoid discrimination, some argue that young people only identify with one group or nationality. As we have seen, it is not always possible to ascribe a positive alterity while being marginalized. This proves that constructing a powerful identity has its limitations contingent on the broader context.

Concluding Comments

Our study adds nuances to the phenomenon of mixedness empirically and theoretically, rather than simply positivizing mixed identity. The history of race and mixed identity within the Danish context contributes to an understanding of contested childhoods and growing up in "partial" migrancy for these children and young people. They negotiate different identities in different settings. They have agency, which they use to claim complex and changeable selves, and they contest the notion of belonging to just one group even though they are still ignored and at times stigmatized by society. Although they are still young individuals, they are not just passive individuals to be cared for. Their mixed identity is plural and dynamic (Tizard and Phoenix 2002, 234) and if supported they have potential to contribute positively to any society.

Although they do experience exclusion and contradictions, the participants in our study still contest the stereotypical notion of being confused and lacking a sense of belonging. They express their simultaneous subjective belonging to several places or cultures, as growing up in sedentariness and in migrancy.

New studies—not only from Denmark, the UK and the U.S.—show that similar identity processes take place on a global scale, in countries like Germany, the Netherlands, France, Japan, and Brazil. While some hide their mixed background due to shame and fear of harassment, others highlight their mixed identity as an advantage (King-O'Riain 2014, 9, 263). A need for new categories is emphasized in Denmark. The young individuals of mixed parentage in Denmark contest being labelled as "Danes," "migrants" or "foreigners"—they are just mixed. As this is becoming increasingly common, the emergence of a new paradigm such as indicated by us is perhaps only to be expected. Though embedded in the Danish context, these findings can be generalized to other Nordic countries as there are commonalities in the way these categories are constructed. The findings can also be generalized to a global context to some extent, based on the methodological analytic generalization.

The present study underpins the need for further investigation on mixed children's and young people's situation, also in Denmark. On the group level, it is crucial to discuss mixedness with their families and the significant others. How are their relationships with peers, teachers, caregivers and other professionals? Much more research in this field is needed, both at the societal, group, and personal level, as a growing mixed community is evolving globally (King-O'Riain 2014, 274). Due to globalization, the population of mixed people will expand to become an increasingly noticeable part of contemporary society. Therefore, we must examine related themes around identity, such as status, resources, privileges, race, ethnicity,

8 Mixed Parentage: Negotiating Identity in Denmark

inclusion, exclusion, stigma, and power. The contested belongings have to be addressed, and we must move beyond simplistic dichotomies, because mixed children and young people are growing up in the context of migrancy, yet they are both ethnic minorities and majorities at the same time. They influence the present and the future of the societies into which they are born and the society which their "migrant" parent comes from originally. They also influence their families as active and mixed persons in context of migrancy. Thus, it is crucial to embrace the mixedness of identity in contemporary societies.

References

Ali, S. (2012). Situating mixed race politics. In R. Edwards, S. Ali, C. Caballero & M. Song (Eds.), *International perspectives on racial and ethnic mixedness and mixing. Relationships and resources*. Abingdon, UK: Routledge.

Aspinall, P., & Song, M. (2013). *Mixed race identities. Identity studies in the social sciences*. London: Palgrave Macmillan.

Backe-Hansen, E., Madsen, C., Kristoffersen, L., & Hvinden, B. (2014). *Barnevern i Norge 1990–2010 En longitudinell studie*. Oslo: NOVA (Norsk institutt for forskning om oppvekst, velferd og aldring) Rapport.

Bang, H. (2010). Negotiating identities among children and adolescents of mixed parentage. Master's thesis, Denmark: Roskilde University.

Barn, R., Das, C., & Sawyerr, A. (1999). *Family group conferences and black and minority ethnic families*. London: Family Rights Group.

Bille, M. (2011) Blandede Børen- I Tyrkiet hedder vi Baru & Kibele in *Børn & Unge 02*, 27 January 2011, 42 årgang. Retrieved February 2016 from www.boernogunge.dk.

Chaudhary, N. (2007). The family: Negotiating cultural values. In J. Valsiner & A. Rosa (Eds.), *The Cambridge handbook of sociocultural psychology*. Cambridge, UK: Cambridge University Press.

Chow, R. (2006). Poststructuralism: Theory as critical self-consciousness. In E. Rooney (Ed.), *The Cambridge companion to feminist literary theory* (pp. 195–209). Cambridge, UK: Cambridge University Press.

Cohrs, J. C., & Kessler, T. (2012). Negative stereotypes, prejudice and discrimination. In A. G. de Zavala & A. Cichocka (Eds.), *Social psychology of social problems, the intergroup context*. London: Palgrave Macmillan.

Conklin, T. A. (2007). Method or madness: Phenomenology as knowledge creator. *Journal of Management Inquiry, 16*(3), 275–287.

Edwards, R., Ali, S., Caballero, C., & Song, M. (Eds.). (2012). *International perspectives on racial and ethnic mixedness and mixing*. Abingdon, UK: Routledge.

Golafshani, N. (2003). Understanding reliability and validity in qualitative research. *The Qualitative Report, 8*(4), 597–607. Retrieved February 2016 from http://www.nova.edu/ssss/QR/QR8-4/golafshani.pdf.

Hall, S. (1992). The question of cultural identity. In T. McGrew, S. Hall, & D. Held (Eds.), *Modernity and its futures* (pp. 274–316). Cambridge, UK: Polity Press in association with the Open University.

Honneth, A. (2004). Organized self-realization: Some paradoxes of individualization. *European Journal of Social Theory, 7*(4), 463–478.

Ifekwunigwe, J. O. (2004). Let blackness and whiteness wash through: Competing discourses on bi-racialization and the compulsion of genealogical erasures. In J. O. Ifekwunigwe (Ed.), *"Mixed Race" studies, a reader* (pp. 183–194). London: Routledge.

Jenkins, R. (2011). *Being danish: Paradoxes of identity in everyday life*. Chicago: University of Chicago Press.

King-O'Riain, R.C. (2014). Global mixed race: A conclusion. In R. C. King-O'Riain, S. Small, M. Mahtani, M. Song, & P. Spickard (Eds.) *Global mixed race*. New York: New York University Press.

Køppe, S. (2008). *En moderat eklekticisme*. *Psyke og Logos, 29*(1), 15–35.

Larsen, A. F. (2008). *Slavernes slægt*. Copenhagen, Denmark: DR.

Mckenzie, L. (2012). Finding value on a council estate: Voices of white working mothers with mixed-race children in St. Anns, Nottingham. In R. Edwards, S. Ali, C. Caballero & M. Song (Eds.), *International perspectives on racial and ethnic mixedness and mixing. Relationships and resources*. Abingdon, UK: Routledge.

Mead, G. H. (1934). The i and the me. In C. W. Morris (Ed.), *Mind, self, and society, from the standpoint of a social Behaviourist*. Chicago: University of Chicago Press.

Mengel, L. (2001). Triples—the social evolution of multiracial panethnicity: An Asian American perspective. In D. Parker & M. Song (Eds.), *Rethinking 'mixed race'* (pp. 99–116). London: Pluto Press.

Meszaros, J. (2013). A desire for the exotic: Racialized desires within the philippines romance tour industry. Paper presented in intimate migrations conference, 3–5 April 2013. Roskilde: Roskilde University.

Nader, L. (2001). Anthropology! Distinguished lecture—2000. *American Anthropologist, 103*(3), 609–620.

Nielsen, A., Trylcova, L., Nohles, N., Gordon-Orr, R., Senniksen S., Javadin S (2016). *Mixedness —a study on Danish-Japanese heritage and its implications*, HIB, 3rd semester project. Autumn 2015, Roskilde University.

Olumide, J. (2002). *Raiding the gene pool*. London: Pluto Press.

Pew Research Center. (2015). *Multiracial in America. Proud, diverse and growing in numbers*. Washington, DC. http://www.pewsocialtrends.org/files/2015/06/2015-06-11_multiracial-in-america_final-updated.pdf.Phoenix.

Rasmussen, J. (2007). Sociologisk subjektteori og socialkonstruktivisme. In B. Karpatschof & B. Katzenelson (Eds.), *Klassisk og moderne psykologisk teori* (pp. 346–364). Copenhagen, Denmark: Hans Reitzels Forlag.

Root, M. P. P. (Ed.). (1992). *Racially mixed people in America*. Newbury Park, CA: Sage Publications.

Root, M. P. P. (1996). The multiracial experience: Racial borders as a significant frontier. In M. P. P. Root (Ed.), *The multiracial experience: Racial borders as the new frontier*. Thousand Oaks, CA: Sage Publications.

Singla, R. (2015). *Intermarriage and mixed parenting, promoting mental health and wellbeing: Crossover love*. London: Palgrave Macmillan.

Singla, R., & Holm, D. (2012). Intermarried couples, mental health and psychosocial wellbeing: Negotiating mixedness in the danish context of "homogeneity". *Counselling Psychology Quarterly, 25*(2), 151–165.

Spickard, P. R. (1992). The illogic of American racial categories. In M. P. P. Root (Ed.), *Racially mixed people in America* (pp. 2–23). Newbury Park, CA: Sage Publications.

Statistics Denmark. (2015). *Indvandrere i Danmark 2015 (immigrants in Denmark 2015)*. Retrieved February 2016 from http://www.dst.dk/Site/Dst/Udgivelser/GetPubFile.aspx?id=20703&sid=indv2015.

Statistics Denmark. (2016). *Indvandrere og efterkommere (immigrants and their descendants)*. Retrieved February 2016 from https://www.dst.dk/da/Statistik/emner/indvandrere-og-efterkommere/indvandrere-og-efterkommere?tab=dok.

Tizard, B., & Phoenix, A. (2002). *Black, white or mixed race? Race and racism in the lives of young people of mixed parentage* (2nd ed.). London: Routledge.

Torngren, O.S. (2011). *Love ain't got no color?—Attitude toward interracial marriage in Sweden*. Ph.D. thesis, Malmo, Studies in International Migration and Ethnic Relations, No. 10.

Twine, F. W. (2010). *A white side of black Britain: Interracial intimacy and racial literacy*. Durham, NC: Duke University Press.
Verkuyten, M. (2005). *The social psychology of ethnic identity. European monographs in social psychology*. East Sussex, UK: Psychology Press.
Williams, T. K. (2004). Raceing and being raced: The critical interrogation of "passing". In J. O. Ifekwunigwe (Ed.), *"Mixed Race" studies, a reader* (pp. 166–170). London: Routledge.
Williams, L. (2010). *Global marriage: Cross-border marriage migration in global context: Migration, minorities and citizenship*. London: Palgrave Macmillan.

Open Access This chapter is licensed under the terms of the Creative Commons Attribution-NonCommercial 2.5 International License (http://creativecommons.org/licenses/by-nc/2.5/), which permits any noncommercial use, sharing, adaptation, distribution and reproduction in any medium or format, as long as you give appropriate credit to the original author(s) and the source, provide a link to the Creative Commons license and indicate if changes were made.

The images or other third party material in this chapter are included in the book's Creative Commons license, unless indicated otherwise in a credit line to the material. If material is not included in the book's Creative Commons license and your intended use is not permitted by statutory regulation or exceeds the permitted use, you will need to obtain permission directly from the copyright holder.

Chapter 9
"I Think of Myself as Norwegian, Although I Feel that I Am from Another Country." Children Constructing Ethnic Identity in Diverse Cultural Contexts in Oslo, Norway

Mari Rysst

Growing up, children contest many issues, including the identities that they and those around them construct. This chapter discusses the ethnic identity construction of Norwegian-born children with foreign parents at a place and school located in the ethnically diverse Grorud Valley east of Oslo, Norway. I write about the school here using the pseudonym Dal. My discussion of children's ethnic identity construction builds on previous research (Rysst 2012, 2013, 2014) which I analyze here in light of the concept of "migrancy" as a social space. This concept is understood as "the socially constructed subjectivity of 'migrant,' or 'foreigner,' which is inscribed on certain bodies by the larger society in general" (Näre 2012, 604). According to Lena Näre, "its subjectivity is very seldom, if ever, embraced by migrants themselves" (Näre 2012, 605). In the present study, however, the children do talk about each other, and themselves, as "foreigners," yet sometimes also as "Norwegians" and mostly in terms of hybrid identities such as "Norwegian-Pakistani." The terms used depend on the social context.

Like many other European countries, Norway has experienced increased ethnic and racial diversity because of immigration since the late 1960s. Today, immigrants and Norwegian-born children with both parents born abroad constitute 15.6 % (roughly five million people) of the total population of Norway (Statistics Norway 2015a). About 25 % of all immigrants in Norway live in Oslo. A growing city of 650,000 inhabitants, Oslo is home to 160,000 immigrants and 48,000 persons born in Norway whose parents were both born abroad. The single largest nationalities represented in the immigrant population are Pakistanis, Poles, Swedes, and Somalis (Statistics Norway 2015b). This situation makes parts of the city of Oslo very ethnically and culturally diverse. In Dal, ethnic Norwegians, here defined in line

---

M. Rysst (✉)
Lillehammer University College, Lillehammer, Norway
e-mail: Mari.Rysst@hil.no

© The Author(s) 2016
M.L. Seeberg and E.M. Goździak (eds.), *Contested Childhoods: Growing up in Migrancy*, IMISCOE Research Series,
DOI 10.1007/978-3-319-44610-3_9

with local usage as persons born in Norway and whose parents and grandparents were all also born in Norway, constitute a minority. The borough of Dal has approximately 9,500 inhabitants; immigrants and their Norwegian-born children make up nearly 70 per cent of this population (Wiggen et al. 2015). The most numerous groups are Pakistanis, Turks, Moroccans, Afghans, Iraqis, Iranians, and Somalis. This diversity challenges the stereotypical notion of Norway as "homogenous people made up of Lutheran peasants and fishermen" (Seeberg 2003, 25).

Based on participant observation and interviews with the children I got to know in Dal, I argue that the childhoods of children living in ethnically diverse contexts are often contested because of conflicting cultural values. As they grow up, these children have to negotiate their parents' cultural values and the cultural values of the Norwegian society regarding ethnic identity construction. "Ethnic identity" can refer to people's sense of historical national belonging, as is the case with Pakistani, Norwegian or Turkish populations. It can also refer to minority groups within a nation state, as with Kurdish populations within Turkey or Iraq. Childhood, which is socially constructed to encompass society's conceptualization of a child and expectations vis-à-vis children of different ages becomes a contested space (Wells 2009, 2). As such, this chapter is written in line with what Seeberg and Goździak write in Chap. 1, page 12, about "national populations that tend to more or less comply with official understandings of what childhood should be like."

In this contested space, children face tensions regarding who they are and aspire to be in relation to age, ethnicity, and gender. For instance, some children—particularly teenage girls from immigrant families—do not return to school after the summer holidays because they are kept behind in their families' countries of origin. This may happen because their parents do not want them to become "too Norwegian," meaning for example that they disapprove of their daughters dressing in clothes that do not cover the body according to their cultural values or date. Parents worry that their daughters will marry against their wishes (Yusuf 2014). This situation is worrisome for both children and school personnel. It is also an illustration of conflicting cultural values, and thus of a contested childhood. It appears hard for children of foreign-born parents to escape the migrancy framework. In this chapter, I address these questions: how do children and youth in Dal construct identity at the intersection of age, gender, ethnicity and religion? How and why do they relate to the ubiquitous categories of "Norwegian" and "foreigner"?

The Field Site and Methodology

The field site and the school where I conducted my research are located in a suburb east of Oslo. This school caters to pupils between the ages of ten and sixteen. Information from the local school administration states that there are approximately 460 students in the school living in families originating in sixteen to eighteen different countries. Ethnic Norwegians constitute a minority, while Pakistanis are the most numerous. Other countries represented include Turkey, Afghanistan, Iraq, Iran, Morocco, Somalia, Gambia, Nigeria, and Vietnam. One boy, David, is of mixed origin, having an ethnic Norwegian mother and West-African father. In 2010–2011, I did research, including long-term participant observation, on consumption and integration in the same school with students in the 5th and 6th grades (Rysst 2012, 2013, 2014). At the time of the present research conducted two years later, these children were thirteen and fourteen years old. These teens constitute the primary informants in my follow-up study. Among these, only Pernille is an undisputed ethnic Norwegian, while David has mixed origin. I wanted to talk again with the children I already knew (Rysst 2012) but I also included two new girls I found particularly interesting because of their gendered presentation of self which I found to be in conflict with the dominant Islam-inspired gender images in Dal.

I was present in the classroom and outside in the schoolyard at breaks once a week for three months in the 8th and 9th grades. I arranged and conducted five informal group interviews with nine children—seven girls and two boys. These groups consisted of friends, that is, children I knew hung out together. In methodological terms, the interviews were in focus groups, which I believe have the potential of bringing forth more information than individual interviews, particularly if the group atmosphere is based on trust among the participants and between the participants and the researcher (Thagaard 2013). One of the methodological advantages of long-term participant observation is a fair chance of achieving relations based on trust and the children included in this study were all happy to participate. They knew each other and myself quite well before the interviews started, which is likely to have increased the reliability of their narratives.

All the interviews were done in the classroom during lunch breaks. The parents had given permission for their offspring to participate in the study and the students were happy to provide consent as well. Three interviews were done when the children were in the 8th grade and two when they had started the 9th grade, which provided longitudinal perspective. The groups consisted of two pairs of girls, one group of three girls, and only one pair of boys. All interviews were tape-recorded and transcribed. All the names used in this chapter are pseudonyms to ensure the children's anonymity.

Youth participate in several social contexts every day, and I observed and partly participated in some of these. I observed them in classes where I had a chance to see how the children related to their teachers and peers, as well as in less formal surroundings around school where I could observe their interactions with peers. In the interviews, we spoke about the broader contexts of their friendships and leisure activities, but less about their families. Two issues took me by surprise. First, the relationship between religion, gender (including sexuality), and ethnic identity, as it emerged from their much-used emic social categories of "Norwegian" and "foreigner." This relationship was more intermingled than I first thought. Second, I was surprised to find that minority youth, often stigmatized in the Norwegian public discourse, did not aspire to be considered Norwegians.

In the following sections, I present my theoretical framework, discuss the empirical findings, and end with some concluding remarks.

Theoretical Framework

Childhood Studies and Children's Perspectives

According to James et al. (1998), conceptualizations of children prior to Freud were dominated by a developmental discourse asserting that "children become future adults" (James et al. 1998, 17–19). Research on children has often been carried out in relation to both psychological and sociological theories of socialization (Kampmann 2003). Although these theories differ, they have a common focus on the child as becoming, not being. The becoming child is viewed as an incomplete adult on its way to adulthood (James et al. 1998; Thorne 1993). The sociological and anthropological research on children initiated during the 1990s focuses on children as agents, as active participants, and as interpreters and creators of their lifeworlds. They are both being and becoming. This way of thinking was termed a "new paradigm" of child research (Kampmann 2003; James et al. 1998). Most importantly, the present-day sociology of childhood embraces studying children from their point of view. This is an experiential and phenomenological approach, taking children's concepts, categories, and experiences as points of departure in the analysis of their everyday lives. I take the same approach in this chapter. I believe a bottom-up approach in studying children is needed, particularly regarding children of foreign born parents, as their voices—or insider's points of view—are not often heard.

Shifting Selves, Subject Positions and Gender

The activities and self-presentations of the children I got to know changed according to situations and social contexts, particularly between home and school. Henrietta Moore, like other post-structuralist researchers, has argued that decentred selves, multiple selves, or multiple identities are acted out in different social contexts (Moore 1994). One distinction between modern and post-structuralist conceptualizations of the self is that the former reads the self as having a core, while the latter views the self as fragmented (Lorentzen and Muhleisen 2006). Moore's theory of subject positions implies that a single subject can no longer be equated with a single individual. Each individual is a multiply constituted subject and "take [s] up multiple subject positions within a range of discourses and social practices" (Moore 1994, 55). This theoretical stance allows the study of intra-cultural variation and the construction of ethnic identities, particularly among foreign-born and their children. As such, in a situation with both parents and friends present, a daughter may position herself differently depending on her understanding of expectations from the persons interacting with her. This is highly relevant for the Norwegian-born girls of immigrants included in this study.

Similarly, ethnic identity construction is understood as presentation of self that includes ethnic cultural values concerning gender, that is, femininity and masculinity, and thus encompasses dress, hairstyle, appearance, and behaviour. This also includes ways of talking, and is relational and something persons do (West and Zimmerman 1987) or perform (Butler 1993), rather than something they are. I understand gendered identity to be embedded in ethnic identity. However, whether gender is activated or not depends on social context (Rysst 2014). Gendered ethnic identity is often constructed and done in relation to the other sex: femininity in relation to masculinity, which presuppose each other (Thorne 1993; Rysst 2008, 2014). This view understands gender as fluid and gendered identities as "shifting hybrids" (Moinian 2009, 33), or shifting selves.

Notions of Hybridity and Social Classification

Hybridity means a cultural blending and reinvention. Previous research theorizing hybridity assumed that children of immigrants occupied a space between two cultures (Anthias 2001; Back 2002, 446). This liminality affected their identity construction, sense of belonging, and well-being. More recent research suggests taking a more positive approach, viewing children of immigrants as creative *bricoleurs* who combine different cultural expressions into something new, becoming competent navigators of culture (Prieur 2004, 101; Jacobsen 2002, 32). Viewing children as creative bricoleurs is in line with the so-called "new" paradigm in childhood research presented above, which views children as having agency, not as passive objects of socialization (James et al. 1998). As such, youth mix cultural styles, values, and trends into hybrids, often related to consumer goods like clothing, which is particularly apparent in relation to gender, as I will show later.

Hybridity is often discussed in relation to globalization and the ways in which contact with different cultures results in "cultural complexity" (Hannerz 1992). Olga Nieuwenhuys argues that the post-colonial theorist Homi Bhabha's notion of "the third space," which is an "in-between space of culture," is "seminal for understanding the dynamics of identity negotiation in minority communities" (Nieuwenhuys 2013, 3). The vast majority of children in Dal were born in Norway to foreign-born parents and are therefore often read as having "one foot in two cultures," or living in a space between two cultures (Back 2002, 446). In line with this conceptualization, I argue that these children participate in and negotiate ethnic identity construction in a "third space."

Social classification, while universal, organizes people differently in different contexts, based on culturally relevant characteristics. The interesting issue, as formulated by Halleh Ghorashi et al., is "*which* categories we use and *how* we use them" (Ghorashi et al. 2009, 11). How people classify their social world tells us something about dominant cultural values in their relevant social contexts. The categories, however, are not something "natural"; they are social constructions that change with time, place, and situation (Ghorashi et al. 2009, 11).

164 M. Rysst

"Norwegian" and "foreigner" are emic classificatory concepts used in all parts of Norway (Rysst 2008; Prieur 2004). In the subsequent sections I will analyze how the children I studied relate to the categories of "Norwegian" and "foreigner" and how this is reflected in what I interpret to be their construction of ethnic identity.

Ethnic Identity Construction Among the Children

"One Foot in Two Cultures"

Despite being born and raised in Norway, the children I interviewed did not appear to aspire to a Norwegian identity. When I asked Fatima, Sahra, and Pernille how they would answer the question "Where are you from?" the following conversation ensued:

Pernille: I say Norway.

Fatima: Norwegian-Pakistani.

Sahra: I say I come from Morocco, but that I was born and raised in Norway. So in a way I am from Norway… and Morocco.

Fatima: I say I am from Pakistan, but I am Norwegian-Pakistani, but in Pakistan I say I am from Norway.

Mari: And the people in Pakistan probably say you are from Norway?

Fatima: Yes…

Mari: And how does it feel to come to Pakistan, to your "homeland" so to speak, as we talk about it in Norway, and you may experience it as not your homeland…?

Sahra: It's like… you are kind of on holiday when you are here too, and when you are in Morocco… you see? We don't have a permanent homeland.

Mari: Don't you think so, is it something in between, or?

Sahra: Yes, but then I don't live in Morocco, I live in Norway…

Fatima: But then all our traditions are from our country of origin…

This conversation illustrates Sahra and Fatima's experience of "having one foot in two cultures," which makes them somewhat ambivalent about their ethnic identity and also makes it contested. They experience having both identities. The one or the other is activated according to social context and indicates shifting selves. In addition to the two identities as Norwegian or Pakistani, they also have a third: the hybrid "Norwegian-Pakistani" (*norsk-pakistaner*). The term "norsk-pakistaner" (Norwegian-Pakistani) is probably chosen rather than "pakistansk nordmann/norsking" (Pakistani-Norwegian) because it is phonetically easier to pronounce. In addition, the term "nordmann" provokes some feminists because of the term "mann" (man). They would favour the gender neutral "norsking," which generally is not preferred in Norway.

The hyphenated "Norwegian-Other" category such as "Norwegian-Pakistani" is probably the most used in everyday peer contexts. They negotiate cultural values from their parents' country of origin with values in Norwegian society in their construction of ethnic identity. This is indicated in what Fatima says about starting to wear a hijab, which, depending on social context, denotes religious and/or ethnic affiliation:

> Mari: Why do you wear a headscarf? Why did you choose to put it on (in the 6th grade)?
>
> Fatima: Because I felt ready for it. And, it is sort of "tradition" in our family to begin wearing a headscarf (starting in puberty), it's not that you have to, but if you want you do, and I wanted to, and after I started wearing it I have become more seriously Muslim and focus more on religion than before.
>
> Mari: So you have become more interested in religion than before?
>
> Fatima: Yes, I think that I cannot abuse the headscarf, sort of.

The reasons why girls and women wear hijabs in Norway are frequently debated in the media, various reasons are presented, and the discourse is highly charged. It goes beyond this chapter to discuss all aspects of this discourse; suffice it to say that among the girls in this study, Fatima started wearing one because her sisters and cousins did, and for her, it symbolized increasingly serious Muslim faith.

Sahra and Fatima also said that they were proud of their heritage and the values from their parents' homeland. However, Sahra added that she would take it as a compliment if somebody thought she was Norwegian. This may suggest that she under-communicates her aspiration to Norwegian identity, as she knows she doesn't look Norwegian because of her very curly hair and other physical characteristics giving "foreign" connotations. In addition, they all know that hijabs do not go with the label "Norwegian." Pernille, however, is fair and blonde and nobody gives it a second thought when she says she is Norwegian. The conversations point to how appearance is part of identity construction and how it is negotiated, developed and contested during adolescence.

The Importance of Appearance: Skin Colour

I found that teachers and other school staff did not focus explicitly on the children's "skin colour" as a marker of racial ethnicity. "Skin colour" is here understood broadly as including all physiological characteristics associated with ethnic or racial origin. Rather, adults working there conceptualized the children themselves as "colour-blind." This was evident when I asked Lisa, a teacher who had worked in the school for twenty years, if the children showed interest and awareness of different skin colours:

Nope. They do when they argue and don't find other words. They don't have a wide vocabulary. So, if they fight and argue, if they don't find other words, they take skin colour, but they have no reason for doing that. So I don't think THAT is a problem. And we (the teachers) have talked about it, and yes, they ARE colour-blind.

In addition, the children themselves said they did not care about skin colours in their school.

Therefore, on the surface, it appeared that skin colour was not an issue. However, observation of various events, one of which I will present below, challenges the assertion of colour-blindness (see also Seeberg 2003).

As part of the fieldwork, I was with the children in a gym and saw Robert lying on the floor, apparently very upset. It turned out that Adine had called him "nigger" (*svarting*, lit. "blackie"). Both Adine and Robert's families come from Africa. Adine's family is from Morocco, while Robert's parents come from South Africa. Adine called Robert *svarting* for no apparent reason; they were not quarrelling or fighting. Her use of the derogatory word may contradict the teacher's assertion that the students used racial terms only in cases of conflict.

The term angered the other boys in the gym. They started whispering excitedly and soon a loud, unified, aggressively repetitive "Racist, racist, racist!" was heard throughout the gym. The boys, led by Abdullah, approached Adine. She tried to hide behind me while I was trying to calm the angry boys down: "Stop, stop, don't make a fuss out of this, just leave it!" "But, listen, she is a racist!" they insisted. I told them to calm down and continue with their games, because I considered this an issue to be dealt with by the teacher, not by a researcher doing fieldwork.

The above event indicates that skin colour did have importance in their everyday life. This is supported by a comment made by Lisa, the teacher, who asserted, "Africans, they are black, they are labelled blacks, they can be called that by Pakistanis, who are labelled brown." It is my impression that the label "black" is more an expression of serious insult, as in the situation with Adine above, than the "brown" label. "Brown" is more of a descriptive classificatory term and it is not part of a legacy of racist terminology in the same way as "black." These colour distinctions may be interpreted as an indication of racialized ethnic hegemony and are also indications of a contested childhood. At Dal school, this hegemony is represented by (light) brown-skinned Asians, for instance the majority group of Pakistanis, together with ethnic Norwegians.

This example indicates that skin colour is important for identity construction among the studied children. The following conversation between Nasreen and Saira, two girls whose families are from Pakistan, further attests to this hypothesis:

Mari: I suppose you often get the question: where are you from?

Nasreen: They see it by the way we look! But people can mix up whether we come from India, Bangladesh, Pakistan… People can see whether you are Norwegian by the way you dress, they dress in "short" clothes…[to be discussed later].

Saira: Because we don't have different skin colour [the nationalities just mentioned].

Mari: But what do you think yourself, you are born in Norway, go to a Norwegian school…

9 "I Think of Myself as Norwegian, Although I Feel … 167

> Nasreen: I say I am Norwegian-Pakistani [and Saira agrees].
>
> Mari: Would you be pleased if somebody classified you as Norwegian?
>
> Nasreen and Saira: No.
>
> Nasreen: Well, I am Norwegian, but not ethnic Norwegian…
>
> Saira: We live in Norway, and have a Norwegian passport…

Like Sahra and Fatima, Nasreen and Saira too have multiple identities: one Norwegian and one Pakistani as well as the hybrid Norwegian-Pakistani. It is worth noting that they mention two Norwegian categories: "Norwegian" and "ethnic Norwegian." They may experience themselves as "Norwegian" in some social contexts, but never "ethnic Norwegian." In order to be labelled "ethnic Norwegian" they believe their parents and grandparents have to have been born in Norway, they must speak only Norwegian at home, and they should have fairer skin. They know they will not pass as ethnic Norwegians because of their physical appearance: dark hair and eyes, brownish skin.

When it comes to boys, Kofi and David were also born and raised in Norway. Both of Kofi's parents are from the Ivory Coast. David's mother is ethnic Norwegian, while his father is from Kenya. David had visited his relatives in Kenya three times during his lifetime. Yet he, like Kofi and the girls above, did not know what it is like to grow up outside Norway. Kofi said he views himself as from the Ivory Coast because his parents are from that country, while David said "I think of myself as Norwegian, although I feel that I am from another country and like to say I am from another country. I like to say that I am from Kenya. I am 'half,' but some people think I am 'whole,' from another country; but most people think I am 'half,' and when people ask I say I am 'half.'"

David said he preferred to say he was from another country because he hung out with people who are not ethnic Norwegian. His choice of friends may also be because he looks "foreign" with dark skin and African curly hair, like many of the others. In his everyday life he navigates and negotiates various cultural values by hanging out with peers having both non-Norwegian and ethnic Norwegian parents. However, an experience of belonging appears more connected to hanging out with children of immigrants. This may be because possible ethnic Norwegian friends are few in this area and children of immigrants look more similar to him. Again, the issue of skin colour appears relevant. The American psychologist Beverly Daniel Tatum, in her book *Why are all the black kids sitting together in the cafeteria?* (2003), argues that it is a necessary step in young people's identity construction to hang out and seek belonging among those with the same racialized ethnic origin. David and other children in Dal appear to support Tatum's claim of youth seeking belonging with others they define as "similar" regarding physical appearance and ethnic identity (Rysst 2014).

As indicated in the case of the girls, the boys' emphasis on non-Norwegian identity may be in part related to the fact that they have given up ever being called "Norwegian" by others because of their appearance. As already mentioned, both Kofi and David are very dark-skinned. Previous research has illustrated the importance of whiteness for successful Nordic identity labelling (Hubinette and Tigervall 2009; Prieur 2004). This may be something these children have experienced in one way or another and, if so, the issue of skin colour and identity may be understood as highly contested. One possibility is that, because they know that their appearances hinder them in passing as ethnic Norwegians, they construct hybrid gendered ethnic identities in a third space marking them off from majority Norwegians.

As these examples indicate, I suggest the expression and question "always a foreigner?" is relevant among the "foreigners" I studied because they appear to claim an identity as "foreigners" rather than "Norwegians." My conversation with Melek, of Turkish origin, and Hadia, of Moroccan origin, also underlines this:

Mari: What do you think about having a Norwegian identity? I know that at this school you classify yourselves as "Norwegians" and "foreigners." How do you think about yourself?

Hadia: I think that I am a foreigner!

Melek: So do I, even though I was born in Norway.

Mari: Do you think that's ok, do you like it that way, your appearance (fair skinned) is after all not obviously foreign?

[Both of them laugh].

Hadia: But I like it…

Mari: You like saying that you are a foreigner?

Hadia: Yes, but it is so common here, it's not something I like or not, it's common, yes. I can say I am a foreigner everywhere in Norway, sort of.

Mari: You too? [I address Melek].

Melek: Yes, it's very common, normal, I don't reflect about it, I just say I am a foreigner, sort of, that I come from Turkey.

Mari: I understand from what you say here, that it's not important for you to be classified and labelled Norwegian?

Both: No.

Mari: And what about David? Would you say he is Norwegian or foreigner?

Melek: Both, he is both really… I really think he is the same as us, because even though we experience ourselves as foreigners, we are Norwegian as well. We were born and raised here, so we are used to this culture, and when we go to Turkey or Morocco, we experience a difference between us and the people living there. They look upon us as more Norwegian than Turkish, I think.

As is indicated in this conversation, physiological characteristics are important. David, although his mother is all white and he has lived his whole life in Norway, is classified as both a foreigner and Norwegian, probably because of his dark skin colour. This suggestion is based on the fact that his African father has not been living with David or the mother for many years; they have no contact. Besides, David has only friends of foreign origin, in addition to one of mixed origin in a higher grade, who is also dark skinned.

The conversation also illustrates the relevance of multiple identities, here from the point of view of others than themselves: they are classified as Norwegian in their "homeland" but as "foreigners" in Norway. They have one foot in two cultures, not two feet in one culture. As such, skin colour, understood broadly, appears as having high relevance in a migrancy perspective. Recall Näre's definition of migrancy described at the beginning of this chapter. In Norway, skin colour appears to decisively illustrate migrancy as something "which is inscribed on certain bodies by the larger society in general" (Näre 2012, 604). The consequence in my study was that children conceptualized themselves as "Norwegian," "foreigner," or the hybrid "Norwegian-Pakistani" depending on the context (they also used other hybrid ethnic combinations).

The Importance of Appearance: Clothes

The importance of appearance for ethnic identity construction also involves clothing, as Nasreen indicated above: "People can see whether you are Norwegian by the way you dress; they [Norwegians] dress in 'short' clothes." This utterance implicitly points to the intermingling of ethnic identity construction and age and gender, as well as religion and sexuality. Among the study participants, Islam was the only religion referred to in relation to clothes and dress. Other options were inspired by main street fashion. Nasreen's statement also points to what I read as an illustration of contested childhood: the negotiation of different, conflicting cultural values regarding what is considered suitable attire, and thus gender construction. Our conversations on clothing, first in the 8th and later in the 9th grade, highlight the importance of a covering-up code, directly informed by cultural interpretations of Islam. "Short" clothes do not cover the body and are thus not acceptable.

In the group interview referred to above with Pernille, Sahra, and Fatima, who wore a hijab, I asked explicitly about clothing styles among their classmates. Fatima said, "The three of us sport almost the same style." I then commented on her hijab, an item not worn by the other two girls. She said that besides for the hijab, "we like the same clothes." The following conversation ensued:

Sahra: We don't like short clothes; we want to hide our bottoms…

Mari: Hmm… I think that is rather usual among Muslim girls… ethnic Norwegians don't think like this?

Sahra: No, she (Pernille) is very influenced by how we… I don't mean to insult by saying this… but one gets influenced by the people one hangs out with and she doesn't socialize with very many Norwegians…

Pernille: In Norway when I wear shorts I have something underneath (tights), but if I am elsewhere, I can go without because there I don't know people. And then I don't get gazes or comments on what I wear. But I can get that here if I only wear shorts…

Mari: But what kind of comments do you risk getting?

> Sahra: She has never got any, but mostly from the boys... they can look at you in a mischievous way and ask "what are you wearing," sort of...

Sahra and Fatima then comment that Pernille once wore shorts to school, at which Pernille underscores that she wore tights underneath, meaning that her legs were acceptably covered. This suggests that Sahra and Fatima believe Pernille lacks the proper skills for dressing acceptably. In their view, wearing shorts to school is just not done, while tights are ok as long as they are combined with a long tunika, shirt or sweater.

They also add that in general, they do not like showing much of their bodies, so they wear long sweaters, jackets, or tunics over jeans or tights. Pernille, in spite of being ethnic Norwegian, still wanted to cover up in situations where she risked comments (Rysst 2014). In other words, her gendered subject position differed according to social context; one among peers of foreign origin and another among people of unknown origins and/or ethnic Norwegians. It is worth noting that, as a 13-year-old, she preferred a style I read as hybrid rather than Norwegian. I interpret Pernille's choice of style, and thus gender construction, as her way of securing her friendships, particularly with Sahra. Sahra, as a Muslim, has internalized and acted according to the covering-up code. Pernille adapted to the Dal majority's dressing norms which probably made it easier for her to experience belonging among her best friend(s) in most of the peer contexts.

Pernille is the only child in this study who explicitly expressed what I interpret as an indication of a shifting self, or variations of subject position according to context. Still, Muslim girls' way of dressing and behaving in family contexts versus school and peers shows the relevance of a "shifting selves" perspective, which I return to at the end of this subsection. Only four of the thirteen girls in the 8th grade wore headscarves. However, the majority of the girls wore very modest clothing, concealing rather than revealing the shapes of their bodies. Only three girls—Melek of Turkish origin, Nasreen of Pakistani origin, and Helen of Thai origin—adopted mainstream Western fashion, usually tight jeans with short blouses or sweaters. I am not sure if Malek or Nasreen wore more traditional clothing proscribed for Muslim girls within their familial context.

We discussed the clothing styles of the other girls in the students' class, and thus gained insight into how the girls felt they presented themselves. The thirteen-year-olds, Sahra, Pernille, and Fatima agreed that there existed an "ethnic-religious style." This included the hijabs and long traditional skirts typical of Somali girls. They also mentioned the three girls in their class who sport the "Norwegian style" of tight jeans with shorter sweaters. Sahra, Pernille, and Fatima, however, are somewhere in between these two. They are *bricoleurs*, or navigators of culture. In line with this, I interpret them as constructing a hybrid gendered ethnic identity, which represents the third feminine position in their peer culture. By positioning themselves in this way, they managed to fit in among Muslims expecting them to hide their bodies, and among Norwegians, because these girls bought their clothes in the same shops as Norwegians. The only difference was that they more often bought longer tops to cover their bottoms if they wore tight jeans, and did not wear shorts to school. This was the general fashion among Norwegian teenagers in 2013–2014. The majority of girls at Dal school are understood to "do gender" through varieties of this hybrid style, which may be with or without hijabs, but which generally had covering up at its core (Rysst 2014).

Kofi and David confirmed that the highly gendered norm of girls covering up is part of their peer context. In contrast to the girls, the boys at Dal did not mark themselves off from ethnic Norwegian boys in the same conspicuous manner. They had no religiously derived dress codes. I therefore did not talk with them about their own ways of dressing, but was curious about the boys' opinions of girls' presentations of self and ways of dressing. I broached the subject by asking who they considered to be the popular girls in their class. David said quickly "Some think they are more popular" (and indicated Nasreen). We commented on the appearances of the girls in general, noting that some girls wore hijabs but otherwise most wore Norwegian (covering up) clothes. Then David said that "girls get a plus if they wear a hijab; it is a good thing." Kofi added "It's a good thing to cover up when young," which was a unanimous opinion, they agreed, at this school.

Against this backdrop, Melek and Nasreen were of particular interest because they wear Norwegian-style clothing despite being Muslim and well aware of the dominant gender hierarchy at Dal. As we have seen, the majority of girls and boys in the 8th grade, irrespective of religious or ethnic background, appeared to agree on the value of covering-up which illustrates the ideological power hierarchy at this school and is also an indication of how their childhood is contested. This hierarchy had Islamic-inspired cultural values at the top, which organized Islamic-inspired femininities to encompass the covering-up dress code. Embedded in this cultural interpretation of Islam is heterosexual normativity. According to Judith Butler, heterosexual normativity refers to an institutionalized assumption that all humans are heterosexual as a basis for the organization of modern life (Butler 1993, 3). The girls construct their gendered ethnic identity according to a factual or imagined heterosexual judging gaze informed by a cultural interpretation of Islam. This gaze may be interpreted as an experience of being uncomfortable when concealment was violated, and appeared in the interviews with most of the girls. The following conversation with Hadia, who has Moroccan parents, and Melek in the 9th grade is particularly interesting, because, as mentioned above, Melek was one of the girls not covering up in the 8th grade:

Hadia: For me it is, like uncomfortable, to wear low necked jumpers and clothes that don't conceal…

Mari: But why is it important to wear long sweaters and such?

Melek: As Hadia said, I don't feel very comfortable either if I wear a very open top, or sweater, I don't feel comfortable, some use long sweaters because they think that is correct in their culture or religion, while others do it because they don't feel comfortable. So… yes.

Nasreen, who did not cover up in the 8th grade either, can now be understood to also position her gender construction in the covering up discourse. The following conversation was part of the interview with Saira and Nasreen cited previously. The conversation on covering up started with religion:

> Nasreen: Our parents would like us to be as religious as they are, but they don't force us, they say that girls should cover up in our religion, but they also say it's up to us. They don't say "cover up," but rather "pray, it only takes you three minutes!"
>
> Mari: But when you shop for clothes, do you choose clothes that cover up?
>
> Saira: Well, I look for clothes that conceal, but if I find something else very nice, I buy it, and put something longer underneath or over the shorter one.
>
> Mari: And what exactly, is it you want to conceal?
>
> Saira: [Laughs] the bottom...
>
> Nasreen: Your skin, hair and bottom...
>
> Mari: Hmm, yes. And last year it was easy to buy fashionable clothes that covered up. But now these are more difficult to find?
>
> Saira: Yes, now the clothes are sort of... shorter... And it is difficult, yes. Because we cannot wear the same old sweaters and dresses every day! The Norwegian girls have a much easier time finding suitable clothes!

The narratives of all these girls indicate that gendered ethnic identity construction at Dal involves the covering up dress code as a vital element. They all have internalized that they are to hide their bottoms and skin. In addition, they are aware of the restrictions they, as Muslim girls, experience compared to ethnic Norwegians, indicating different parental practices and thus contestations of childhood. There is some implicit envy, or at least ambivalence, in what they say:

> Saira: I think that the Norwegian girls, it's not difficult for them to choose clothes and such, because they can wear what they want, the parents don't say anything, they don't have to cover up...
>
> Mari: So you think that Norwegian girls have an easier time?
>
> Nasreen and Saira: Yes, because we have some simple rules, that we have to wear certain clothes, we have to think twice, it takes time for us to get dressed properly.
>
> Nasreen: But it's not that we very much want to dress "Norwegian," it's sort of ok for us, we create our own style. And when we are going to a party with only girls, we don't dress according to the "rules"!! [she laughs loudly].

This also indicates how their construction of gendered ethnic identity is influenced by values deriving from both their parents' country of origin and from Norway where they were born. Nasreen and Saira reflect on how they experience their own situation regarding socially acceptable clothes compared to how they consider ethnic Norwegian girls' situation. They negotiate cultural values of gender in order to comply with the existing cultural norms in their various social contexts. The conversation also illustrates contested childhood and shifting selves related to the dominant Islam-inspired discourse of covering up and conflicting Norwegian values: "And when we are going to a party with only girls, we don't dress according to the 'rules'!!" One subject position is to follow parental-imposed gender rules of covering up and modesty when they are in public contexts with both genders and in family contexts. The other is to break these rules when they are in the company of female peers, because they appear irrelevant from a heterosexual normative standpoint.

The heterosexual male gaze is also part of how girls construct gender through clothes. The girls related to this in an ambiguous and interesting manner. In the 8th grade, the boys said they thought it a good idea for girls to cover up. When I confronted Fatima, Pernille, and Sahra about this, they laughed, and Sahra said: "If that was so then, this has changed now! They like girls that show their bottoms... we notice that they look at us..." Nasreen and Saira reacted in a similar manner, and even said that they felt the boys to be hypocrites. Saira commented: "Fuck, no!" And Nasreen continued: "Well, they can probably say to you and older people that they like girls who cover up, but we know what they really mean inside... they tell us about nice girls elsewhere who have attractive bottoms and bodies..." It appears that the girls did care about the boys' views on attractiveness. So when I asked if they dress and act in accordance with what they believed the boys like (heteronormativity), Saira said: "Yes, in a way, because we want them to like us..." This dialogue may point to how the boys relate, unconsciously, to the whore and Madonna discourse: respectable girls cover up, while uncovered girls are more exciting. The girls accordingly experienced contradictory and ambiguous expectations in their construction of gendered ethnic identity as Muslim Turkish-Norwegians, Muslim Moroccan-Norwegians and Muslim Pakistani-Norwegians girls.

The varieties of femininities were more difficult to distinguish in the 9th grade compared to the 8th. The hybrid dressing style of simultaneous concealment and fashion was stretched to its limits when mainstream fashion dictated even shorter skirts than last year. The covering up code met structural restrictions by way of the latest fashion design. This meant girls had to combine older, longer clothes with new, shorter ones. It also meant they had to show more of their bottoms than before. They knew the boys preferred this, but their parents probably did not. I frequently observed girls desperately pulling down and stretching their sweaters as far as they would go in order to hide more of their bottoms. The result was the same femininity positions as before, but the hybrid had come closer to the Norwegian way of not covering up (Rysst 2014).

The Importance of Language

An interesting, related issue is the development of spoken language among Norwegian-born children and youth of immigrant parents. Norwegian integration and school policy underlines the importance of learning the Norwegian language. This is prioritized in Dal from a very early age, as kindergartens have reduced their fees in order to help children of immigrant parents to learn Norwegian before entering school. Even though all my informants were born and raised in Norway, they still speak with a recognizable accent. This applies to girls and boys of all ethnic backgrounds and their particular way of speaking is widespread in the area. For instance, it dominates at the Club, a free leisure time youth programme organized by the local school authorities. The Club offers a programme for children of all ages (10–16) and both sexes, and constitutes a third space in the sense that most of the young people who use the Club regularly have parents of various foreign origins. Hybrid cultural expressions like rap music fill this place. The Norwegian language is mixed with English and words from Urdu and other languages into what has been termed "kebab-Norwegian"—a hybrid, "cool" social dialect understood as part of their identity construction. It may be read as an effort to increase their dignity and self-respect. The dialect does not only include new words, but also "incorrect," unconventional grammar and new intonation. This makes their spoken language sound "foreign" compared to other Norwegian dialects and underlines their understanding of themselves as "foreigners." Most interestingly, the ethnic Norwegians use this social dialect as well, illustrating how a minority group adapts to the norms of the majority. When I confronted the girls when they had entered the 9th grade about this particular way of speaking, they were astonished:

Mari: Are you aware of the fact that you talk with a different intonation than people do in other parts of Oslo?

Fatima, Sahra and Pernille: Do we??

Fatima: I haven't noticed. I think we talk the same all of us…

Mari: No, you don't. It is also audible during Norwegian classes, when you are to perform something in class, you have this special dialect.

Sahra and Fatima: We haven't noticed it.

Mari: You haven't thought about it?

Both: No. But Melek talks a bit more adult like when she presents something, she has a richer vocabulary.

Mari: So you don't know that you have a special intonation, your own dialect…

Sahra: Do you mean kebab-Norwegian?? We know THAT!

Mari: Do you talk that way as well?

Sahra: Not as a language, but when we are making jokes and fooling around…

Pernille: Just a few words.

Sahra: Our language is not like that [meaning kebab-Norwegian].

Mari: But is there anyone in this class using such a language?

Sahra: The boys!

Mari: Do you mean that the boys use kebab-Norwegian more than you do?

All: Yes, they really only speak that way.

Pernille: They don't speak proper Norwegian, sort of, they talk with big words, that's how they always talk to each other.

Before this interview, I had wondered if kebab-Norwegian was more advanced and ordinary among the boys. I wondered if the dialect served as a more important identity marker among them because clothes did not have the same role as markers of belonging as among the girls. The girls above confirmed this assumption. According to them, the boys mostly speak in this fashion and have a wider vocabulary, while the girls use this dialect (the words) only occasionally. However, the intonation was constant for both girls and boys. The dialect is an indication of how particular hybrid expressions develop in a third space to ensure social inclusion and dignity within a contested childhood and migrancy framework.

Concluding Remarks: Contesting Ascribed Ethnic Identities in Migrancy

This chapter has shown and discussed the challenges children of foreign-born parents face in their ethnic identity constructions in Norway, which includes contesting and navigating cultural values of both their parents' country of origin and the country in which they are born. As *bricoleurs* and competent navigators of culture, the boys' and girls' identity constructions move beyond the emic dichotomous social categories of "Norwegian" and "foreigner." The children construct hybrid identities such as Norwegian-Pakistani, which may or may not include an Islamic-inspired feminine dress code of covering up, in addition to a particular social dialect.

The complex relationship between gender, ethnicity, age, and religion regarding identity construction has been shown to have various expressions depending on social context. This suggests that future studies of migrancy and hybridity may fruitfully be combined with postcolonial theory emphasizing both the phenomenon of "third spaces" and the importance of "shifting selves" depending on social contexts. These theoretical perspectives combined may allow us to elucidate how ascribed ethnic identities and migrancy frameworks may be approached in order to reduce the intensity of future contestations of childhood.

References

Anthias, F. (2001). New hybridities, old concepts: The limits of "culture". *Ethnic and Racial Studies, 24*(4), 619–641.

Back, L. (2002). The fact of hybridity: Youth, ethnicity, and racism. In D. T. Goldberg & J. Solomos (Eds.), *A companion to ethnic and racial studies*. Massachusetts: Blackwell Publishing.

Butler, J. (1993). *Bodies that matter*. New York: Routledge.

Ghorashi, H., Eriksen, T. H., & Alghasi, S. (2009). Introduction. In S. Alghasi, H. Ghorashi, T. H. Eriksen, & S. Alghasi (Eds.), *Paradoxes of cultural recognition*. Farnham: Ashgate.

176 M. Rysst

Hannerz, U. (1992). *Cultural complexity: Studies in the social organization of meaning.* New York: Colombia University Press.

Hubinette, T., & Tigervall, C. (2009). To be non-white in a colour-blind society. *Journal of Intercultural Studies, 30*(4), 335–353.

Jacobsen, C. M. (2002). *Tilhørighetens mange former. Unge muslimer i Norge.* Oslo: Unipax.

James, A., Jenks, C., & Prout, A. (1998). *Theorizing childhood.* New York: Teachers College Press.

Kampmann, J. (2003). Barndomssosiologi. *Dansk Sosiologi, 2.*

Lorentzen, J., & Muhleisen, W. (2006). *Kjønnsforskning.* Oslo: Universitetsforlaget.

Moinian, F. (2009). I'm just me! Children talking beyond ethnic and religious identities. *Childhood, 16*(1), 31–48.

Moore, H. L. (1994). *A passion for difference.* Cambridge: Polity Press.

Näre, L. (2012). Migrancy, gender and social class in domestic labour and social care in Italy: An intersectional analysis. *Journal of Ethnic and Migration Studies, 39*(4), 601–623.

Nieuwenhuys, O. (2013). Theorizing childhood(s): Why we need postcolonial perspectives. *Childhood, 20*(1), 3–8.

Prieur, A. (2004). *Balansekunstnere.* Oslo: Pax Forlag A/S.

Rysst, M. (2008). *I want to be me, I want to be kul.* Ph.D. thesis, University of Oslo.

Rysst, M. (2012). Lyden av hudfarge blant barn i Groruddalen. In S. Alghasi, T. H. Eriksen, & E. Eide (Eds.), *Den globale drabantbyen.* Cappelen Damm Akademisk: Oslo.

Rysst, M. (2013). The social importance of consumption for inclusion and exclusion among children in a multi-ethnic suburb of Oslo. *Nordic Journal of Migration Research, 3*(1), 19–26.

Rysst, M. (2014). Friendship and gender identity among girls in a multicultural setting in Oslo. *Childhood,* National Institute for Consumer Research. Retrieved May 22, 2015, from http://chd.sagepub.com/content/early/2014/09/12/0907568214549081.

Seeberg, M.L. (2003). *Dealing with difference: Two classrooms, two countries: A comparative study of Norwegian and Dutch processes of alterity and identity, drawn from three points of view.* Ph.D. thesis, University of Bergen.

Statistics Norway (2015a). Innvandrere og norskfødte med innvandrerforeldre, 1 January–March 4 2015. Retrieved May 22, 2015, from http://www.ssb.no/befolkning/statistikker/innvbef.

Statistics Norway (2015b). Retrieved March 3, 2016, from https://www.oslo.kommune.no/politikk-og-administrasjon/statistikk/befolkning/landbakgrunn/.

Tatum, B. D. (2003). *Why are all the black kids sitting together in the cafeteria?* New York: Basic Books.

Thagaard, T. (2013). *Systematikk og innlevelse.* Oslo: Fagboklaget.

Thorne, B. (1993). *Gender play.* New Jersey: Rutgers University Press.

Wells, K. (2009). *Childhood in a global perspective.* Cambridge: Polity Press.

West, C., & Zimmerman, D. H. (1987). Doing gender. *Gender & Society, 1*(1), 125–151.

Wiggen, K. S., Dzamarija, M.T, Thorsdalen, B., Østby, L. (2015). *Innvandreres demografi of levekår i Groruddalen, Søndre Nordstrand, Gamle Oslo og Grünerløkka.* Oslo: Statistisk sentralbyrå, 2015/43.

Yusuf, K. (2014). Når ferien blir et mareritt. *VG Meninger.* Retrieved May 22, 2015, from http://www.vg.no/nyheter/meninger/naar-ferien-blir-et-mareritt/a/10130210/.

Open Access This chapter is licensed under the terms of the Creative Commons Attribution-NonCommercial 2.5 International License (http://creativecommons.org/licenses/by-nc/2.5/), which permits any noncommercial use, sharing, adaptation, distribution and reproduction in any medium or format, as long as you give appropriate credit to the original author(s) and the source, provide a link to the Creative Commons license and indicate if changes were made.

The images or other third party material in this chapter are included in the book's Creative Commons license, unless indicated otherwise in a credit line to the material. If material is not included in the book's Creative Commons license and your intended use is not permitted by statutory regulation or exceeds the permitted use, you will need to obtain permission directly from the copyright holder.

Chapter 10
Looking Ahead: Contested Childhoods and Migrancy

Elżbieta M. Goździak and Marie Louise Seeberg

At the beginning of this volume, we explained how our interest in globalization's changing ideas and practices of childhood led us to propose 'contested childhoods' and 'growing up in migrancy' as twin conceptual tools. The purpose was to understand the migration, governance, and identity processes currently involving children and ideas of childhood. In this final chapter, we return to this conceptual pair and reflect on some of the theoretical and policy implications of the concepts as emergent throughout the book. *Whose children are we talking about?* This question, raised in our first chapter, pinpoints the link between 'contested childhoods' and 'growing up in migrancy'. Whose children are trafficked, seeking refuge, taken into custody, active in youth organisations, struggling and juggling in identity work? Which societies can claim them as their own, and build individual and societal futures accordingly? These are questions with far-reaching implications of a theoretical as well as a practical and policy-oriented nature. In this final chapter, we draw out and discuss some of these implications.

Theoretical Implications

Marie Louise: All these children and young people are growing up in migrancy, which is the main reason why their childhoods are contested. The very notion of migrancy appears to give non-migrants the right, or the feeling that they have the right, to decide who these children are, and define what is best for them now and in

---

E.M. Goździak
ISIM, Georgetown University, Washington, DC, USA
e-mail: emg@georgetown.edu

M.L. Seeberg (✉)
NOVA, Oslo and Akershus University College, Oslo, Norway
e-mail: marie.l.seeberg@nova.hioa.no

© The Author(s) 2016
M.L. Seeberg and E.M. Goździak (eds.), *Contested Childhoods: Growing up in Migrancy*, IMISCOE Research Series,
DOI 10.1007/978-3-319-44610-3_10

the future. The space of migrancy allows majority populations to question the capabilities and qualifications of migrants: Are these children, as minors, capable of exerting agency? Are their families qualified to make life choices on their behalf? Or should they be protected against their own and their families' attempts at exerting (misguided) agency, for their own and society's good? Elzbieta's chapter on trafficking is the only one that explicitly poses these questions, but they are also applicable to the other chapters. Running through the whole book is a conflict between paternalism on the part of powerful, non-migrant societies in the countries of residence, and resistance against such paternalism from the children and young people themselves and, to some extent, from their families. Without notions of migrancy that open up the space for ostensibly legitimate paternalism and subsequent contestation, such struggles would have been much more limited. Other forms of paternalism—class or gender based, for instance—also form similar processes. It is clearly a matter of "power"; it is concomitantly a matter of what is usually referred to as "structure" and "agency". Our combining "migrancy" with "contested childhoods" exposes how power travels in all directions, in all these very different settings.

Let me try to set out some of the theoretical implications of this insight. I've always been a bit of a theory geek, so let me reach for some of the kinds of thinking that have fascinated me in the past and try to explain how I think they may help us understand the lives and contexts of children growing up in migrancy. First out was Gregory Bateson and his cybernetic systems theory. As a young student, I read and re-read his *Mind and Nature* (Bateson 1979) several summer holidays in a row, as well as his essays on the double bind, schismogenesis, and many other topics (Bateson 1972/2000). Running through Bateson's work is what he calls "the pattern which connects," and he sums up his central thesis as follows: "The *pattern which connects is a metapattern*. It is a pattern of patterns. It is that metapattern which defines the vast generalization that, indeed, *it is patterns which connect*" (Bateson 1979, 11). This means, I believe, that rather than studying social objects separately, we should be looking for their interconnections and relationships. Moreover, we should be looking for systematic patterns in relationships and for what seemingly different forms of relationships and interconnections have in common. For example, rather than trying to understand what "childhood" or "migrancy" mean in a particular setting, we would learn much more about reality by studying how ideas and practices of childhood and of migrancy are interconnected with each other and with other parts of the context in which migrant children and children of immigrants live. However, Bateson continued, "We have been trained to think of patterns, with the exception of those of music, as fixed affairs... In truth, the right way to begin to think about the pattern which connects is to think of it *primarily* (whatever that means) as a dance of interacting parts and only secondarily pegged down by various sorts of physical limits" (Bateson 1979, 13). Primarily, then, our concern should be on how patterns of relationships move, evolve, and change in similar ways and in on-going dynamics with their environments. This means that not only should we try to understand how our objects of study are interconnected: our attention should mainly be directed toward, or tuned into, the dynamics and processes that form the moving patterns of connection. Ideas and practices of childhood and ideas and practices of migrancy are not fixed but moving relatively to each other and to other parts of their environments, and this dynamic movement creates and changes the patterns that connect.

Although I still do not understand everything Bateson writes, he has certainly contributed strongly to shaping the way I think. His writings have also guided me through some of the more recent, related theories such as critical realism and complexity theory, both of which provide an alternative to conventional social theoretical perspectives (e.g. Morin 2008; Potter and López 2001; Walby 2007). These theorists regard social phenomena as interconnected systems rather than as structures versus agency—what's more, they argue that social systems are always open, which means that parts of one system will always be interacting with parts of other systems (Danermark et al. 2002; Sayer 2010; Smith 1998). I also find relevant their emphasis on the historical embeddedness and "path dependency" of agency, so evident in the variety of ideas and practices of childhood worldwide as well as within national and local communities. So many practices and choices are simply not conceivable in other contexts. For instance, look at Ada's chapter on "protecting" Roma children in Norway—although the Roma do experience and respond to control and oppression in many other national settings, these play out in other, particular ways for particular historical reasons. Adaptation strategies that have worked well in the past may no longer give the intended results, because the present is always different and always changing.

Critical realism as well as complexity and dynamic systems theories provide ways of thinking about society that dissolve the structure-agency dichotomy, replacing it with an approach foregrounding the dynamics of practice and process, as immanent in individuals as well as in larger social entities. The issue of whether social phenomena and events should be understood primarily in terms of structure, or primarily in terms of individual agency constitutes an ongoing challenge to the social sciences. While existing literature has tended to favour structural explanations at the expense of agency, or the other way around, I am much more interested in exploring how structure and agency interplay with each other and with power processes. "Pure" structure and "pure" agency are theoretical constructs that have little resonance with empirical research. If you focus on processes and systems, questions about where structure ends and agency begins just seem like a dead end— at least to me, they do. Is it not more interesting to explore identity processes *as processes*, rather than trying to pinpoint whether a young person is part of one or the other static social structure through individual choices? If we regard Czech, or Danish, or Norwegian, or any national society as open and dynamic systems, and the individuals as smaller open systems adapting to and thereby also changing the larger systems, to me that comes much closer to understanding what identity processes are all about. It also shows how influence and power are multi-directional. Even when relationships are clearly power asymmetrical, such as in all the chapters in this book, people don't just sit there and let things happen. That's not how people are and that's not how power works.

So how may these approaches enable a new take on the links between power and the structure/agency problem? Well, that depends. Conventionally, power is understood either predominantly in terms of competing individual agency, or predominantly in terms of agency as determined by structures. Which one of the two it will be depends not only on the taste of the beholder, but also on the nature of the evidence. Looking at my own chapter about child refugees in this light, the structural perspective may seem to dominate. After all, to what extent do refugees in general and child refugees in particular influence their own situation? A great deal, I'd say: Enough to create action in the systems around them. In spite of their plight, and in spite of our habit of thinking of refugees (and of children!) as powerless, the very existence of children who are refugees means that national states are forced to respond, even to the extent that a lack of response—ignoring them—is also a form of response that may in turn lead to action, for instance from civilians who feel that they are filling a void left open by the state's failure to act. In most cases, how refugee children attempt to cross national boundaries prompts reactions from agents of the state. Border fences have been raised, refugee boats turned away, schools opened and closed, politicians confronted, laws changed, civilians arrested. Some of these actions lead to changes in the state systems, others reinforce existing characteristics, but the systems do not remain untouched. What connects these two systems, the child to the state, is what always connects systems: agency. If the heavy structure of the state does not make itself felt through the practices of its agents, the child will not feel it. If the child does not attempt to cross national boundaries, the state will have no such attempts to respond to. And in whichever way the state responds through its agents, this will create a new response from the child. I talk now as if there were only the state and the child, but this process involves other systems too. Families, the media, and party politics—it's really an important empirical question: Which are the systems involved here? It's the problem of context all over again: How does the scholar separate the relevant from the irrelevant? Where are the boundaries of the object of study? I think systems thinking helps here, too: follow human agency as it manifests itself in action and creates events. Who does what, and which systems does this action involve? Small systems and large systems all include both their own immanent structures and their own immanent agency, and this insight makes away with the dichotomous logic of structure vs. agency.

Agency is often understood as equal to the individual potential to act, or to the realization of that potential. However, what constitutes an individual is not self-evident either, and groups may be said to possess agency. To Bateson, acts and agency are inextricable parts of the systems in which they take place (Bateson 2000 [1972], p. 338). Maybe some inspiration from his theory of the double bind situation could serve as another way to bring together our conceptual twins. A double bind situation, loosely described, is a sort of damned-if-you-do and damned-if-you-don't scenario—say, the dilemma of trying to live up to the ostensibly conflicting demands of transnationalism and integrationalism at the same time. Therefore, if you are growing up in migrancy because you or your family originated "somewhere else", your childhood will be a contested space. However, taking into account the larger system of which both the diaspora and the country of residence are part may contribute to resolving this kind of locked situation,[1] much as Bateson indicated that communicating about a double bind—not *within* it but *about* it, on a higher logical level of communication, would help resolve the situation. That really brings into light the importance of theory to policy and practice.

Policy and Programmatic Implications

Elżbieta: Having lived in Washington, DC for over 30 years, having been a policy-maker in the U.S. Office of Refugee Resettlement, and having worked as a practicing anthropologist for decades, I bring to our debate a very pragmatic and policy-oriented perspective. While I appreciate theory as much as Marie Louise does, I am always anxious to find practical applications for theoretical concepts. Since migration studies are data driven, at least on this side of the Atlantic, I am also interested how empirical data—both quantitative and qualitative—can inform policy decisions and program design. Being a migrant and a first generation U.S. citizen, I am also very concerned with facilitating migrants' participation in decision-making processes. Finally, I am also fascinated—and sometimes annoyed —with the language we use to describe children who are growing up in migrancy. The language deployed to discuss young migrants is not a matter of pure semantics but an important element of the discourse on identity and rights.

I come from a country where identity is viewed through a primordial lens. One is Polish only if one's social existence is characterized by immediate contiguity and kin connections with other Poles, by being born into a homogenous Polish ethnic community, Roman Catholic congregation, by speaking Polish as a mother tongue, and by following Polish social practices (whatever those are!) (Kempny 2010). In contrast, I live in a country where anybody can become American and where identity is not some static "given" (Geertz 1973), but a dynamic process of "becoming" (see Jenkins 1996). In this volume, several contributors show how children contest or oscillate between these two approaches to identity construction, and how laws and policies on citizenship sometimes deprive them of the choice to assert their own identity and place them squarely in the "migrancy" framework even when the children have never migrated.

As the case studies in this volume attest, in many European countries both policy makers and the general public do not commonly distinguish between immigrant children and children of immigrants; both are referred to as "children from immigrant background". The label of "migrancy" does not go away even when we are talking about children born in Norway or Denmark to immigrant parents. Ironically, as Helene and Rashmi show, the identity of children born in Denmark to a native Danish and an immigrant parent is commonly linked to the foreign-born parent not

---

[1]In fact, Erdal and Oeppen (2013) argue convincingly in favour of this view.

to the white Danish parent. In the United States where the Constitution guarantees birthright citizenship to all children born in the country's territory, regardless of parentage, we take great care to distinguish these two cohorts of children. In the U.S. we have also replaced the label "native language" with "heritage language" when talking about the young people growing up in migrancy and the children's facility in the native language of their parents. Reading Marianne and Guro's chapter I wondered whether and when the youth, born in Norway or having grown up in the country from an early age, engaged in building ethnic community-based organization, will start contesting the status quo of the public funding streams that force the youth to pay more attention to their cultural heritage then to civic and political participation in the mainstream society. Call me naïve but despite the rise of xenophobia I am hopeful that as more and more countries become de facto countries of immigration both the rhetoric and the laws will change to reflect the fact that children of immigrants belong as much to their family as to the society into which they were born. This belonging ought to translate into inclusive language and full complement of rights bestowed on the children when they are born not at some later point in their lives when the government decides that they are worthy of being treated as full-fledged citizens.

Meaningful participation of migrant, refugee, and trafficked children is essential in research, policy-making, and practice. Following the 1989 UN Convention on the Rights of the Child (CRC), "listening to children's voices has become a powerful and pervasive mantra for activists and policy makers worldwide. However, despite such representations of the 'voices of children,' children themselves may nonetheless, continue to find their voices silenced, suppressed, or ignored in their everyday lives" (James 2007, p. 261). In my studies of trafficked children I have seen time and time again how the "best interest of the child" principle deployed to guide service provision to trafficked adolescents contradicted their right to participate in determining what was best for them (Goździak 2016). Indeed, there is consensus in literature that Western policy makers and caretakers tend to prioritize the children's perceived best interests over the children's right to express their wishes and feelings (Bluebond-Langner and Korbin 2007). Service providers often justify their predisposition to decide the child's best interest rather than advocating for her wishes and respecting her feelings by invoking the age of the youngsters they assist. They habitually treat all minors under the age of 18 as children and do not make distinctions between very young children and older adolescents. This conceptualization of young people under 18 years of age as passive and unknowing dependants without the ability to make independent decisions (see Christensen and James 2000; Jenks 1996), especially decisions regarding labour migration, contradicts the "evolving capacity" principle enshrined in the CRC.

Don't get me wrong, there are tremendous examples of immigrant youth asserting their agency and bringing about important political and social change, often against all odds. In the United States, the DREAMers, a movement of undocumented high school students aspiring to attend college, transformed the national immigration debate and resulted in two important national immigration policies: Deferred Action for Childhood Arrivals (DACA) and Deferred Action for Parents of Americans and Lawful Permanent Residents (DAPA). DACA is an American immigration policy that allows certain undocumented immigrants who entered the country before their 16th birthday and before June 2007 to receive a renewable two-year work permit and exemption from deportation. DAPA is an immigration policy that grants deferred action status to certain undocumented immigrants who have lived in the United States since 2010 and have children who are U.S. citizens or lawful permanent residents. At the state level, the DREAMers advocated for legislation allowing unauthorized students access to in-state tuition. Several states, including Arkansas, California, Colorado, Florida, Illinois, Kansas, Maryland, Nebraska, New Jersey, New Mexico, New York, Oregon, Texas, Utah, Washington, and Wisconsin, have passed such laws or DREAM Acts. These achievements are not insignificant; all came about because undocumented students staged occupations, hunger strikes, and demonstrations to get their voices heard. The adults, including policy-makers at the federal and state level as well as advocates in cities, towns, and neighbourhoods, recognized the youngsters' ability to fight for their own rights and started taking their demands seriously. The DREAMers' achievements ought to be seen as building blocks towards societal understanding that young people know best what is in their "best interest".

Unfortunately, in many instances decisions regarding migrant children are made without consultations with the young people or in an empirical vacuum. Both Ada and I write about our struggles to get access to the children we wanted to study. Ada ended up consulting secondary sources to carry out her analysis of the protective regimes deployed to care for Roma children in Norway. I persevered and managed to talk to quite a number of children and youth trafficked to the United States. We remain optimistic that policy makers and service providers will ultimately realize the benefits stemming from research with and about migrant and minority children. I am particularly hopeful that funders will support innovative participatory action research with migrant children.

Implications for Further Research, Practices, and Policies

Accounts about children and adolescents on the move are often rooted in humanitarian narratives (Boyden and de Berry 2004). These narratives have focused mainly on *protection* of child migrants from harm and *provision* of needed resources, and less on *participation* (Bluebond-Langner and Korbin 2007). These narratives are often based on a single universal definition of childhood enshrined in international humanitarian and human rights law and ignore the fact that there is no universal experience or understanding of childhood. They conceptualize "child migrants," "child labourers," "trafficked children", and "child soldiers" as products of adult agency and presuppose that children are dependent, exploited, and powerless (Rosen 2007, p. 297). These common assumptions of child migration as an inevitably exploitative phenomenon reflect views of children as incapable of independent economic or political agency. Such views were prevalent in European and North American scholarship until the 1990s and are still historically embedded in these societies. However, first in academia and—slowly and erratically—in other parts of society they have gradually been replaced by the new paradigm in childhood studies, where the agency and subjectivity of children takes front stage. We are concerned, however, that this development is uneven so that policy makers and practitioners are not necessarily appreciative of this paradigm shift—and, ironically, that the conditions for foregrounding children's subjectivity may be laid down by adults. We are also apprehensive of any foregrounding of the agency of children at the cost of social structures that have real impact on children's experiences, opportunities, and spaces for navigation and agency.

Our aim is that research on migrant children, such as the case studies included in this volume, will continue to enhance our understanding of their multifaceted experiences. Enhanced partnership between and among researchers and practitioners will help develop models of good practice. Several contributors to this volume have already shown examples of good practice in research with children and youth by employing innovative data collection methodologies focused on eliciting narratives from the point of view of the youth, not just by talking to their teachers, social workers, and parents. Without a doubt, more is needed both in research and in praxis. We are optimistic that empirical research presented in this and similar volumes will result in culturally appropriate and effective policies for migrant children and children who are growing up in migrancy. We are already seeing positive effects of Elzbieta's research with trafficked adolescents, and more recently newly arrived Central American youth, on how services to young migrants expanded to include not just basic education, but also vocational training and employment placement. These efforts are directly related to the recognition that young migrants—especially those living in non-welfare states—need to find suitable livelihoods. The social workers who were co-researchers on the study of trafficked children took the results of the research and implemented training programs to explore the nexus of resiliency.

Acknowledging that migrant children do not speak with one single voice, this volume bears testimony to the enormous diversity and complexity of child migration and of children who are growing up in migrancy. This complexity offers a remarkable potential for scholarly advancement, but also poses difficulties to practitioners and policymakers seeking standardized responses. Indeed, building fruitful bridges between research-based evidence and action on behalf of children is one of the most pressing challenges facing those working to improve the lives of

10 Looking Ahead: Contested Childhoods and Migrancy

migrant children worldwide. Protection, provision and participation, the three interlocking principles of the Convention on the Rights of the Child, are indispensable in addressing contested childhoods—in scholarship, policy-making, and practice. The key feature of contested childhoods is that children growing up in migrancy have agency, yet are also vulnerable in important ways.

References

Bateson, G. (1979). *Mind and nature: A necessary unity*. London: Wildwood House.

Bateson, G. (2000). Steps to an ecology of mind (New York: Ballantine, 1972; reissued with an introduction by Mary Catherine Bateson, Chicago).

Bluebond-Langner, M., & Korbin, J. E. (2007). *Children, childhoods, and childhood studies*. University of California Press.

Boyden, J., & de Berry, J. (2004). *Children and youth on the front line: Ethnography, armed conflict and displacement* (Vol. 14). New York: Berghahn Books.

Christensen, P., & James, A. (2000). *Research with children: Perspectives and practices*. London: Falmer Press.

Danermark, B., Ekstrom, M., & Jakobsen, L. (2002). *Explaining society: Critical realism in the social sciences*. London: Routledge.

Erdal, M. B., & Oeppen, C. (2013). Migrant balancing acts: Understanding the interactions between integration and transnationalism. *Journal of Ethnic and Migration Studies, 39*(6), 867–884.

Geertz, C. (1973). *The interpretation of cultures/selected essays*. New York: Basic Books.

Goździak, E. M. (2016). *Trafficked children and youth in the United States: Reimagining survivors*. New Brunswick, NJ: Rutgers University Press.

James, A. (2007). Giving voice to children's voices: Practices and problems, pitfalls and potentials. *American Anthropologist, 109*(2), 261–272. doi:10.1525/aa.2007.109.2.261.

Jenkins, R. (1996). *Social identity*. New York: Routledge.

Jenks, C. (1996). Childhood (Key Ideas). Routledge: London.

Kempny, M. (2010). *Polish migrants in belfast: Border crossing and identity construction*. Cambridge: Cambridge Scholars Publishing.

Morin, E. (2008). *On complexity*. Cresskill, New Jersey: Hampton Press.

Potter, G., & López, J. (2001). *After postmodernism: An introduction to critical realism*. London: Athlone.

Rosen, D. M. (2007). Child soldiers, international humanitarian law, and the globalization of childhood. *American Anthropologist, 109*(2), 296–306. doi:10.1525/aa.2007.109.2.296.

Sayer, A. (2010). *Method in social science: A realist approach*. London: Routledge.

Smith, M. J. (1998). *Social science in question*. London: Sage Publications.

Walby, S. (2007). Complexity theory, systems theory, and multiple intersecting social inequalities. *Philosophy of the Social Sciences, 37*(4), 449–470.

Open Access This chapter is licensed under the terms of the Creative Commons Attribution-NonCommercial 2.5 International License (http://creativecommons.org/licenses/by-nc/2.5/), which permits any noncommercial use, sharing, adaptation, distribution and reproduction in any medium or format, as long as you give appropriate credit to the original author(s) and the source, provide a link to the Creative Commons license and indicate if changes were made.

The images or other third party material in this chapter are included in the book's Creative Commons license, unless indicated otherwise in a credit line to the material. If material is not included in the book's Creative Commons license and your intended use is not permitted by statutory regulation or exceeds the permitted use, you will need to obtain permission directly from the copyright holder.

Erratum to: Contested Childhoods: Growing up in Migrancy

Marie Louise Seeberg and Elżbieta M. Goździak

**M.L. Seeberg and E.M. Goździak (eds.), *Contested Childhoods: Growing up in Migrancy*, IMISCOE Research Series,
DOI 10.1007/978-3-319-44610-3**

This book was inadvertently published with the incorrect license type CC BY 4.0. This has now been amended throughout the book to the correct license type CC BY-NC 2.5.

The updated online version of this book can be found at 10.1007/978-3-319-44610-3

M.L. Seeberg (✉)
NOVA, Oslo and Akershus University College, Oslo, Norway
e-mail: marie.l.seeberg@nova.hioa.no

E.M. Goździak
ISIM, Georgetown University, Washington, DC, USA
e-mail: emg@georgetown.edu

© The Author(s) 2017
M.L. Seeberg and E.M. Goździak (eds.), *Contested Childhoods: Growing up in Migrancy*, IMISCOE Research Series,
DOI 10.1007/978-3-319-44610-3_11

Index

A

Abuse, 33, 89, 90, 95, 96
  sexual, 28
Adolescence, 121, 122, 124, 126
Adolescent(s). *See* Youth
Adult(s), 3, 7, 9, 14, 26, 30, 52, 56, 65, 66, 68, 74, 89, 133, 166, 185
  age of majority, 25, 26
Afghanistan, 11, 96, 161
African American, 2, 130
Age, 6, 9, 11, 18, 26, 33, 73, 88, 101, 107, 143, 161
Agency, 7, 14, 29, 33, 39, 66, 181–183, 185, 186
  and structure, 4, 5, 14
Alienation, 65, 148
Anglican Church, 50
Anti-Trafficking in Persons Program, 24
Appearance, 144, 149, 163, 167, 168
  clothes, 159, 169
  skin colour, 159, 166
Asian Americans, 126
Asylum seekers, 43, 46, 51–53, 55, 56
Austin, Texas, 2
Azerbaijan, 100, 101, 107, 109

B

Banana child, 122
Bateson, Gregory, 180
Bhabha, Homi, 164
Bloods (gang), 72
Boundaries, 45, 47, 56, 182
  cognitive, 131
  ethnic, 141
  national, 15, 43–45, 56, 182
  social, 45, 54
Bricoleurs, 17, 164, 171, 175
Britain. *See* united Kingdom
Butler, Judith, 172

C

Cairo, 62
Canada, 66, 105
Caseworkers, 24, 26, 37
Child/children, 2, 7, 15, 23, 25, 34, 38, 46, 47, 49, 51, 70, 82, 84, 90, 96, 99, 110, 125, 133, 140, 143, 152, 159, 179, 186
  as refugees, 15, 43, 44, 47, 51, 55, 56, 182
  Child Protection Laws, 16
  exploitation, 30
  forcible trafficking of, 15, 24
  labour, 28, 30, 186
  perspectives of, 143, 162
  transnational, 7
Childhood, 2, 4, 5, 13, 30, 38, 46, 47, 56, 69, 82, 87, 91, 93, 126, 152, 160, 172, 180, 186
  and globalization, 4
  approaches to, 3, 86
  contested, 1, 2, 14, 64, 82, 154, 159, 161, 170, 175, 179, 180
  defined, 43, 44, 83
  hegemonic regime of, 82, 86
  normal, 3
  studies, 3, 4, 15, 75, 159
Child Protection Services (CPS), 81, 82, 84, 91, 92, 94, 96
Christianity, 146
Citizenship, 2, 45, 88, 100, 102, 184
Civil society, 6, 49, 100, 102
Community, 100, 101, 107, 110, 111, 152, 183
  Community Based Organizations(CBOs), 99, 101, 105, 108, 113, 114
Complexity theory, 181
Conflict(s), 1, 6, 14, 50, 70, 74, 84, 89, 113, 161, 166
Constructivist perspective, 125
Contestation, 1, 5, 6, 18, 139, 173, 180
Contested childhood(s). *See* Childhood

© The Author(s) 2016
M.L. Seeberg and E.M. Goździak (eds.), *Contested Childhoods: Growing up in Migrancy*, IMISCOE Research Series,
DOI 10.1007/978-3-319-44610-3

Convention Concerning the Status of Refugees
  Coming from Germany, 48
Convention on the Rights of the Child (CRC),
  6, 25, 27, 32, 56, 81, 85, 91, 93, 187
Copenhagen, 10, 139, 143
Corporal punishment, 73
Council of Europe, 92
Court, 27, 31, 82, 84
  cases, 83, 92
  documents, 10, 12, 13, 25
Coyote ("smuggler"), 27
Crips (gang), 72
Critical realism, 181
Culture, 16, 29, 38, 66, 70, 82, 103, 110, 113,
  122, 125, 128, 133, 146, 151, 164, 171
  activities, 99, 104, 108, 109
  culture brokers, 121
  heritage and preservation of, 114
Czechoslovakia, 50, 123
Czech Republic, 10, 14, 17, 121, 122, 124,
  129–131, 133
  lifestyle in, 127

D

Deep hanging out, 10
Denmark, 10, 14, 17, 100, 140, 141, 145, 151,
  154, 184
Deportation, 53, 55, 89, 185
Depression, 36
Diaspora, 11, 61, 63–65, 67–69, 74, 183
  South Sudanese, 65, 68, 71, 74
  studies, 63
Dickens, Charles, 32
Dinka, 67, 69, 72, 74
Disidentification, 130, 132
Drugs, 27, 51, 72, 131

E

Economic crisis 2007, 51
El Salvador, 35
Employment, 28, 36, 66, 123, 186
English language. *See* language, English
Ethiopia, 62, 66
Ethnic identity. *See* identity, ethnic
Ethnicity, 125–127, 132, 133, 141, 144, 152,
  161
  ethnic revival, 132
  situational ethnicity, 132
Ethnography, 10
European Convention for the Protection of
  Minorities, 16
Exile, 11, 64–66, 74, 75
Experiential approach, 162
Exploitation, 25, 27, 28, 33, 34

F

Facial markings (gaar), 69
Family, familiesand state
  as traffickers, 27
  conflicts or tensions, 6, 94
  foster, 11, 16, 24, 26, 32, 44, 50, 82, 95, 96
  gender roles in, 68
First generation. *See* Generation
Fordelingsutvalget (Distributive Committee),
  102
Foster families. *See* Family,foster
Foucault, Michel, 86, 96

G

Gambia, 11, 161
Gangs, 16, 63, 70, 72
Gardner, Katy, 7
Gateway Programme, 51
GBLOCK (gang), 72
Geertz, Clifford, 10, 134
Gender, 18, 26, 69, 75, 87, 93, 122, 159,
  161–164, 170, 171, 173, 180
Generation, 9, 48, 54, 64, 71, 75, 134, 151
  first,second,critique of, 2, 3, 6, 8, 9, 64, 68,
  70, 126
Gentleman, Amelia, 51
Germany, 16, 48, 50, 52, 88, 89, 105, 154
Ghorashi, Halleh, 164
Girls, 12, 27–29, 31, 32, 35–37, 51, 147, 159,
  161, 171–175
  trafficking of, 34
Globalization, 2, 4, 10, 17, 140, 155, 164, 179
Goffman, Erving, 130
Governance, 16, 86, 179
  and pastoral power, 86
  instruments of, 16
  of childhood, 15
  of migration, 1, 179
  of minorities, 87
Grorud Valley, Oslo, 17, 160
Guatemala, 31, 34

H

Haiti, 38
Hall, Stuart, 64
Headscarf, 165
Hijab. *See* Headscarf
Hinduism, 148
Hitler, Adolf, 48
Hoare, Samuel, 48
Hoffman, Dianne, 38
Holocaust, 47, 49
Home Office (UK), 52
Honduras, 26, 31, 35

Index 191

Human trafficking, 15, 23, 28
Hybridity, 63, 159, 163, 176
   hybrid identities, 159, 175

I

Ideas oflife
   obligations, 127
   transnational, 64
Identity
   development of, 68, 121, 125, 126, 128
   ethnic, 17, 125, 132, 159, 160, 163, 165,
      168, 169, 173, 175
   identification, 16, 18, 64, 65, 68, 90, 122,
      132, 134, 143
   negotiation of, 145, 152
   outcomes, 121, 122
   processes, 1, 12, 75, 179, 182
IMISCOE, International Migration, Integration
   and Social Cohesion, 8
Immigrants, 1, 2, 6, 9, 14, 17, 46, 66, 68, 72,
   73, 87, 96, 100, 102, 105, 107, 111,
   121–123, 132, 140, 160, 164, 184, 185
   children of, 8, 9, 14, 99, 100, 107, 110, 114,
      121, 122, 124, 163, 168, 174, 181, 184
Immigration and Customs Enforcement (ICE),
   27, 29, 31
Immigration and Naturalization Service (INS),
   31
Incarceration of family members, 32
India
   Indian festivals, 148
   Indian religions, 148
Integration
   as supported by community organisations,
      70
   of immigrants, 1, 8, 9, 105, 122, 174
Interview(s), 10, 11, 13, 25, 29, 47, 65, 83,
   101, 108, 124, 143, 160, 161
Iran, 11, 44, 51, 161
Iraq, 11, 108, 160, 161
Islam, 6, 161, 170, 172, 173
Itang refugee camp, 66
Ivory Coast, 167

J

Japan, 148, 151, 154
Jewish, 44, 47–49, 55
Jewish Refugee Committee, 48, 55, 57
Journal of Ethnic and Migration Studies, 7

K

Kebab-Norwegian, 174, 175
Kenya, 62, 66, 73, 167
Khartoum, 62, 66
Kindertransport(e), 44, 47–49, 56
Kurdistan, 99–101, 107, 109, 113

L

Labour
   exploitation, 25
   forced, 25, 31
   trafficking, 25, 28
Language
   Czech, 121–123, 126, 131, 133, 182
   Danish, 10, 13, 140, 141, 143, 145–148,
      150, 151, 154, 184
   English, 8, 46, 50, 55, 143
   kebab-Norwegian, 175
   Norwegian, 174
   Romanes, 84, 85, 90
   Urdu, 174
   Vietnamese, 10, 109, 121–124, 126–128,
      130–132, 146
League of Nations, 47, 56
Lithuania, 107
Loans, 68
Longitudinal Immigrant Student Adaptation
   Study, 71

M

Majority, 11, 17, 36, 65, 67, 89, 102, 104, 130,
   134, 164, 171, 174, 180
Marginalization, 82, 88, 126
Marital tensions, 68
Marriage, 17, 83, 90, 94, 140, 142
Mead, Margaret, 8, 151
Medicaid, 27
Mengistu, Haile, 66
Methodologies, 10, 186
Mexico, 31
Mickelsen, Mick, 31
Migrancy, 8, 9, 16, 65, 99, 100, 110, 130, 134,
   143, 150, 154, 159, 161, 169, 176, 180,
   181, 187
   as social space, 122, 134, 143, 160
   defined, 100
   growing up in, 2, 8, 16, 63, 99, 123, 131,
      144, 179, 180, 183, 184, 186, 187
Migrant(s), 2, 5, 8, 16, 63, 67, 70, 122, 123,
   130, 144, 154, 160, 183, 186
   backgrounds, 17, 122
   status as, 14, 16
Migration, 1, 3, 4, 7, 14, 28, 30, 37, 65, 70,
   121, 122, 179
   child, 7, 28, 186, 187
   histories, 109, 110, 114
   labour, 28, 35, 185
   studies, 3, 6, 13, 15, 34
Minority, 9, 46, 53, 81, 82, 87, 92, 94, 102,
   124, 134, 160, 185
Mixedness, 12, 140–142, 153–155
   mixed parentage, 17, 142, 153
MJ (gang), 72

MOB (gang), 72
Mobility, 2, 8
  new paradigm of, 2
Moore, Henrietta, 163
Morocco, 11, 161, 166, 169
Multiple subjectivities, 63
Muslim(s), 57, 171
  countries, 57

N

Nansen, Fridtjof, 47
Nansen International Office for Refugees, 48
Narayan, Kirin, 10
Netherlands, the, 48, 154
New Zealand, 66
Nigeria, 11, 69, 161
Norway, 10, 13, 16, 17, 44, 47, 50, 53, 55–57,
    81, 83, 84, 87–89, 92–95, 99, 100, 102,
    107, 109, 110, 113, 160, 164, 165, 167,
    169, 173, 181, 185
Norwegian Children and Youth Council,
    Landsrådet for Norges barne- og
    ungdomsorganizasjoner (LNU), 103
Nuer, 67, 69, 72, 74

O

Omaha, Nebraska, 10, 11, 15, 61–63
Organizations. *See* Youth organizations
Oslo, 13, 83, 88, 90, 108, 160, 161

P

Pakistan parenting, 107
Parentage. *See* mixed parentage
Parliament (British), 48
Participant observation, 10, 11, 24, 160, 161
Participation, 24, 83, 99, 101, 102, 104, 105,
    112, 114, 184, 187
  democratic, 16, 99, 113
  in research, 11, 24
Partner choice, 129, 130
Passport, 48, 88
Pathologization, 17, 139
Pennsylvannia, 25, 27
Phenomenological approach, 143, 162
Phenotypes, 141, 149
Policy, 2, 13, 18, 28, 39, 48, 99, 105, 113, 114,
    174, 183, 185
  and practice, 139, 183
  immigration, 48, 185
  implications, 179
  integration, 114, 174
  on ethnic organizations, 102
Political opportunity structures, 101, 102, 113,
    114

Post-structuralism, 143, 145
Post-traumatic Stress Disorder (PTSD), 36
Poverty, 30, 32, 34, 50, 70, 85, 93, 152
Power, 4, 14, 56, 86, 93, 155, 181
Prague, 128
Pregnancy, 32
Prejudice. *See* racism
Prostitution, 23, 27, 28, 31
Protective regimes, 16, 81–83, 85, 96, 185
Puberty. *See* Adolescene

R

Race, 132, 140–142, 146, 150, 153, 155
  racial stereotypes, 71, 130
  racism, 68–71, 149, 150
Ramirez, George, 31
Rape, 27
Refugees, 15, 37, 45, 46, 48, 51, 53, 55, 56,
    61–63, 66, 68, 70, 74, 182
  child refugees, 15, 43, 45, 51, 53, 55, 182
Rehabilitation of the Norwegian Gypsies
    (programme), 88
Remittances, 35
Resilience, 37, 64
Restavek children, 38
Romania, 13, 83, 89
Rom, Roma, 16, 81–83, 85, 87–90, 92, 94, 95,
    181
  community, 83, 89, 95
  conception of childhood, 3
  cultural values, 90
  discrimination against, 16, 89, 92, 96
  family, 85, 88–90, 95
Root, Maria, 144

S

Schengen, 52
School, 26, 36, 53, 55, 69, 72, 73, 83, 84, 89,
    90, 94, 106, 127, 145, 146, 148, 149,
    160–163, 166, 170, 171, 185
  access to, 55, 70
  behaviour of children at, 91
Second generation. *See* Generation
Second World War, 17, 55, 83
Selassie, Haile, 66
Seminars, 103, 112
Sex, 29, 32, 163
  age of consent, 33
  assault and abuse, 84, 95
  exploitation, 29
  sexualized behaviour, 84
  trafficking, 28
  work, 29
Shifting selves, 159, 163, 165, 171, 173, 176

Index 193

Slavery, 25, 141
Socialization, 17, 18, 121, 162, 164
Social workers, 25, 26, 33, 34, 36, 51, 52, 186
Somalia, 11, 107, 161
Sri Lanka, 100, 101, 107, 108, 113
Stalin, Joseph, 48
Stereotypes, 13, 71, 130
  of Vietnamese in the Czech Republic, 130
  racial. *See* race
Stigma, 95, 130
  stigmatization, 73, 149
Structure. *See* Agency and structure
Subject positions, 159, 163
Sudan
  civil war, 61, 62
  lost boys of, 15, 61
  south, 11, 62, 65, 67, 69, 70, 73
  South Sudan Soldiers(gang), 62
  Sudanese-American, 61–63, 68, 74
  Sudan People'sLiberation Movement
    (SPLM), 74
Sweden, 50, 66, 100, 107
Syria, 57
Systems theory, 180

T
Tatum, Beverly Daniel, 168
Teenagers. *See* Adolescents
Texas, 25, 27, 31, 185
Thailand, 145
Therapeutic interventions, 36
Third spaces, 159, 176
Trafficking. *See* Human trafficking
Trafficking Victims Protection Act (TVPA),
  25, 33
Transnational families. *See* Families
Trauma, 36, 37
Traveller problem, 88
TripSet (gang), 72
Tunisia, 73
Turkey, 11, 51, 52, 100, 107, 141, 160, 161

U
Uganda, 62
UK. *See* United Kingdom
United Kingdom, 14, 141
United Nations, 56, 62

Declaration of Human Rights, 85, 91
High Commissioner for Refugees
  (UNCHR), 51, 66
protocol to prevent,supress and punish
  trafficking in persons,especially women
  and children, 25
United States of America, 2, 130
Uprootedness, 75
US, USA, 15, 25, 27, 31, 35, 62, 63, 66, 67, 69,
  141, 183

V
Victims, 7, 11, 26, 30, 33–35, 56
  victimhood, 5, 7, 34
  victimization, 34, 36, 38, 56
Vietnam, 11, 100, 101, 107, 109, 121, 123,
  126, 129, 131, 161
Vietnamese, 17, 121, 123–128, 130, 132, 147
  culture, 121, 127, 148
  migration to the Czech Republic, 123
Violence, 1, 6, 34, 37, 63, 71, 72, 74, 96
  as punishment, 73
  domestic, 68
  gang, 72
Visa, 27, 46, 48
Vocational training, 186
Voluntary organizations. *See*
  Community-based organizations
Vulnerability, 7, 13, 15, 23, 24, 30, 34, 38

W
Walby, Sylvia, 181
Waters, Mary, 130
Welfare, 14, 38, 46, 68, 82, 86, 88, 91, 105
  state, 14, 86, 92, 186
Wells, Karen, 4, 96
White, Susan, 96
Work permits, 36
World War II. *See* Second World War

Y
Youth, 6, 10, 16–18, 24, 28–31, 33, 37, 63, 70,
  75, 89, 99–101, 105, 109, 111, 113,
  114, 121, 134, 162, 168, 184–186
  organizations, 10, 101–103, 107

Printed in the United States
By Bookmasters